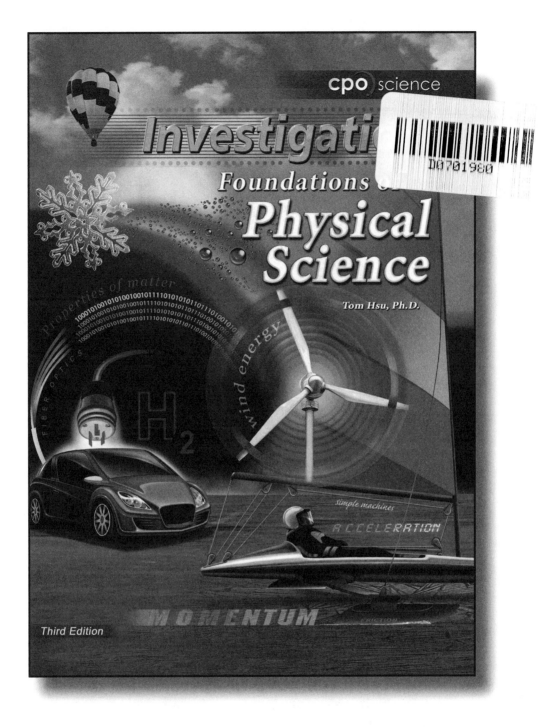

cpo science

Investigation

Foundations of
Physical Science

Tom Hsu, Ph.D.

Third Edition

cpo science

School Specialty
Science

Foundations of Physical Science Investigations

Third Edition

PRINCIPAL WRITERS

Thomas C. Hsu, PH.D – Author
Nationally recognized innovator in science and math education and the founder of CPO Science. Holds a Ph.D. in Applied Plasma Physics from the Massachusetts Institute of Technology (MIT), and has taught students from elementary, secondary and college levels. Tom has worked with numerous K–12 teachers and administrators and is well known as a consultant, workshop leader and developer of curriculum and equipment for inquiry based learning in science and math.

Erik Benton – Principal Investigation Editor and Writer
B.F.A., University of Massachusetts with minor in Physics
Taught for eight years in public and private schools, focusing on inquiry and experiential learning. Erik brings extensive teaching and technical expertise, ranging from elementary and adult education to wildlife research. As a naturalist for the Web of Life Field School in Santa Cruz, California, he participated in a worldwide amphibian population study. Currently he is involved in bird population studies in Massachusetts. Erik is our investigation writer and conducts national content presentations.

Scott Eddleman – Co-Author, Curriculum Manager
B.S., Biology, Southern Illinois University; M.Ed., Harvard University
Taught for 13 years in urban and rural settings. Developed two successful science-based school-to-career programs. Nationally recognized teacher trainer in inquiry-based and project-based instruction. Participated in a fellowship at Brown University where he conducted research on the coral reefs of Belize. Worked on National Science Foundation-funded projects at TERC. Scott has been a principal writer and curriculum developer for CPO Science for the last seven years.

Mary Beth Abel – Writer, Curriculum Specialist
B.S., Marine Biology, College of Charleston; M.S., Biological Sciences, University of Rhode Island.
Taught science and math at an innovative high school and at the college level. Has expertise in scientific research, inquiry-based teaching methods, and science curriculum development. Mary Beth has been a principal writer with CPO Science since 2000.

Patsy Eldridge – Writer
B.S., Biology, Grove City College; M.Ed., Tufts University.
Experienced science teacher and national hands-on science trainer and presenter. As an adjunct professor for Endicott College in Beverly, MA, and the College of Charleston, developed content-intensive Physical Science courses for educators. Partners with Dr. Tom Hsu to create and deliver innovative science lessons on interactive DVDs for students and teachers. Patsy has developed curriculum and training materials with CPO Science since 2000.

CONTRIBUTING WRITERS

Alyson Mazza
B.A., Environmental Biology and Education, Houghton College

Experienced science teacher with inquiry-based science teaching expertise. Alyson has worked with the PROBE K-12 project through the Leitzel Center at the University of New Hampshire to research and practice inquiry-based teaching strategies. She currently teaches science at Salem High School in Salem, NH.

Laura Preston
B. S. Geology and teaching certification, University of Texas, Arlington
Has thirteen years of science and math teaching experience for grades 5–12. Currently teaching at Salem High School in Salem, New Hampshire. Worked as a geologist in the early 1990's, and as a geophysicist in 2007. Laura participated in a research cruise aboard the R/V "Atlantis" collecting data on the East Pacific Rise. Member of the New Hampshire Geologic Society. Laura joined the CPO Science curriculum writing team as a consultant in 2007.

Michael Vela
Ph.D., Inorganic Chemistry, Brandeis University
Teaches 10th– and 11th–grade chemistry at Concord-Carlisle High School in Concord, Massachusetts. Taught 11th–grade chemistry at Lexington High School, Massachusetts.

Melissa Vela
B.A., Earth and Environmental Science, Lehigh University; M.S., Agricultural and Biological Engineering, Cornell University; M.Ed., Curriculum/Instruction, Boston College
Melissa has taught six years of 9th grade Earth and space science at Lexington High School in Massachusetts. She also taught 6th grade physical science and 8th grade algebra at Weston Middle School in Massachusetts.

SENIOR EDITOR

Lynda Pennell – Executive Vice President
B.A., English; M.Ed., Administration, Reading Disabilities, Northeastern University; CAGS Media, University of Massachusetts, Boston.
Nationally known in high school restructuring and for integrating academic and career education. Served as the director of an urban school for 5 years and has 17 years teaching/administrative experience in the Boston Public Schools. Lynda has led the development for CPO Science for the past eight years. She has also been recognized for her media production work.

EDITORIAL CONSULTANT

Christine Golden
B.A., Psychology, Gordon College: M.B.A., Rivier College
Project manager at *Imperial Communications* since 1999, with 22 years publishing experience. Owner and managing editor of *Big Dog Publishing Services*. Christine's work centers on editing of K-12 textbook material.

ART AND ILLUSTRATION

Polly Crisman – Graphics Manager/Illustration
B.F.A., University of New Hampshire
Worked as a designer and illustrator in marketing and advertising departments for a variety of industries. Polly has worked in the CPO Science design department since 2001, and is responsible for organizing workflow of graphics and file management. She created the CPO Science logo and supervises the graphic design image for CPO publications and media products.

Jesse Van Valkenburgh – Illustration/Photography
B.F.A. Illustration, Rochester Institute of Technology
Worked in prepress and design. Was responsible for creative design and prepress film production for computer catalogs, brochures and various marketing materials. Jesse completes photography and illustrations as a graphic designer for CPO book and media products.

Bruce Holloway – Senior Designer/Illustrator
Pratt Institute, N.Y., Boston Museum of Fine Arts
Expertise in illustration, advertising graphics, exhibits and product design. Commissioned throughout his career by The National Wildlife Federation's Conservation Stamp Campaign. Other commissions include the New Hampshire State Duck Stamp campaigns for1999 and 2003. Bruce has worked as senior designer with CPO Science since 2000 and collaborated with various teams to create all CPO book covers.

EQUIPMENT DESIGN

Thomas Narro – Senior Vice President
B.S., Mechanical Engineering, Rensselaer Polytechnic Institute
Accomplished design and manufacturing engineer; experienced consultant in corporate reengineering and industrial-environmental acoustics.

Danielle Dzurik
B.S., Industrial Design, Auburn University
Focuses her efforts in product development on creating new products and improving upon older designs.

MATERIAL SUPPORT

Kathryn Gavin – Purchasing and Quality Control Manager
Responsible for all functions related to purchasing raw materials and quality control of finished goods. Works closely with product development and design.

PROJECT AND TECHNICAL SUPPORT

Susan Gioia – Educational CPO Science Administrator
Expertise in office management. Oversees all functions necessary for the smooth product development of CPO products, including print and media.

Lynn L'Heureux
Owner of M&M Composition, LLC. Has worked in textbook composition for 10 years and specializes in math, computer, and science texts.

REVIEWERS

How to Read an Investigation

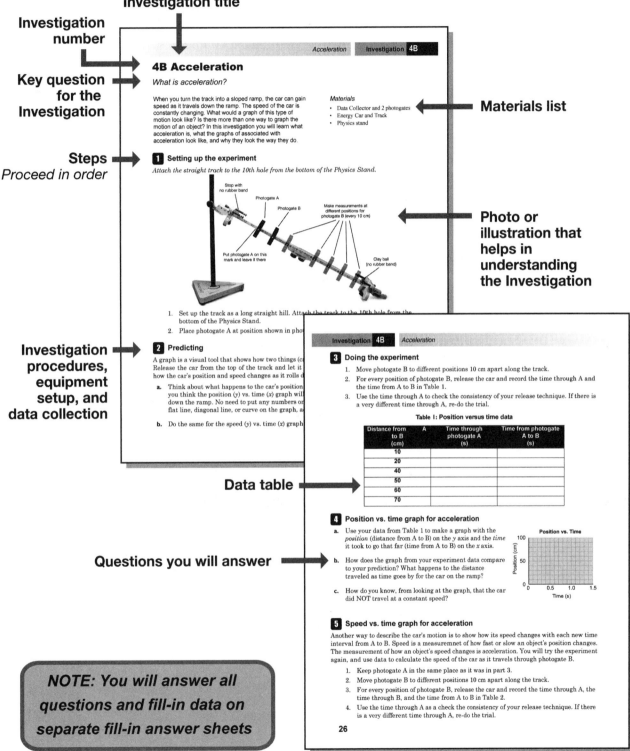

Investigation title

Investigation number

Key question for the Investigation

Steps
Proceed in order

Investigation procedures, equipment setup, and data collection

Materials list

Photo or illustration that helps in understanding the Investigation

Data table

Questions you will answer

NOTE: You will answer all questions and fill-in data on separate fill-in answer sheets

LAB SAFETY

Observing safety precautions is an extremely important practice while completing science investigations. Using science equipment and carrying out laboratory procedures always requires attention to safety. The purpose of learning and discussing safety in the lab is to help you learn how to protect yourself and others at all times.

The investigations in this book are designed to reduce safety concerns in the laboratory. The physics investigations use stable equipment that is easy to operate. The chemistry investigations use both household and laboratory chemicals. Although these chemicals might be familiar to you, they still must be used safely.

You will be introduced to safety by completing a skill sheet to help you observe the safety aids and important information in your science laboratory. In addition to this skill sheet, you may be asked to check your safety understanding and complete a safety contract. Your teacher will decide what is appropriate for your class.

Throughout this book, safety icons and words and phrases like "caution" and "safety tip" are used to highlight important safety information. Read the description for each icon carefully and look out for them when reading your book and doing investigations.

	General safety: Follow all instructions carefully to avoid injury to yourself or others.
	Wear safety goggles: Requires you to wear eye protection to prevent eye injuries.
	Wear a lab apron or coat: Requires you to wear a lab apron or coat to prevent damage to clothing and to protect from possible spills.
	Wear gloves: Requires you to protect your hands from injury due to heat or chemicals.
	Poisonous chemicals: Requires you to use extreme caution when working with chemicals in the laboratory and to follow all safety and disposal instructions from your teacher.
	Skin irritant: Requires you to use extreme caution when handling chemicals in the laboratory due to possible skin irritation and to follow all safety and disposal instructions from your teacher.
	Respiratory irritant: Requires you to perform the experiment under a laboratory hood and to avoid inhaling fumes while handling the chemicals.
	Laser: Requires you to use extreme caution while using a laser during investigations and to follow all safety instructions.

Lab safety is the responsibility of everyone! Help create a safe environment in your science lab by following the safety guidelines from your teacher as well as the guidelines discussed in this document.

Table of Contents

Optional Investigations

Lab Skills and Equipment Setups

1A Measurement

Are you able to use scientific tools to make accurate measurements?

In everyday life we use tools to make our work easier. For example, it is difficult to pound a nail without a hammer, to wrap a gift without tape, or to open clear plastic packages without scissors. In science, it is important to be able to correctly choose and use laboratory equipment to make measurements. During the "Measurement Games" you and a partner will practice choosing the correct tool to make measurements accurately. The group with the best averages overall wins the Measurement Games!

Materials (per group)
- Paper cup
- Pebbles
- Water
- Masking tape
- Graduated cylinder
- Electronic balance
- Meter stick
- CPO DataCollector

1 Stop and think

a. Are you familiar with the tools necessary to make measurements of length, mass, and volume? Look at the list of materials above and write down a tool used for measuring each property.

Property	Tool Used
Length	
Mass	
Volume	

b. Do you understand what metric units coincide with length, mass, and volume? Discuss this with your partner and write an appropriate unit that corresponds to each property.

Property	Unit Used
Length	
Mass	
Volume	

c. Read about the events listed below in Part 2 and predict the outcome of each event for yourself before you actually perform the task.

Olympic Event	Prediction
Straw Javelin	
Paper Cup	
Pebble Grab	
Side Step	
Hoppity Hop	

2   Doing the activity

A. Perform the event, collect, and record data

1. **Straw Javelin:** During this event, you will be throwing a straw as far as you can, like it is a javelin. Your front foot may not cross the start line, and you must throw the straw like a javelin with only one hand. Measure the distance of your throw in meters and centimeters.

2. **Paper Cup Challenge:** How much water can you move from a tank to a beaker in 10 seconds using just one paper cup? Use a graduated cylinder to measure the volume of water you successfully transferred. Be careful so you don't spill any water!

3. **Pebble Grab:** Who can grab the greatest mass of pebbles? Use *only one hand* to grab as many pebbles as you can out of a container. Transfer them to an *electronic* balance to measure the mass. Be sure the balance is measuring *in the correct units* before you begin!

4. **Side Step:** How far is your leg span? From a starting point step as far as you can to the side. Your partner will measure the length of your step in meters and centimeters.

5. **Hoppity Hop:** Who can hop 10 meters the fastest on one foot? Mark 10 meters on the floor with the masking tape. To use the timer, plug the power cord into an outlet, and then into the side of the electronic timer. Turn the timer on by sliding the small, black button on the side of the timer. To start the clock, push the "A" button; push it again to stop the clock. Push the "reset" button to reset the clock. Time how long it takes your partner to hop 10 meters on one foot!

B. Game results

1. Record your results below. Any result with missing or incorrect units will be automatically disqualified from the Measurement Games!

2. After you have recorded your results there will be a class discussion to see who the winners are in each event. Decide within your group who has the best score for each event. Use that score for the class data set. Record the data in the data table your teacher has drawn on the board. Determine the best overall score for the group winner. Record the individual winner's results for each event in the data table below.

Olympic Event	My Results	Winner's Results
Straw Javelin		
Paper Cup Challenge		
Pebble Grab		
Side Step		
Hoppity Hop		

3 Thinking about what you observed

a. Calculate the difference between the winner's results and your results for each event. (Don't forget units!)

Olympic Event	Difference
Straw Javelin	
Paper Cup Challenge	
Pebble Grab	
Side Step	
Hoppity Hop	

b. In which event were you closest to the winner?

c. In which event were you the farthest away from the winner?

d. How close were you to your predictions?

e. Which measurement were you most familiar with before the games? Why?

f. Which measurement did you find easiest to make during the games? Why was it so easy for you?

g. Which measurement did you find to be the most difficult during the games? Why?

4 Exploring on your own

a. Scientists work hard to be precise in their measurements when experimenting. In real life, most of us are accurate enough, but hardly precise, every time we perform a task that involves a measurement. Do you know the difference? Look it up and draw several examples that represent the difference between accuracy and precision.

b. Create a "quiz" that your classmates could "take" regarding the different tools used in a science lab and their appropriate units. Include an answer key.

c. Find a real science article from a magazine, newspaper, or internet website where scientists are measuring something. Explain in a one-paragraph summary what they are measuring, what tools they are using or could use to make the measurements, and the units associated with the measurements.

1B Conversion Chains

How can you use unit canceling to solve conversion problems?

$$115 \text{ km} \times \frac{1 \text{ mi}}{1.6 \text{ km}} = 72 \text{ mi}$$

Suppose you are traveling in Canada or Mexico, and you see a sign that says the next city is 115 kilometers away. How many miles is that? You could use the dimensional analysis process to figure it out. Dimensional Analysis is a method of using conversion factors and unit canceling to solve unit conversion problems. In this activity, you will use conversion chains to start and solve conversions.

Materials

- CPO Conversion Chain card deck
- Conversion chain table for recording chains and solutions
- Calculator

1 Conversion Chain cards

The deck of cards contains:

12 START cards, 12 SOLVE cards, 36 conversion factor cards

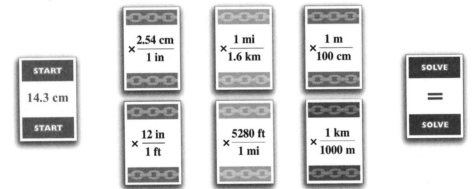

1. Look at the cards to identify what START, SOLVE, and conversion factor cards look like.
2. Shuffle the cards thoroughly!

2 Creating Conversion Chains

The object of the game is to have the most points after solving six conversion chains.

1. Deal four cards to each player (works best with three to five players).
2. Choose a player to go first. This player must play a START card draw one from the deck. If the player draws a START card, it may be played; otherwise play passes to thr next player. Play passes until a START card has been played. Anytime a START card is played the player scores 5 points. (Each group must assign a scorekeeper.)
3. The next player may play another START card or a conversion card that will continue the conversion chain. That means that the card must have a denominator unit that matches a START card unit, to cancel the starting unit and continue the chain. Only six START cards can be played in a game.

4. If the player has more than one card that could be played on multiple START cards, the player must choose only *one* card to play on each turn.

5. After playing a card, the player *must* draw a card.

6. If the player does not have a suitable card, the player must draw one card from the deck. If the card will play, he can play it. If the card won't play, he must pass his turn.

7. The next player plays a conversion factor card, plays a START card, or draws a card, and play continues.

8. A team can have as many as three conversion chains going at once.

9. After a minimum of three conversion factor cards have been played on any particular START card, any player is allowed to play a SOLVE card on her turn, and the player *immediately scores 5 points for each conversion chain card in the chain*.

3 Solving a chain and scoring points

1. Anytime a SOLVE card is played on any conversion chain, all players must record the chain on the answer sheet and calculate the answer with the correct number of significant digits and unit.

2. Players compare answers and determine who has the correct answer. Consult your teacher if there are disagreements.

3. *Any* player with the correct answer scores 25 points.

4. Keep playing until your team has created and solved six conversion chains.

5. At the end of the game, after six conversion chains have been scored, players must subtract 5 points per card for unplayed cards remaining in the hand.

6. Total up the points, subtract the unused cards, and determine the winner.

4 Reminders and strategy

1. Whenever you play a START card, you score 5 points! If you draw a START card after six chains have already been started, you must keep that card in your hand, and it will cost you 5 points in the end.

2. Remember: you always draw a card at the end of *every* turn.

3. When a conversion chain has been solved, place the START, chain, and SOLVE cards to the side in a pile. You might want to look at a solved chain later in the game. Also, this will help your team keep track of how many conversion chains have been solved (the goal is to solve six).

4. You can play a SOLVE card only after there are at least three conversion factor cards in any chain. For beginners, a SOLVE card should be played after three chain cards are in a chain. For advanced players, a SOLVE card can be held back and played after the chain is much longer. The SOLVE card player benefits, since 5 points are awarded for each chain card in the chain to that player!

5. Record each conversion chain your team creates in Table 1. There are blanks for recording six conversion factors per chain. If a chain has less than six, just leave remaining boxes blank. If you need more than 6, continue on the back of the page.

6. The first row of Table 1 shows an example chain.

Table I: Conversion Chains

START card							Answer with correct sig figs and unit	Points scored
46.3 m	$\times \dfrac{1\ km}{1000\ m}$	$\times \dfrac{1\ mi}{1.6\ km}$	$\times \dfrac{5280\ ft}{1\ mi}$	$\times$ ——	$\times$ ——	$\times$ ——	153 ft	
	$\times$ ——	$\times$ ——	$\times$ ——	$\times$ ——	$\times$ ——	$\times$ ——		
	$\times$ ——	$\times$ ——	$\times$ ——	$\times$ ——	$\times$ ——	$\times$ ——		
	$\times$ ——	$\times$ ——	$\times$ ——	$\times$ ——	$\times$ ——	$\times$ ——		
	$\times$ ——	$\times$ ——	$\times$ ——	$\times$ ——	$\times$ ——	$\times$ ——		
	$\times$ ——	$\times$ ——	$\times$ ——	$\times$ ——	$\times$ ——	$\times$ ——		
	$\times$ ——	$\times$ ——	$\times$ ——	$\times$ ——	$\times$ ——	$\times$ ——		
							TOTAL	

5 Thinking about the game

a. The conversion chains you create for this game could be quite long, and the actual conversions could be solved with fewer conversion factors. What is the least number of conversion factors you would need to make these conversions, given the cards you have in the deck?

- converting ft to cm

- converting mi to m

b. Because of the limitations of the cards in the deck, to convert from km to cm, you would have to go through English units. What is a much easier way to convert from kilometers to centimeters? Explain.

c. Explain the math reasoning behind why you are able to "cancel" like units that appear in the numerator and denominator of conversion factors in a conversion chain.

2A Mass, Volume, and Indirect Measurement

How can you find the mass of a single rice grain?

In this investigation you will find the average mass of a single grain of rice. One grain of rice is too small to register a mass value on your electronic scale. There are many situations like this where scientists need to measure something that is too small or too large to measure directly. In these situations, scientists use methods of indirect measurement. To do this, you calculate the measurement you can't make from other measurements that you can make.

Materials (per group)

- About 1/4 cup of rice
- Cellophane tape
- Electronic scale (or triple-beam balance)
- Scissors
- Index card

1 Getting started

To find the average mass of a single grain of rice, you will measure the mass of a 1-cm box filled with rice. You will then estimate how many grains there are in the cube. By dividing the mass of the cube by the number of grains in the cube, you will get a good indirect measurement of the average mass of a single grain of rice.

The first thing we need to do is find out how many grains of rice there are in a cubic centimeter.

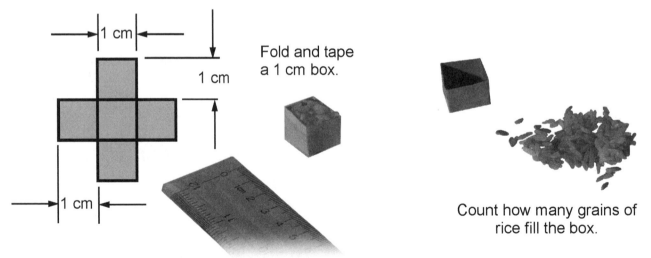

1 cm

1 cm

1 cm

Fold and tape a 1 cm box.

Count how many grains of rice fill the box.

1. Cut out and fold up the small cube (made out of an index card) as shown in the diagram. Use tape to hold the cube together. This cube has a volume of 1 cubic centimeter (1 cm^3 or 1 cc).

2. Fill the cube level with rice.

3. Carefully empty the rice in the cube onto the table. Count how many grains fit into the cube and record the value in Table 1.

4. Calculate the number of grains of rice per cubic centimeter and record this value in Table 1. Use this formula: *number of grains / volume of cube = grains per cubic centimeter*

Table 1: Data on number of rice grains per cubic centimeter

Volume of cube (cm³)	1
Number of grains of rice	
Calculated grains per cubic centimeter	

2 Accuracy, precision, and resolution

No instrument in science makes perfect measurements. A single cubic centimeter of rice is a very small mass and difficult to measure precisely with an ordinary balance. For example, suppose you want a measurement that is precise to 1 percent. A typical electronic balance has a resolution of 0.1 grams. That means the smallest mass you can measure with this balance is 100 times as large as its resolution (100 × 0.1 g = 10 g), therefore 10 grams is the smallest mass you can measure to a precision of 1 percent. Since the mass of one cubic centimeter of rice is less than 10 grams, we will use a much larger amount of rice.

3 Making a precise measurement

1. Cut out and fold up the 3-centimeter cube as shown in the diagram. Use tape to hold the cube together.

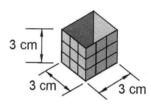

3 cm

3 cm   3 cm

Make and fill a 3 cm box with rice.

2. Calculate the cube's volume and record in Table 2.

3. Place the cube on the balance and reset the balance to zero. The balance display should now read 0.0 grams.

4. Remove the cardboard cube and fill it level with rice. Place the filled cube back on the balance and record the mass.

5. Calculate the number of grains of rice in the cube based on the value of grains per cubic centimeter you calculated in Table 1.

6. Use the mass of rice in the large cube and the calculated number of rice grains to find the average mass of one grain of rice.

Table 2: Data on the mass of a grain of rice

Volume of cube (cm³)		Number of grains of rice in 3 cm cube	
Mass of rice in cube (g)		Calculated mass of 1 grain of rice (g)	

4 **Stop and think**

a. Why did the balance show a small negative mass when you removed the empty cardboard cube at the beginning of step 4?

b. Why does this experiment measure the *average* mass instead of the *actual* mass of a grain of rice?

c. Why is the average mass a more-useful quantity than the actual mass of any single grain of rice?

d. Compare your average mass of one grain of rice with other groups' results. How do your results compare? Discuss.

2B Density

How is an object's density related to its volume, mass, and tendency to sink or float?

You may be familiar with the trick question "Which is heavier: a pound of feathers or a pound of bricks?" The answer, of course, is that they have the same weight. However, the pound of feathers has a much greater volume because feathers have a much lower density than bricks. The brick material is squeezed together tightly, while the feathers contain a large amount of empty space. In this investigation you will study the relationship between mass, volume, and density. You will also determine how an object's density affects whether it sinks or floats in water.

Materials

- Balance
- Displacement tank
- Disposable cup
- 250-milliliter beaker
- Set of six identical objects
- 100-milliliter graduated cylinder
- Graph paper
- Density cubes
- Metric ruler
- Water
- Paper towels

1 Measuring mass and volume

1. Each lab group has a unique set of six objects. Find the mass and volume of one of your objects. Add a second object and find the total mass and volume of both objects. Then find the total mass and volume of three, four, and five objects. Record your data in Table 1. Note: Although your objects look identical, there may be small differences. Do not obtain your data by multiplying the mass or volume of one object by the number of objects you have. Use the displacement method for measuring density.

Table 1: Mass and volume data

	one object	two objects	three objects	four objects	five objects
mass in grams (g)					
volume in milliliters (mL)					

2. Plot your data on graph paper. Label the *x*-axis "volume" and the *y*-axis "mass." Be sure use the entire space on your graph paper for making your graph.

2 Analyzing your results

a. Is there any pattern to the data points on your graph? For example, the points might form a smooth curve, a straight line, a random scattering, or a cluster in a certain region. Describe any pattern you see.

b. Line up your ruler along the points on your graph so it is as close as possible to all of the dots. The line may not touch all of the dots, but should have an equal number of dots on each side of it. This line is called the "line of best fit." Draw the line.

c. Find the slope of the line of best fit. To do this, choose any two points on the line. These will be represented as (X_1, Y_1) and (X_2, Y_2). Use the formula below to calculate the slope of the line.

$$\frac{(Y_2 - Y_1)}{(X_2 - X_1)} = \text{slope}$$

The slope tells how many grams of matter are contained in each milliliter of material. Some substances, like lead, have quite a few grams of matter packed into each milliliter. Other substances, like styrofoam, have less than a single gram of matter packed into each milliliter.

d. Compare your slope with the result obtained by other groups. Are your slopes similar or different?

e. The relationship between a substance's mass and volume is called its density. What is the density of the material you tested?

3 Using your knowledge

a. Your graph shows data for five objects. Use your graph to predict the mass of *six* objects.

b. Next, use the balance to find the total mass of all six objects.

c. How does your value from your graph compare to the mass obtained using the balance?

d. Use the mass that you found in step b. Find that number on the *y*-axis of your graph. Now find the point on the line with that *y*-value. What is the *x*-value of the point?

e. Now, find the volume of six objects experimentally.

f. How does the *x*-value from the graph compare with the measured volume?

4 Comparing class data

Collect data from each group in the class to fill in Table 2.

Table 2: Class data for density of objects

	Group1	Group 2	Group 3	Group 4	Group 5	Group 6
volume of one object (mL)						
type of material						
density (g/mL)						

Using the data from Table 2, answer the following questions.

a. Does density depend on the size of the material? Give evidence to support your answer.

b. Does density depend on the type of material? Give evidence to support your answer.

c. Using what you have observed in this lab, do you suppose that density depends on the shape of the material? Why or why not?

5 Using a different method to find volume

You used the displacement method to find the volume of your objects in the first part of the investigation. The displacement method works because an object's volume is equal to the volume of water it displaces, or pushes aside. This method is useful for objects with complicated shapes.

If an object has a simple shape, such as a cube, its volume can be found by measuring its dimensions. The volume of a cube is found using the formula:

Volume = length × width × height

When length, width, and height are measured in centimeters, volume is in cubic centimeters or cm^3. A 1 cm × 1 cm × 1 cm cube displaces 1 milliliter of water, so 1 cm^3 = 1 milliliter.

1. Use the method demonstrated in the diagram on the right to measure the length, width, and height of the steel cube in centimeters.

2. Record your measurements in Table 3.

3. Calculate the volume of the steel cube. Record your volume calculations in cubic centimeters in Table 3.

4. Repeat steps 1–3 for the other 4 cubes.

Table 3: Cube volume table

Material of solid cube	Length (cm)	Width (cm)	Height (cm)	Volume from calculation (cm^3)
Steel				
Oak				
Aluminum				
Copper				
PVC				

6 Calculating the density

Each cube's volume is almost exactly the same, but their masses are different because they are all made of different materials. Use Table 4 to calculate the density of each cube.

1. Use a balance to determine the mass of the steel cube, and record it in Table 4.
2. Divide the mass by the volume of the steel cube to calculate its density: density (g/cm^3) = mass (g) / volume (cm^3). Record the density value in Table 4.
3. Repeat steps 1 and 2 and calculate the density of each cube.

Table 4: Cube density data

Material of solid cube	Mass (g)	Volume (cm^3)	Density (g/cm^3)	Prediction (sink or float)	Result (sink or float)
Steel					
Oak					
Aluminum					
Copper					
PVC					

7 Stop and think

a. How do the volumes compare to each other? Why do you think they might be different?

b. Pick up and hold each cube. Predict whether it will sink or float in water. Record your predictions in Table 4. What did you base your predictions on?

c. What is the density of water in g/cm^3?

d. Compare the density of water to the density you calculated for each cube. Take another look at your sink/float predictions. Make any changes you need to based on density.

e. What rule did you use to make your prediction? Write the rule down in one sentence.

8 Testing the hypothesis

Your predictions from part 7d, and the rule from part 7e, represent a hypothesis. Test the hypothesis by dropping each cube in a beaker of water. Record your results in Table 4.

9 Thinking about what you learned

a. Describe two different ways you can find the density of a regularly-shaped object like a cube.

b. Explain why two different objects can have equal volumes but different masses.

c. Which method of prediction was better, testing the weight of the cube in your hand, or comparing the density of the cube to the density of water? Why?

3A Measuring Time

How is time measured accurately?

A measurement is a quantity with a unit that tells what the quantity means. For example, 3 seconds is a measurement of time that includes a quantity (3) and a unit (seconds). This investigation will explore time measurement.

Materials

- DataCollector and 2 photogates

1 Using the DataCollector as a stopwatch

A stopwatch measures a *time interval*. The Data Collector stopwatch shows time in seconds up to 60 seconds. The display shows *min:sec:hundredths* for times longer than 1 minute.

1. Select the DataCollector's stopwatch mode from the home screen.
2. Practice starting and stopping the stopwatch.
3. Reset the stopwatch to zero.

2 Observing reaction time

The time it takes a signal from your brain to move a muscle is called *reaction time*.

1. This experiment takes two people. One person (the watcher) watches the stopwatch and the other person (operator) pushes the buttons without looking at the display. The watcher selects a time between 5 and 10 seconds and keeps the time secret.
2. The operator starts (and stops) the stopwatch *without looking at the display*. The watcher looks at the display and says STOP at the secret time. For example, if the secret time is 6 seconds, the watcher should say STOP when the display reaches 6.00 seconds.
3. Repeat the experiment several times, record your results in Table 1, and calculate reaction time by taking and average of the difference in times for all five trials.

Table I: Reaction Time

Trial	Secret time (s)	Measured time (s)	Difference (s)	Avg. Difference Reaction time (s)
1				
2				
3				
4				
5				

3   Mixed units for time

In physical science, you are usually going to measure time in seconds. However, time is often given in mixed units, which may include hours, minutes, and seconds. Consider the following three time intervals.

    1.   16,000 seconds

    2.   250 minutes

    3.   4 hours, 23 minutes, and 15 seconds (4:23:15)

a.   Which one is in mixed units?

b.   Can you tell which time is longest or shortest?

c.   If 1 minute = 60 seconds, how many seconds is 250 minutes?

d.   If 1 hour = 60 minutes, how many minutes are in 4 hours?

e.   Use your answer from question d. to figure out how many seconds are in 4:23:15.

f.   Arrange the three measurements from smallest to largest.

4   Using the photogates

A photogate allows us to use an infrared light beam to start and stop the DataCollector. When the CPO timer mode is on the interval function, it uses photogates to control the clock.

    1.   Connect a single photogate to the Photogate A input with a cord.

    2.   Select *interval function* in the CPO timer mode of the DataCollector.

    3.   Try blocking the infrared beam with your finger and observe what happens on the timer display.

Try your own experiments until you can answer the following questions. Be very specific in your answer. Someone who has never used the DataCollector before should be able to read your answer and know what to do with the infrared beam to make the clock start and stop.

a.   How do you start the clock?

b.   How do you stop the clock?

c.   What time interval has the clock measured?

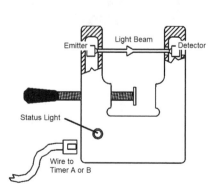

5 Using two photogates

1. Connect a second photogate to the DataCollector.
2. Make sure the light on each photogate is green and press the reset button. Pressing reset clears the clocks and also tells the DataCollector to look at its inputs to see which photogates are connected.
3. Do your own experiments and fill in the rest of Table 2.

Table 2: Timer and photogate rules

t_A

How do you start the t_A clock?	
How do you stop the t_A clock?	

t_B

How do you start the t_B clock?	
How do you stop the t_B clock?	

t_{AB}

How do you start the t_{AB} clock?	
How do you stop the t_{AB} clock?	

3B Experiments and Variables

How do you design a valid experiment?

Experiments help us collect evidence so we can unlock nature's puzzles. If an experiment is well-planned, the results can provide an answer to a scientific question like "What would happen if I did this?" If the experiment is not well-planned, you will still get results, but you may not know what they mean. In this investigation, you will experiment with a car on a ramp. Only by paying careful attention to the variables can you make sense of the results.

Materials

- CPO Energy Car and Track
- DataCollector and photogates
- CPO Phyics Stand

1 Setting up the experiment

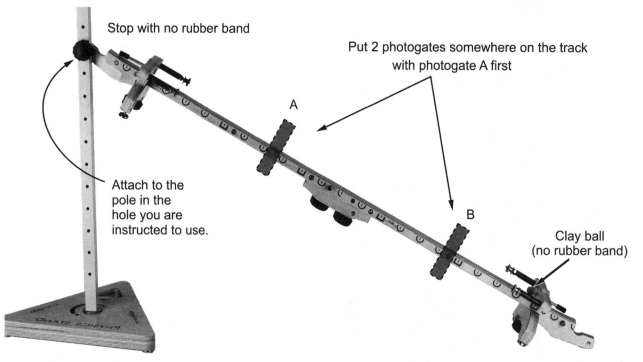

Stop with no rubber band

Put 2 photogates somewhere on the track with photogate A first

A

Attach to the pole in the hole you are instructed to use.

B

Clay ball (no rubber band)

1. Set up the track as a long straight section. Your teacher will tell you which hole in the stand to attach the track. Each group will have a different angle.
2. Put a clay ball on the stop at the bottom.
3. Place two photogates on the track with photogate A higher than photogate B.
4. Release the car and record the time it takes the car to pass between the photogates (t_{AB}).

2 Stop and think

a. Which track should have the fastest car? Which track should have the shortest time between photogates?

b. Write a one-sentence hypothesis that relates the time between photogates to the angle of the track.

c. Use Table 1 to record the results from each group in your class. Record the times in the column labeled "First Trial." Leave the column labeled "Second Trial" blank. How do the results compare with your hypothesis? Can you give a reason why they did or did not behave as you expected?

Table 1: Photogate times from A to B

Attachment hole (holes from bottom)	First Trial Time from A to B (s)	Second Trial Time from A to B (s)

3 Variables

a. List at least six variables in your system which affect the time between photogates.

b. Which variable is the experimental variable in your class? How do you know?

c. What should be done with the other variables (other than the experimental variable)? Why should this be done?

d. Name two variables that should not be included in your system. These variables should not have much (or any) influence on the time from photogate A to B.

4 A controlled experiment

1. With your teacher and the rest of your class, decide on how to control the variables other than the experimental variable.
2. Practice rolling the car until you can get three consecutive times within 0.0010 seconds of each other.
3. Repeat the experiment using the experimental and controlled variables you discussed and decided upon. Record the new data in the column titled "Second Trial."

5 Applying what you have learned

a. Does the second trial of the experiment produce results that agree with your hypothesis?

b. Why does the second trial produce better agreement with your hypothesis than the first trial did?

c. If something does not work, discuss what you should do to try and find the problem. List at least three steps that relate to variables, experiments, and controls.

4A Speed

Can you predict the speed of the car as it moves down the track?

What happens to the speed of a car as it rolls down a ramp? Does the speed stay constant or does it change? In this investigation you will measure the speed of a car at different points as it rolls down a ramp. Then you will make a graph that describes the motion, and predict the speed of the car somewhere on the ramp.

Materials

- CPO DataCollector and 1 photogate
- CPO Energy Car and Track
- CPO Physics Stand

1 Describing speed

Suppose you ran in a race. What information do you need to describe your speed? Saying that you ran for 20 minutes would not be enough information. To describe your speed, you need two things:

1. The *distance* you traveled, and

2. The *time* it took you to travel that distance.

Example	Distance	Time	Speed
10 seconds 100 meters	100 meters	10 seconds	10 m/s
1 hour 50 miles	50 miles	1 hour	50 mi/hr
15 seconds 10 feet	10 feet	15 seconds	0.67 ft/s

Based on the examples above, fill in the boxes to complete the *equation* for calculating speed.

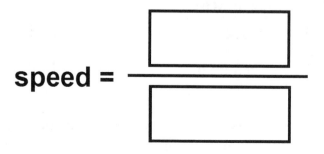

speed =

2 Making a hypothesis

Where is the car going the fastest on the ramp? Is it going fastest at the top, middle, or bottom?

a. Create a hypothesis about the car's speed on the ramp–where is it the fastest, and why do you think so?

3 Setting up the experiment

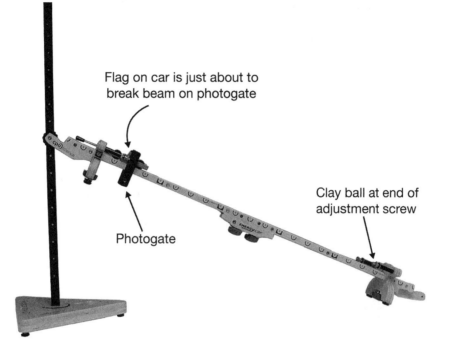

Flag on car is just about to break beam on photogate

Clay ball at end of adjustment screw

Photogate

1. Join the two ends of the ramp that say "Energy Car" to each other. The ramp should be straight, without a bend in the middle. Use two threaded knobs to connect the two parts.
2. Attach the ramp to the physics stand using one threaded knob. Your teacher will tell your group which hole on the stand to use. Hole where ramp is attached: _____
3. Place a bumper at each end of the ramp. Place a clay ball on the end of the thumb screw at the bottom of the ramp to stop the car. The thumb screw at the top of the ramp will be the place where you start the car.
4. Attach a photogate to the Photogate A input of the DataCollector.
5. Place the photogate so its screw is on the round mark that is closest to the front of the car.

4 Using the photogate to measure speed

As the car passes through the photogate, the DataCollector clock starts and stops. The DataCollector measures the length of time that the light beam is broken. Speed is equal to the distance traveled divided by the time taken. What distance do you use?

If you look at the car you will see a small "flag" on one side. This is the part of the car that blocks the photogate's light beam. The distance the car moves while the light is blocked is the width of the flag, 1 centimeter.

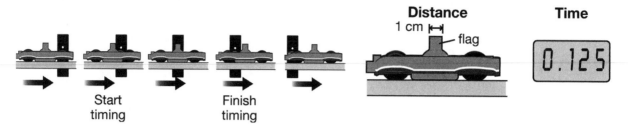

Distance
1 cm ⊢⊣ — flag

Time

0.125

Start
timing

Finish
timing

a. What is the *distance* traveled by the car in the example?

b. What is the *time* taken by the car in the example?

c. What is the *speed* of the car in the example?

5 Doing the experiment

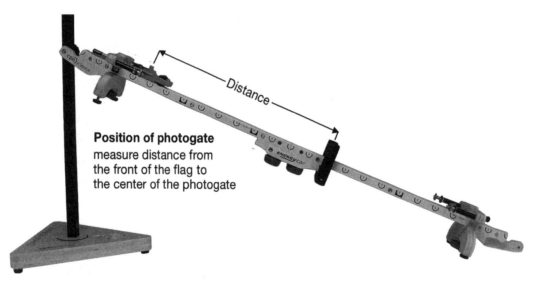

Distance

Position of photogate
measure distance from
the front of the flag to
the center of the photogate

1. Place the car at the top of the ramp. Place the photogate 10 centimeters downhill from the car. Measure the distance from the front edge of the car's flag to the middle of the screw that holds the photogate to the track. If you line up the car's flag over one of the circular markings, measuring is made easier, since each mark is 5 centimeters away from each other. Record the photogate's position in Table 1.

2. Release the car without pushing it. Record the time through photogate A in the table.

3. Calculate the speed of the car using the distance traveled (1 cm) and the time at photogate A.

4. Move the photogate 10 centimeters down the track. Record the position, time, and speed.

5. Repeat the measurements of position, time, and speed for six different places spaced along the ramp. You will have to skip some places in the middle of the track where the photogate won't attach.

Table 1: Position, time, and speed data

Position of photogate A (cm)	Time through photogate A (s)	Distance traveled by the car (cm)	Speed of the car (cm/s)
		1.00	
		1.00	
		1.00	
		1.00	
		1.00	
		1.00	

6 Analyzing the data

a. From your measurements, what can you say about the car's speed as it moves down the ramp?

b. Use your data to make a graph which shows how the car's speed changes as it rolls down the ramp. Put speed on the *y-axis* and position of the photogate on the *x-axis*. Be certain to label the axes with the correct variable and the proper unit of measurement. Give the graph a descriptive title. Include the number of the hole you used to connect the ramp to the stand in your title.

c. Describe what the graph shows about how the speed of the car is changing as it moves down the ramp.

d. Compare your graph with that of students who connected their ramps at different heights on the stand. Explain any differences you see.

7 Using your graph

Now that you have gathered, organized, and analyzed your data, it is time to use it to make a prediction. You measured the speed of the car at several places on the ramp as it rolled to the bottom. Now you will predict what the speed of the car will be at a place you did not measure. There is a way to do this with the information represented by your graph.

1. In Table 2 record a position on the ramp where you did not measure the speed of the car. The position should be between two places where you did measure the speed.

Table 2: Predicted speed data

Selected position (cm)	Predicted speed at selected position (cm/s)	Actual speed at selected position (cm/s)	Percent correct of prediction

2. Use your graph to find the predicted speed of the car at the selected position. To do this, start on the *x*-axis at the position you have selected. Draw a line straight up until it interesects with the speed vs. position line on your graph. At the intersection point, draw a line horizontally over to the *y*-axis where the speed is recorded. This is the speed that corresponds to your predicted location. The graph to the right uses a position of 55 centimeters as an example. Use a different position. Record your predicted speed in Table 2.

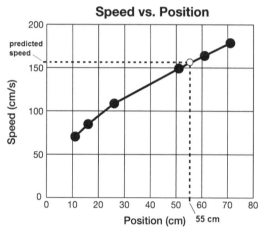

3. Place the photogate at the position you selected in step 1 and record the time it takes for the car to pass through the photogate.

4. Use the wing length (1.00 centimeter) and the time to calculate the speed. Record the actual speed in Table 2.

5. How does the predicted speed compare with the actual measured speed? What does this tell you about your experiment and measurements?

8 Calculating percent error

a. Find the difference between the predicted speed and the actual, calculated speed.

Predicted speed – Actual speed = Difference

b. Take this difference and divide it by the predicted speed, then multiply by 100.

(Difference ÷ Predicted speed) × 100 = Percent error

c. Use the percent error to calculate percent correct. Record percent correct in Table 2.

100 – Percent error = Percent correct

d. What do you think can account for any error you may have had?

4B Acceleration

What is acceleration?

When you turn the track into a sloped ramp, the car can gain speed as it travels down the ramp. The speed of the car is constantly changing. What would a graph of this type of motion look like? Is there more than one way to graph the motion of an object? In this investigation you will learn what acceleration is, what the graphs of associated with acceleration look like, and why they look the way they do.

> **Materials**
> * CPO DataCollector and 2 photogates
> * CPO Energy Car and Track
> * CPO Physics Stand

 1 **Setting up the experiment**

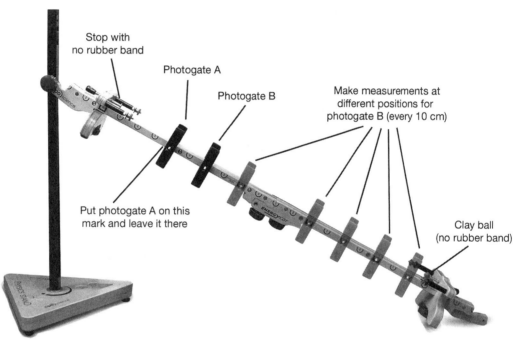

Stop with no rubber band

Photogate A

Photogate B

Make measurements at different positions for photogate B (every 10 cm)

Put photogate A on this mark and leave it there

Clay ball (no rubber band)

1. Set up the track as a long straight ramp. Attach the track to the 10th hole from the bottom of the Physics Stand.
2. Place photogate A at the position shown in the photo. Keep photogate A in this position.

2 **Predicting**

A graph is a visual tool that shows how two things (called variables) are related to one another. Release the car from the top of the track and let it roll down the track a few times. Observe how the car's position and speed changes as it rolls down the track.

a. Think about what happens to the car's position as it rolls down the track. Sketch what you think the position (y) vs. time (x) graph will look like for the Energy Car as it moves down the ramp. No need to put any numbers on the axes, just label the axes and place a flat line, diagonal line, or curve on the graph, according to your prediction.

b. Do the same for the speed (y) vs. time (x) graph prediction.

3 Doing the experiment

1. Move photogate B to different positions 10 cm apart along the track.
2. For every position of photogate B, release the car and record the time through A and the time from A to B in Table 1.
3. Use the time through A to check the consistency of your release technique. If there is a very different time through A, redo the trial.

Table 1: Position versus time data

Distance from A to B (cm)	Time through photogate A (s)	Time from photogate A to B (s)
10		
20		
40		
50		
60		
70		

4 Position vs. time graph for acceleration

a. Use your data from Table 1 to make a graph with the *position* (distance from A to B) on the y-axis and the *time* it took to go that far (time from A to B) on the x-axis.

b. How does the graph from your experiment data compare to your prediction? What happens to the distance traveled as time goes by for the car on the ramp?

c. How do you know, from looking at the graph, that the car did *not* travel at a constant speed?

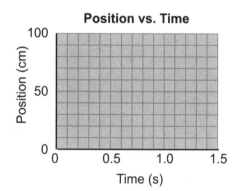

5 Speed vs. time graph for acceleration

Another way to describe the car's motion is to show how its speed changes with each new time interval from A to B. Speed is a measuremnet of how fast or slow an object's position changes. The measurement of how an object's speed changes is acceleration. You will try the experiment again, and use data to calculate the speed of the car as it travels through photogate B.

1. Keep photogate A in the same place as it was in part 3.
2. Move photogate B to different positions 10 cm apart along the track.
3. For every position of photogate B, release the car and record the time through A, the time through B, and the time from A to B in Table 2.
4. Use the time through A as a check the consistency of your release technique. If there is a very different time through A, redo the trial.

Table 2: Speed vs. Time Data

Distance from A to B (cm)	Time through photogate A (s)	Time through photogate B (s)	Time from photogate A to B (s)	Speed at photogate B (cm/s)
10				
20				
40				
50				
60				
70				

5. How fast is the car going as it travels through B each time? Calculate the speed of the car at each position of photogate B. Record your speeds in Table 2.

$$v = \frac{d}{t} \qquad v = \frac{1.00 \text{ cm}}{\text{time B}}$$

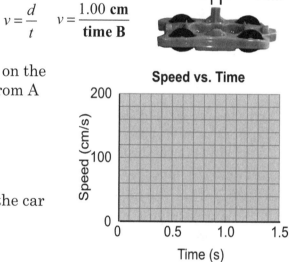

Speed vs. Time

a. Draw a graph with the *speed* (speed through B) on the *y*-axis and the *time* it took to go that far (time from A to B) on the *x*-axis.

b. How does the graph from your experiment data compare to your prediction?

c. What happens to the speed as time goes by for the car on the downhill ramp?

6 Applying what you've learned

a. Did the car accelerate as it traveled down the hill? Justify your answer.

b. Use the formula for acceleration to find the average acceleration of your car. Use data from the trial in Table 2 where photogate B was 70 cm from A. The unit for acceleration will be cm/s/s.

$$acceleration = \frac{final\ velocity - initial\ velocity}{time\ elapsed} \qquad acceleration\ of\ car = \frac{speed\ \textbf{B} - speed\ \textbf{A}}{time\ \textbf{A to B}}$$

c. Use your speed vs. time graph to predict how much time would elapse for the car to reach a speed of 200 cm/s.

d. Use your position vs. time graph to predict where on the track the car would reach a speed of 200 cm/s.

e. Test your predictions with a photogate at your predicted location on the track. Were your predictions accurate? Record your observations.

5A What is a Newton?

What is force and how is it measured?

You can think of force as a push or pull. Objects interact with each other (and you) through forces. It takes force to start an object's motion, and also force to stop an object in motion. This investigation will explore the precise definition of force and measure the strength of forces.

Materials

- Spring scale (0–5 N)
- 15 round metal washers (1/2 inch inner diameter)
- Loop of string
- Electronic scale (or triple beam balance)

1 Measuring forces

Forces have two important properties: strength and direction. In the English system of units, the strength of a force is measured in pounds. When you measure your own weight in pounds, you are measuring the force of gravity acting on your body. In the metric system, the strength of a force is measured in newtons (N). A quarter-pound hamburger has a weight of about 1 newton (1 lb = 4.448 N).

1. You can measure force with a spring scale. Before using the spring scale however, you must be sure it correctly starts at zero. Calibrate the spring scale by turning the nut on the top until the plunger lines up with the zero mark.

2. Pull on the hook so the spring extends. When you pull, you are applying a force. Can you make a force of 2 newtons (2 N)?

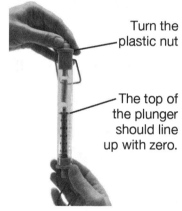

Turn the plastic nut

The top of the plunger should line up with zero.

2 Weight: the force of gravity

Weight is a common force that you may be familiar with. Objects that have mass also have weight. Weight comes from the action of gravity on an object's mass.

1. Attach three steel washers to a loop of string.

2. Use a calibrated spring scale to measure the weight of the washers in newtons (N).

3. Use an electronic scale or triple beam balance to measure the mass in grams (g). Convert each mass in grams to kilograms (divide by 1,000 or move decimal point three places to the left).

4. Repeat the experiment for 6, 9, 12, and 15 washers.

Table 1: Weight and Mass Data

Number of washers	Weight (N)	Mass (g)	Mass (kg)
3			
6			
9			
12			
15			

3 Stop and think

What do the results of your experiment tell you about the relationship between weight in newtons and mass in kilograms? Create a graph as described below to answer this question.

a. Make a graph of your data from Table 1. Place weight in newtons on the vertical (y) axis and mass in kilograms on the horizontal (x) axis.

b. Describe the graph. What does it tell you about the relationship between mass and weight?

c. Calculate the slope of your graph. The slope is equal to the strength of gravity (g) on Earth, measured in newtons per kilogram (N/kg).

d. Write an equation that relates weight in newtons, mass in kilograms, and the strength of gravity (g). It should be in the form: weight = _____

e. If an object has a mass of 10 kilograms, how much does it weigh in newtons?

4 Applying what you have learned

a. Explain how you could estimate the weight and mass of seven of your steel washers.

b. Find the weight and mass for seven of your steel washers. How close is the actual value to your estimated value? Explain some reasons why your value may not be perfectly accurate.

5B Friction

How does friction affect motion?

Friction is always present. Sometimes we want friction. For example, friction between tires and the road allows a car to be steered safely and maintain its direction when moving. Other times we want to reduce friction. Putting oil on a bicycle chain allows it to work more efficiently with the gears. This investigation explores different effects of friction.

Materials

- CPO Energy Car and Track (including the sled)
- CPO Physics Stand
- CPO DataCollector and photogates
- Tongue depressor
- Large paper plate
- Tape

1 Control setup

The first kind of friction you will be investigating is air friction. You will begin by finding out how the car moves before you add extra air friction.

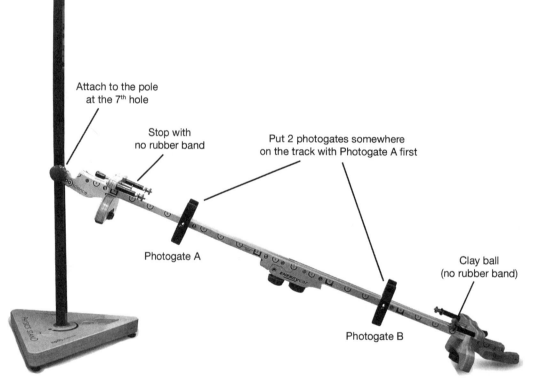

1. Set up the track as a long straight ramp as shown above.
2. Attach the track to the stand at the seventh hole from the bottom.
3. Place one photogate near the top of the track and one near the bottom of the track.
4. Put a steel ball in the middle pocket of the car.
5. Let the car roll down the ramp, and record the time from A to B.
6. Measure the distance between the photogates.
7. Use the distance to calculate the average speed of the car.
8. Repeat two more times, for a total of three trials.
9. Calculate the average speed from your three trials.

Table 1: Control speeds

Trial	Time A to B (s)	Distance between A and B (cm)	Speed (cm/s)
1			
2			
3			
		Average Speed	

 2 Create the "sail" car

A paper plate "sail" adds air friction (drag) to the car.

1. Tape a tongue depressor to the flag on the side of the car.

2. Tape a paper plate to the tongue depressor. Use enough tape to make sure it is securely attached.

3 Your hypothesis

a. Write a hypothesis that compares the speeds of the "sail car" and the normal car.

b. Explain the reasoning behind your hypothesis.

4 Do the experiment

1. The track and photogates should be set up as in part 1.
2. Put a steel ball in the middle pocket of the car.
3. Let the sail car roll down the ramp, and record the time from A to B.
4. Calculate the average speed of the car.
5. Repeat two more times, for a total of three trials.
6. Calculate the average speed from your three trials.

Table 2: Experimental speeds; sail car

Trial	Time A to B (s)	Distance between A and B (cm)	Speed (cm/s)
1			
2			
3			
		Average Speed	

5 Stop and think

a. Did your results confirm your hypothesis? Explain.

b. How did air friction affect the car's motion?

6 Applying what you have learned

a. Friction is a force that opposes motion. Explain where the friction force on the sail comes from.

b. How could you increase the air friction on the car? How could you decrease it?

c. Is the sail the only source of friction? Does the car have any friction forces acting on it other than air friction? Explain.

7 Setting up to measure rolling and sliding friction

Track set up

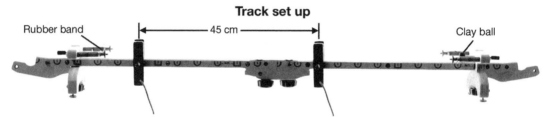

Rubber band · 45 cm · Clay ball

1. Set up the track so is exactly level. Put a clay ball on the stopper at one end of the track. Put a rubber band on the other end of the track. As you attach it, twist it once so it makes an *X*. You will be using the rubber band to launch the car and sled.

2. Adjust the stopper near at the launching end of the track so it is approximately 4 cm from the rubber band.

3. Place the sled on the track so the nose of the sled is touching the rubber band.

4. Place photogate A on the mark just ahead of the flag on the sled. The flag should not be blocking the photogate beam. Place photogate B 45 centimeters from photogate A.

8 Do the experiment

1. Launch the sled by resting your hand on the wooden track support and placing your index finger on the finger grip near the front of the sled. Practice a few times.

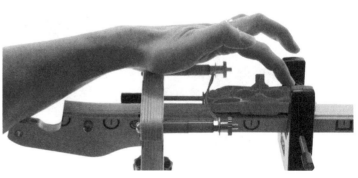

2. The sled should make it through both photogates. If it stops too soon, adjust the stopper so you can pull the rubber band back farther.

3. Record the time through each photogate and the time from photogate A to B.

4. Repeat for a total of three trials.

Table 3: Sliding friction data—sled

Trial	Time through A (s)	Time through B (s)	Time from A to B (s)	Speed through A (cm/s)	Speed through B (cm/s)	Acceleration (cm/s^2)
1						
2						
3						
					average	

5. The speed of the sled through photogate A is the width of the flag (1 cm) divided by the time through A. Calculate the speed through A. Repeat for photogate B.

6. Use the two speeds and the average time from A to B to calculate the acceleration. Then find the average acceleration.

7. Repeat steps 3 through 6 using the car instead of the sled.

Table 4: Rolling friction data—energy car

Trial	Time through A (s)	Time through B (s)	Time from A to B (s)	Speed through A (cm/s)	Speed through B (cm/s)	Acceleration (cm/s^2)
1						
2						
3						
					average	

9 Thinking about your data

a. Were your accelerations positive or negative. Why is this?

b. Which decelerated more, the sled or the car?

c. What does your answer to the previous question tell you about the rolling friction of the car compared to the sliding friction of the sled?

d. How could you increase the sliding friction between the sled or track? How could you decrease it?

e. How could you increase the rolling friction between the car and track? How could you decrease it?

f. Compare rolling friction, air friction, and sliding friction. Which do you think has the greatest effect on the car's motion? Which has the least effect?

6A Newton's First and Second Laws

What is the relationship between force and motion?

The relationships between force and motion are known as Newton's laws. These are among the most widely used relationships in all of physics. The first law explains what happens when there is *no* net force on an object, and the Second Law explains what happens when there *is* a net force. The two laws are closely related. We will focus in this investigation on what happens to the Energy Car's motion when you change the force and the mass separately. Both laws apply!

Materials

- CPO Energy Car and Track
- CPO DataCollector and 1 photogate
- Three same-size rubber bands
- Three steel marbles
- Electronic scale (or triple-beam balance

1 Making predictions

Newton's second law explains what happens to the acceleration of an object when you change the force applied or change the mass of the object. For this first part of the investigation you will use different amounts of force to launch the car. You will not measure the resulting acceleration, because you would have to measure it while the car is still being acted upon by the rubber band, and this is impossible. Instead, you will measure the *result* of the acceleration caused by the force of the rubber band. The *result* will be measured by looking at changes in the car's speed as it rolls along the track after the launch.

a. Make a prediction: What will happen to the speed of the car as the force gets larger?

2 Changing force with constant mass

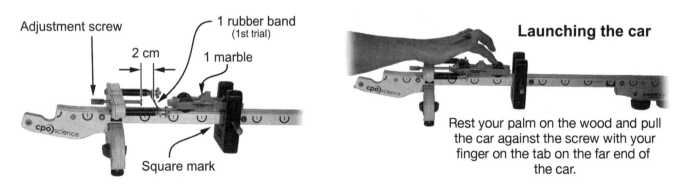

Adjustment screw | 1 rubber band (1st trial) | 1 marble | Square mark

2 cm

Launching the car

Rest your palm on the wood and pull the car against the screw with your finger on the tab on the far end of the car.

1. Set up the long straight track with a rubber band on one end and a clay ball on the other end. Adjust the screw so the rubber band deflects about 2 centimeters. Be sure to stretch the rubber band once or twice before using.

2. Put one photogate on the first square mark after the rubber band.

3. Put one marble in the center of the car. Use the screw to launch the car using the same deflection of the rubber band each time. This means the same force is applied to each launch. Try to get three launches with times that are within 0.0015 seconds. Average these times and record the result in Table 1.

4. Repeat the experiment with two and three rubber bands. Stretch before using!
5. Calculate the car's speed. Remember to use the tab width, 1.00 cm, for the distance.

Table 1: Changing force data

Number of rubber bands	Time through photogate (s)	Speed (cm/s)

3 Stop and think

a. During which portion of the car's motion is the rubber band affecting its speed?

b. Make a graph showing the speed of the car on the *y*-axis and the number of rubber bands on the *x*-axis. As the force was increased, what happened to the speed of the car?

c. Why was the same mass used for all trials (with different force)?

4 Changing mass with constant force

Use 1 rubber band to launch cars with 0, 1, 2, and 3 marbles.

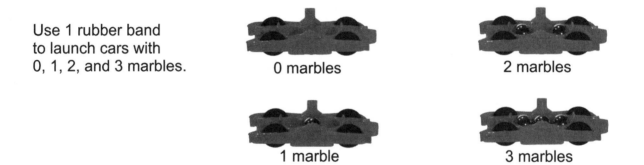

0 marbles

2 marbles

1 marble

3 marbles

1. Put a single rubber band on the launching end of the track. Stretch it before using. Leave the photogate in the same place as it was (on the first square mark after the rubber band).
2. With the screw in the same place, launch cars of four different masses. Record the times in Table 2.
3. Measure the mass of the car with zero, one, two, and three steel marbles.
4. Calculate the car's speed. Remember to use the tab width, 1.00 cm, for the distance.

Table 2: Changing mass data

Mass of car (g)	Time through photogate (s)	Speed (cm/s)

5 Applying what you have learned

a. Use Table 2 to graph the speed of the car (y) against the mass (x). Does your graph show a direct relationship or an inverse relationship?

b. Why did the speed change when the same launching force from the rubber band was applied to cars of different mass? How do your observations support your answer?

c. Newton's first law is often called "the law of inertia." How does this law apply to the car's motion when you changed the mass but kept the force constant?

d. Do you think the force applied to an object causes speed itself or causes changes in speed? Support your answer with at least one sentence of explanation for why you believe your answer is correct.

When an object's speed changes we say the object *accelerates*. Acceleration occurs whenever speed changes. To be precise, acceleration means the "change in speed divided by the change in time."

$$\text{Acceleration} = \frac{\text{change in speed}}{\text{change in time}}$$

e. Based on your experimental results, propose a mathematical relationship between the variables F (force), a (acceleration), and m (mass).

6 Fun challenge

Try this additional mini-experiment to see something interesting. You will launch the car with one rubber band and no marbles. Then you will launch the car with *two* rubberbands and *two* marbles in the car. This means you will double both the force and the mass at the same time. How will the times compare? Make a prediction.

1. Launch the car with one rubber band. Stretch the rubber band before using. There should be no marbles in the car. Get three times that are within 0.0015 seconds of each other and average. Record the time average in Table 3.

2. Launch the car with two rubber bands (be sure to stretch first) and two marbles (placed in front and back of car). Get three times that are within 0.0015 seconds of each other and average. Record the time average in Table 3.

Table 3: Doubling Force and Mass

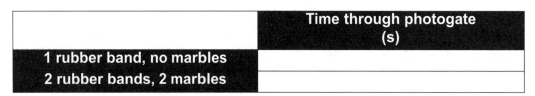

	Time through photogate (s)
1 rubber band, no marbles	
2 rubber bands, 2 marbles	

a. What do you notice about the times?

b. Explain your result. How does it compare to your prediction?

6B Newton's Third Law

What happens when equal and opposite forces are exerted on a pair of Energy Cars?

When you apply a force to throw a ball you also feel the force of the ball against your hand. That is because all forces come in pairs called *action* and *reaction*. This is Newton's third law of motion. There can never be a single force (action) without its opposite (reaction) partner. Action and reaction forces always act in opposite directions on two different objects. You can set up two Energy Cars to study Newton's third law.

Materials

- CPO Energy Car and Track
- CPO DataCollector and 2 photogates
- One rubber band
- Two steel marbles
- CPO Energy Car Link

1 Setting up and starting the experiment

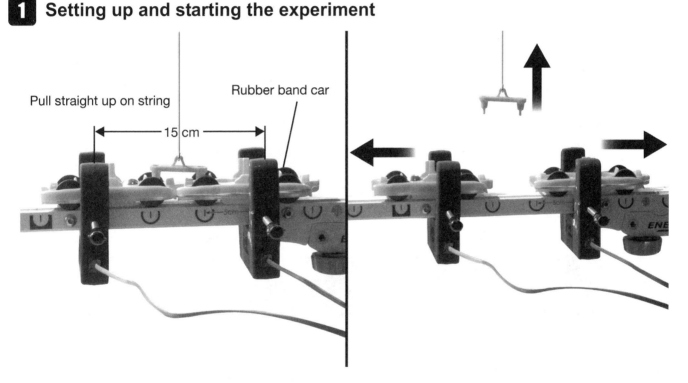

Pull straight up on string · Rubber band car · 15 cm

1. Set up the long straight track with a ball of clay on each stop. Use the bubble level to set the track level.
2. Place one steel marble in each car, and wrap one car with a rubber band.
3. Place two photogates 15 centimeters apart as shown in the photo.
4. Place the two cars "nose to notch" between the photogates.
5. Squeeze the cars together and attach them with the Energy Car link.
6. Center the attached car pair between the photogates so each is about to break the photogate's beam, but do not actually break the beam. Check that both photogate indicator lights are still green. Make sure all four wheels of both cars are on the track.
7. With a *very quick* upward motion, pull the link *straight up* and out from the cars. ***CAUTION: Wear eyeglasses or safety glasses to avoid injury.***
8. Observe the time through each photogate. Repeat several times.

2 Thinking about what you observed

a. What caused the two cars to move when you took out the link?

b. According to Newton's third law, the cars experienced equal and opposite forces. How can you tell this is true by looking at the time through each photogate?

c. If one car was twice the mass of the other, would the cars still experience equal and opposite forces? Why or why not?

3 Changing the masses

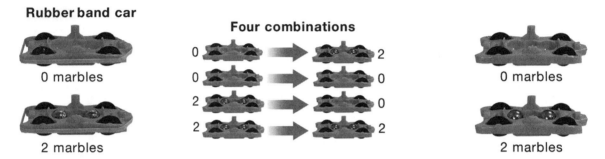

Rubber band car

0 marbles

2 marbles

Four combinations

0 marbles

2 marbles

NOTE: Adding two steel marbles to the Energy Car doubles its mass.

1. Try the experiment with the four combinations of mass shown above. Take the average of three trials for each and record your data in Table 1. *CAUTION: Wear eyeglasses or safety glasses to avoid injury.*

2. Calculate the average speed for each trial and record in Table 1.

Table 1: Energy Car action/reaction data

Marble pairings for connected cars		Time through photogate (s)		Speed (cm/s)	
A	B	A	B	A	B
0 marbles	2 marbles				
0 marbles	0 marbles				
2 marbles	0 marbles				
2 marbles	2 marbles				

4 Applying what you have learned

a. How does the speed of each car pair compare when masses are equal?

b. How does the speed of each car compare when one of the pair has twice the mass?

c. Explain how your speed data supports the idea that there are equal and opposite action and reaction forces acting on the cars.

d. If the action and reaction forces are equal in strength, when the cars separate, why does one car move at a different speed than the other car when the masses are unequal? (*Hint*: The answer involves the Second Law of Motion.)

7A Energy in a System

How is energy related to motion?

A system is a group of objects that interact with each other. Energy measures the ability of a system to change itself or other systems. This investigation is about systems and energy.

Materials

- CPO Energy Car and Track
- CPO DataCollector and 1 photogate
- Rubber band
- CPO Physics Stand

1 Making a system

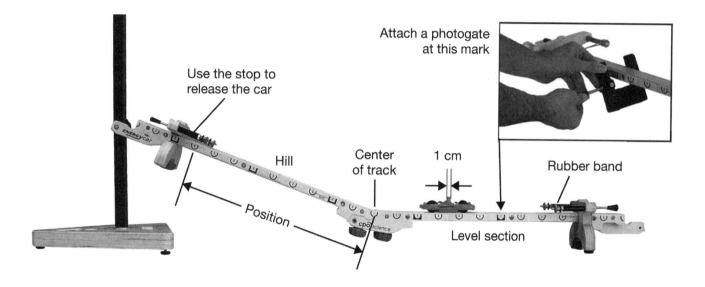

1. Set up the track with a steep incline and a level section as shown above.
2. Place a rubber band on the thumb screws at the bottom of the track.
3. Attach a photogate near the middle of the level section at the spot marked with a square.

2 Collecting data

1. Measure the distance between the center of the track and the stopper at the top of the track as shown above. Record this distance (the drop position) in Table 1.
2. Hold the car against the stopper and release it without giving it a push.
3. Record the time through the photogate before and after the car bounces off the rubber band. You will have to use the memory button to get the time before the bounce.
4. Calculate the speed of the car before and after it bounces. The speed is the width of the flag (1 centimeter) divided by the time it takes the flag to pass through the beam of the photogate. Record the speeds in the table.
5. Move the wooden track stop part of the way down the hill. Measure the distance from the center of the track to the metal stopper.

6. Drop the car as you did before. Measure the times and calculate the speeds.

7. Repeat for several drop positions along the hill.

Table I: Speed data

Drop position (cm from center)	Before bouncing		After bouncing	
	Time through photogate (s)	Speed (cm/s)	Time through photogate (s)	Speed (cm/s)

3 Thinking about what you observed

a. How high did the car climb up the hill after bouncing? Did it go higher, lower, or the same height as the drop position?

b. How is the drop position related to the speed of the car the first time it passes through the photogate (before bouncing)?

c. How do the speeds before bouncing compare to the speeds after bouncing? Is this the same for all five trials?

d. What could you do to make the car travel farther up the hill after bouncing?

e. In one paragraph, explain how the answers to a, b, c, and d are explained using the idea of energy.

7B Conservation of Energy

What limits how much a system may change?

A car launched up the hill at a given speed will never go higher than a certain point. A car rolling downhill will only reach a certain speed. Why? The answer is that nature keeps an exact balance of energy. Speed uses one form of energy and height uses another. This investigation explores the exchange of energy.

Materials

- CPO Energy Car and Track
- CPO Physics Stand
- CPO DataCollector and 2 photogates
- Electronic scale (or triple-beam balance)
- Clay
- String
- Meter stick

1 Energy exchange from potential to kinetic

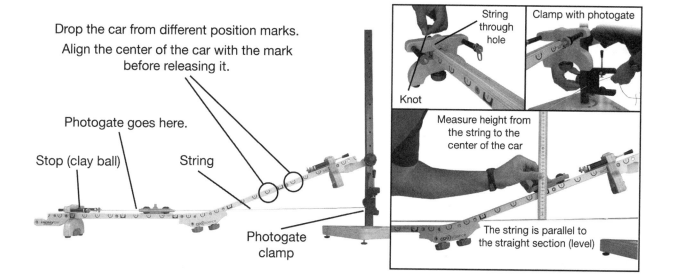

1. Set up the track with the steeper hill and a level section. Make the level section as level as you can. Attach a photogate at the bottom of the hill on the level section.

2. Thread a string though the hole in the lower stop and use a photogate to clamp the other end of the string to the stand. Adjust the string so it is parallel to the level section of the track.

3. Drop the car from each 5-centimeter mark on the hill and measure the speed with the photogate. Measure the height of the car from the string to the center of the car.

4. Measure the mass of the car and record it in the table.

Table 1: Height and speed data

Drop Height (m)	Mass of car (kg)	Photogate time (s)	Speed (m/s)

2   Thinking about what you observed

a. Graph the speed of the car versus the height.

b. What does the graph tell you about the relationship between speed and drop height?

3   Analyzing the data

a. Use the formula for potential energy to fill in the second column of Table 2.

b. Use energy conservation to derive a formula for the speed of the car in terms of the energy it has at the start. (*Hint*: Your formula should include only two variables, velocity and height.)

c. Use the formula you just derived to fill in the column for the predicted speed of the car.

d. Plot the curve for the predicted speed on the same graph as you made in part 2a above.

Table 2: Energy data and predicted speeds

Drop Height (m)	Potential energy (J)	Predicted speed (m/s)	Measured speed from Table 1 (m/s)

4 Thinking about what you observed

a. Explain the relationship between speed and height using the idea of energy conservation.

b. Explain any difference between the predicted and measured speeds. If there is a difference, what does it tell you about the energy of the car as it rolls along the track?

c. Let the car roll downhill, bounce off the rubber band, and go back up hill again. Does it reach the same height as it was dropped from? Explain why or why not using the idea of energy conservation.

d. Challenge experiment. Use a rubber band to launch the car uphill so it goes through the photogate with the same speed as it had going down. You won't be able to get it precisely the same, but come as close as you can. If the speeds are the same, the car's kinetic energy is also the same. Does the car reach the same height on the hill that it was dropped from to get the same speed in part 1? Explain any difference using the idea of energy.

8A Manipulating Forces

How do simple machines work?

Would you believe that a small child could lift an elephant? It can be done by building a simple machine out of ropes and pulleys. In this investigation, you will learn how to build machines that allow you to lift large weights with small forces. You will also learn how to measure the input and output forces of these machines.

Materials
- CPO Ropes and Pulleys kit
- Spring scales (2.5, 5, and 10 N)

1 Setting up the ropes and pulleys

Throughout this investigation you will be measuring forces with a spring scale. To get the most accurate readings, always use a spring scale with the smallest maximum force without going over the limit of the scale. For example, using a 2.5-N scale to measure a force of 1 N will give you a more accurate result than using a 10 N-scale.

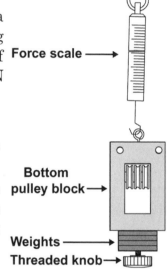

1. Attach four weights to the bottom pulley block. Use a spring scale to obtain the weight of the bottom block after you attach the weights. Record the weight of the bottom block: _____ N

2. The output force of this simple machine will be used to lift the bottom block. Attach the top block near the top of the physics stand. The yellow string can be clipped to either the top block or the bottom block. Start with the yellow string clipped to the bottom block.

Why all the strings?

- The yellow string will be used to move the bottom pulley block with the weights up and down. You will pull on one end of the yellow string. There is a clip at the other end of the yellow string for attaching to the pulley blocks.

- The yellow string may have several strands that directly support the bottom pulley block. These are called the supporting strands.

- The red string is the safety string. It holds up the bottom block while you rearrange the yellow string.

Safety Tip: Don't pull sideways or you can tip the stand over!

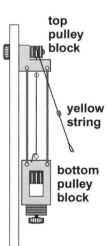

2 Investigating the ropes and pulleys

1. Clip the end of the yellow string to the bottom pulley block. Pass the string over the middle pulley of the top block. Use the marker stop (cord stop) to hook the force scale to the string.

2. Measure the force it takes to slowly lift the bottom pulley block.

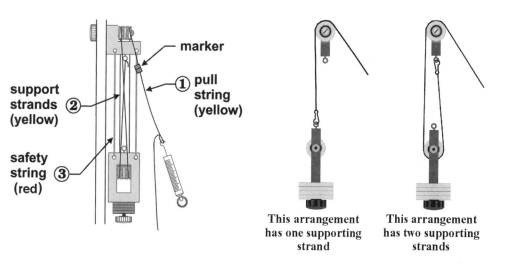

This arrangement has one supporting strand

This arrangement has two supporting strands

1. This arrangement has one strand supporting the bottom pulley block. Record the force in the table below in the row corresponding to one strand.

2. Unclip the yellow string from the bottom block and pass it around the middle pulley in the bottom block as shown in the picture above. Clip the yellow string to the top block.

3. Move the marker and measure the force it takes to slowly lift the bottom pulley block. Record this force in the row for two supporting strands.

4. Rearrange the yellow strings so that you get three, four, five, and six supporting strands. Measure and record the force it takes to lift the bottom pulley block for each new setup.

Table 1: Force to lift pulley block

Number of support strands	Force to lift bottom pulley block (N)
1	
2	
3	
4	
5	
6	

a. As you add more supporting strands, what happens to the force needed to lift the bottom block?

b. How does the amount of input force required to lift the bottom block change with the string arrangement? Can you identify a mathematical rule?

What did you learn?

a. How are all simple machines alike? How is a lever different from a machine made with ropes and pulleys? (Think about input and output force.)

b. What is the relationship between the number of strings on the ropes and pulleys, and the amount of input force required to lift the bottom block?

8B Work

How can a machine multiply forces?

Simple machines such as ropes and pulleys and levers can create large output forces from small input forces. In this investigation you will explore the nature of work and come to an interesting conclusion that is true for all machines.

Materials

- Top and bottom pulley block
- CPO Physics Stand
- Four weights
- Spring scale (0–10 N)
- Yellow string with clip and cord stop
- Knobs (one threaded, one regular)

Setting up the experiment

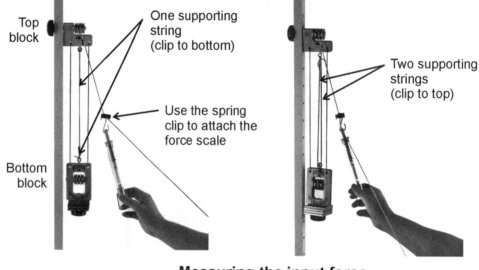

Top
block

One supporting
string
(clip to bottom)

Use the spring
clip to attach the
force scale

Bottom
block

Two supporting
strings
(clip to top)

Measuring the input force

1. Attach four weights to the bottom pulley block. Use a spring scale to measure the weight of the block in newtons. Record this value in column five of Table 1. This value is the *output force* and does not change in the experiment.

2. Using a ropes and pulleys set, clip the end of the yellow string to the bottom block. Pass the string over the middle pulley of the top block as shown.

3. Use the plastic cord stop to mark where the string leaves the top pulley.

4. Lift the bottom block a fixed height (h). The holes in the stand are 5 centimeters apart and you can use the holes as a height reference. Use at least 20 centimeters as your lifting height.

5. Measure how much string length (L) you must pull to lift the block the chosen distance. You can measure this using the cord stops and a ruler.

6. Using the spring scale, measure the force needed to lift the block in newtons (N). This is the *input force*.

7. Record the input force, height difference for the block (h), and string length (L) in Table 1.

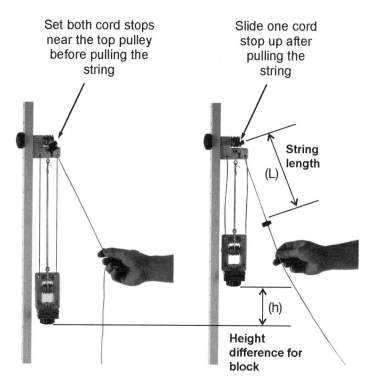

Measuring string length and height difference

8. Unclip the string from the bottom block, and clip it onto the underside of the top block. Pass the string around the middle pulley on the bottom block, and loop it up over the middle pulley of the top block as shown. Pull the string to lift the bottom block the same height (h) that you used for the first set-up. Measure the string length (L) that you must pull the string. Record the values in the second row of Table 1.

9. Rearrange the yellow string so it passes over 3, 4, 5, and 6 pulleys. You should always be pulling down on the string to raise the block, and you should always lift the bottom block the same height.

10. For each combination, record the input force and string length (L).

Table 1: Force and distance data

Number of pulleys	Height difference for block	String length	Input force	Output force (weight of block)	Work done on block (work output)	Work done by you (work input)
	(m)	(m	(N)	(N)	(J)	(J)
1						
2						
3						
4						
5						
6						

2 Analyzing the data

a. Calculate the work done on the block. This work is equal to the output force (weight of the block in newtons) times the height difference. The work done on the block should be the same for all configurations of the strings because the weight of the block and the height it was lifted did not change.

b. Next, calculate the work you did as you pulled on the string to lift the block in each trial. Your work is found by multiplying the input force by the string length.

c. As the number of supprting strings increased, what happened to the input force needed to lift the block?

d. As the number of supprting strings increased, what happened to the length of string that was pulled to raise the block?

e. As the number of supprting strings increased, what happened to the amount of work you had to do (work input) to lift the block?

f. Use your answers to the last three questions to explain the meaning of the statement, "Nature does not give things away for free."

9A Levers

How does a lever work?

How can you lift up a car—or even an elephant—all by yourself? One way is with a lever. The lever is an example of a simple machine. What variables can you change to make a lever do things like lift a car or an elephant?

Materials

- CPO Lever
- CPO Physics Stand
- Steel Weights
- String loops
- Short thumbscrew
- Knob

1 Setting up the lever

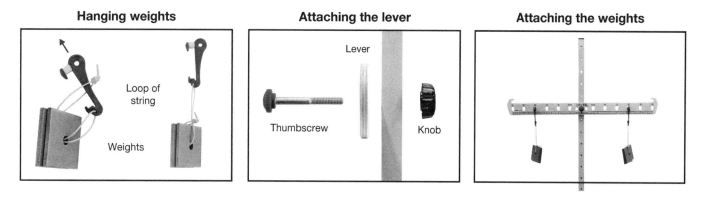

Hanging weights   **Attaching the lever**   **Attaching the weights**

1. Attach weights to hangers. You can put more than one weight on a single string.
2. Slide the loop of string through the hole in the weight.
3. Pull the knotted end through the loop itself and tighten by pulling on the knot.
4. Slide a short thumbscrew through the hole in the middle of the lever.
5. Attach the lever to the physics stand by sliding the short thumbscrew through one of the holes on the front of the stand.
6. Use a knob to secure the lever and thumbscrew onto the back of the stand.
7. The knob should be tightened snugly on the thumbscrew and press lightly against the back of the stand.
8. The weights can be hung from the lever by inserting the hanger key into the numbered key holes along the lever. Also, the hanger key may be clipped on to the top of the lever.

2 Levers in equilibrium

a. The lever is in equilibrium when all the weights on one side balance all the weights on the other side. Hang the weights as shown below. Does the lever balance? (*Note*: When the lever is in equilibrium, the lever arm is not necessarily perfectly horizontal.)

b. What variables can be changed to balance a lever?

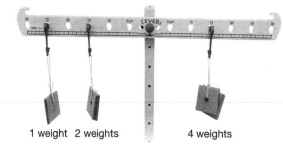

1 weight 2 weights   4 weights

3 Trying different combinations to balance the lever

Make different combinations of weights and positions that balance. Use the chart below to write down the numbers of weights you put in each position. If you want to conduct more than four trials, write your results on a separate sheet of paper

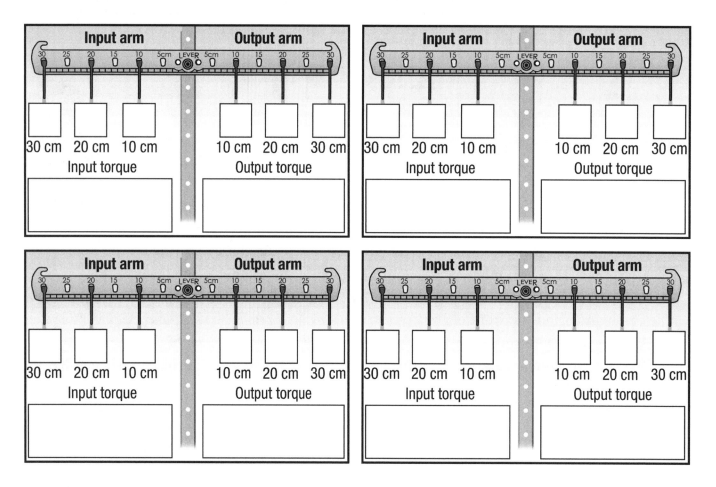

4 Determine the mathematical rule for equilibrium

a. Draw a lever and label these parts: fulcrum, input arm, output arm, input force, and output force.

b. Using the data in the chart above, determine a mathematical rule for levers in equilibrium. Use these variables: input force, output force, length of input arm, and length of output arm. First, make some calculations, then write your rule as an equation. The equation will have two variables on each side, with an equal sign in the middle.

5 What did you learn?

a. There are two ratios that can be used to determine mechanical advantage in levers. What are the two equations? What is the relationship between the two equations?

b. What could you do to the input side of a lever to increase the amount of output force? (*Hint*: There are two different things you could do.)

9B Levers and the Human Body

What types of levers does your body have?

Arms, legs, fingers, toes, the jaw, even the head and neck work like levers. Contracting and extending muscles provide the force to move our levers. Our joints are the fulcrums around which these levers pivot and move. Our bones are the levers themselves. In this investigation, you will look at the human arm and examine how it works like a lever.

Materials

- CPO Lever
- CPO Physics Stand
- Force scales
- Steel Weights

1 The human body

Let your left arm hang down by your side. Place the hand of your right arm into the inner part of your elbow. Slowly lift your left arm (palm up) until it is level with the floor. Feel that tissue in your elbow tightening up with your right hand? That is the connective tissue that joins your biceps muscle to the bones of your forearm, the radius and ulna. We can use the physics stand and the lever to make a model of the human arm and measure the forces involved when we lift something.

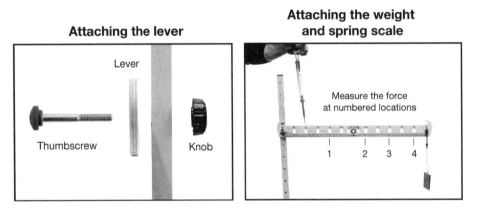

Use what you have learned about lever terms to record your answers in the appropriate columns in Table 1. You will need to include units for each entry you record.

1. Attach the lever to the stand, but this time use the hole on the left-most side of the lever. Use one of the short thumbscrews. Do not tighten the knob all the way. Leave a little room so the lever can still pivot.

2. Use a loop of string to hang one weight on the right-most side of the lever. Measure its weight in newtons using a force scale (the green one). Record it in Table 1.

3. Measure this distance from the pivot point to the position of the hanging weight and record it in Table 1

4. Measure the distance from the pivot point to the next hole on the lever. This is where we will apply force to lift the lever. Record the distance in Table 1.

Table 1: Input and output data

Output force (N)	Input arm (cm)	Output arm (cm)	Mechanical advantage	Predicted input force (N)	Measured input force (N)

2 The lever arm model

a. Calculate the mechanical advantage of the lever. Record your result in Table 1.

b. Based on the mechanical advantage, predict the force required to lift the lever up and keep it horizontal. Record it in Table 1.

c. The connective tissue in your arm attaches your biceps to your forearm at the inside of the elbow. Since the muscle provides the lifting force close to the elbow joint, we will provide the lifting force for the lever close to the pivot point. Hook a force scale (the red one) to the lever at the hole just to the right of the pivot point and lift up until the lever is horizontal. Keep it horizontal and record the force needed to keep it there in Table 1.

d. How does your predicted value match your measured value? Why do you think this is?

e. Test your reason why the values are different. What did you find?

f. Draw a diagram showing how the lever setup models an arm lifting a weight.

10A Pure Substance or Mixture?

How can observing the melting point identify a pure substance or a mixture?

Matter can be divided into two main categories: mixtures and pure substances. *Pure substances* are homogeneous throughout. They have the same chemical properties no matter where the sample is obtained or how large the sample is. *Mixtures* are combinations of two or more substances, with each substance retaining its chemical identity.

In this lab, you will obtain four test tubes containing unknown solids. The melting point, or the temperature at which the matter changes from a solid to a liquid, will be measured to determine if the matter is a mixture or a pure substance. Any given pure substance will always have the same melting point. Pure substances usually melt over a small temperature range while mixtures often melt over a very wide temperature range.

Materials

- Four test tubes with unknowns
- Hot plate
- Stirring rod
- One 250-mL beaker
- Water
- Safety goggles
- Lab apron
- CPO DataCollector
- Temperature Sensor

WARNING — This lab contains chemicals that may be harmful if misused. Read cautions on individual containers carefully. Not to be used by children except under adult supervision.

 1 **Thinking about what you will do**

Why do you think a pure substance will melt over a smaller range of temperatures than a mixture?

2 **Doing the experiment**

1. Attach the temperature probe to the DataCollector and set it to meter mode for the entire experiment. Record your sample label (A–D) in Table 1.

2. Add approximately 200 mL of cold water to a 250 mL beaker. Place the beaker on the hot plate, and turn the hot plate on to medium.

3. Place the first sample into the water bath and have one group member hold the temperature probe about halfway in the water.

4. Another group member should stir the contents of the test tube with a stirring rod as it heats.

5. Watch the contents of the test tube carefully. At the moment the contents begin to melt, measure and record the temperature in Table 1.

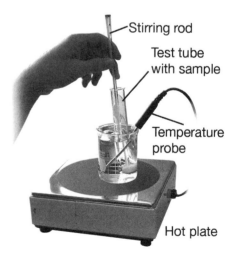

Stirring rod

Test tube with sample

Temperature probe

Hot plate

6. Continue stirring the contents of the test tube and watching the contents until the entire sample is liquefied. Once the last solid particle melts, measure and record the temperature in Table 1.

7. Return your sample to your instructor.

8. Pour out the hot water in the beaker.

9. Repeat steps 2–8 for each of the remaining samples. Be sure to start with a fresh sample of cold water for the water bath.

Table 1: Melting data

Sample label	Temperature melting starts (°C)	Temperature melting ends (°C)
A		
B		
C		
D		

3 Analyzing the data

a. How would you know which test tubes contain pure substances and which contain mixtures?

b. If a sample contained 1 gram of pure substance A and another test tube contained 4 grams of pure substance A, how would the melting points differ? How would the experiment differ?

c. Name two possible sources of error for this experiment. How would they affect your data?

4 Applying your knowledge

A white, waxy substance is heated in a test tube. Part of the substance melts almost immediately, and is poured off into a seperate test tube after a minute of further heating, leaving a little more than half or the original sample behind.

a. Explain why you think the original sample was a pure substance or a mixture.

b. Is the melted portion that was poured off a pure substance or a mixture? What evidence do you base your answer on?

c. Can you be sure that the remaining portion left behind in the test tube is a pure substance or a mixture? How could you know for sure?

10B Determining Freezing/Melting Point

How do you determine the freezing/melting point of cetyl alcohol?

A cooling/heating curve is a plot of temperature versus time. It illustrates the effect on a substance as the temperature decreases/increases through a phase change. In this experiment, you will study the effects of cooling and heating cetyl alcohol through a phase chage. The data will be recorded using a DataCollector and then plotted on graphs. Based on your observations, measurements, and graphs you will be able to determine the freezing/melting point of cetyl alcohol.

Materials

- CPO DataCollector
- Temperature Sensor
- Test tube, 22 × 150 mm
- Cetyl alcohol
- Hot water
- Safety goggles
- Lab apron
- Heat resistant gloves or hot mitts
- 250 mL beaker
- 400–600 mL beaker

> **WARNING** — This lab contains chemicals that may be harmful if misused. Read cautions on individual containers carefully. Not to be used by children except under adult supervision.

1 Thinking about what you will do

a. The cetyl alcohol you will be using is a pure substance. What do you expect to observe in terms of the temperature range for the freezing/melting point?

b. Suppose your cetyl alcohol sample became contanimated with another substance. How would this affect the freezing/melting point?

2 Melting cetyl alcohol

1. Fill a 250-mL beaker with cold water.

2. Fill a 400- to 600-mL beaker with approximately 250 mL of hot water (75–80°C).

3. Measure out approximately 4–5 grams of cetyl alcohol in a test tube.

4. Measure the temperature of the hot water to make sure it is within the range in step 2.

5. Quickly immerse the temperature probe into the cold water. Then remove and dry it making sure it is cooled to room temperature.

6. Make sure the DataCollector is in data collection mode. Place the temperature probe into the test tube and put the test tube containing the solid into the water bath and press start on the DataCollector. View the experiment in graph mode.

7. Stir the solid vigorously with the temperature probe.

8. Continue to stir as long as some solid remains.

9. Once all of the material is liquid, stop and store the experiment. Record the experiment name assigned by the DataCollector.

10. Leave the sample in the warm water for use in Part 4.

3 Stop and think

a. Predict the effect of sample size on the melting/freezing point.

b. Describe and carefully sketch the shape of the graph from Part 2.

4 Freezing cetyl alcohol

1. Observe the cetyl alcohol in the test tube to make sure it is still all liquid. If some solid has formed, pour out the water in the warm beaker and add more warm water.

2. Remove the test tube from the warm beaker and start a new experiment on the DataCollector.

3. Stir the liquid vigorously with the temperature probe as the solid begins to form.

4. Continue to stir until all of the liquid turns into a solid. (*Note*: If you need to repeat any part of the experiment, you may reuse your sample.)

5. When you are finished recording data, return your sample of cetyl alcohol to your teacher.

6. Record the name of the experiment from the DataCollector in your notebook.

5 Thinking about what you observed

a. Describe and carefully sketch the graph from Part 4.

b. Referring to both of your graphs, determine the melting and freezing point of cetyl alcohol. Are they the same? Should they be?

c. Based on the shapes of your curves, which data do you think is more reliable: the heating or cooling data? Why do you think this is so?

d. What is happening to the molecules of cetyl alcohol during the diagonal portions of the heating curve? What about the plateau?

e. Your graph from Part 2 shows that during a change from solid to liquid, the temperature stays the same. Explain why the temperature does not increase, even though energy is being added.

11A Temperature and Heat

How are temperature and heat related?

Hot and cold are familiar sensations. What happens when something hot comes in contact with something cold? Think about putting some ice cubes in a drink. Things don't remain the same, changes occur, and these changes have to do with the movement of energy from one material to the other. This investigation will explore the difference between temperature and thermal energy, and how the movement of thermal energy relates to the concept of heat.

Materials

- Temperature probe
- CPO DataCollector
- Electronic scale (or triple-beam balance)
- Aluminum cube from density kit
- Three 12-oz. foam cups
- Ice
- Hot water
- Tongs
- 100-mL graduated cylinder
- Safety goggles
- Lab apron

1 Making a prediction

Suppose you mix equal masses of water. One sample is at 0°C and the other is at 50°C. What do you think the final temperature of the mixture will be? Why?

2 Mixing hot and cold water

1. You will need three 12-ounce foam cups for this experiment. Label two of the cups as follows: *HOT* and *COLD*.

2. Prepare an ice bath by placing approximately 250 mL of water in the unlabeled cup and add four or five ice cubes.

3. Connect the temperature probe to the DataCollector and select Meter mode for this experiment.

4. Place the temperature probe in the ice water bath.

5. Use a graduated cylinder to measure 100 mL of very hot tap water. Pour the hot water into the hot cup.

6. Use a graduated cylinder to measure 100 mL of the ice water. Pour the cold water into the cold cup.

7. Place the temperature probe into the cold cup, wait until the reading stabilizes and record the temperature in Table 1.

8. Place the temperature probe into the hot cup. Wait until the reading stabilizes and record the temperature in Table 1.

9. Immediately pour the hot water into the cold water. This is the mixture.

10. Stir well using the temperature probe and measure the final temperature (when it has stabilized). Record your data in Table 1.

11. Do not throw away your ice water. You will be using it again in the second part of the investigation.

Table 1: Temperature data for mixing equal masses of water

Cold water temp. (°C)	Hot water temp. (°C)	Mixture temp. (°C)

3 Thinking about what you observed

a. Did the result of your experiment agree with your prediction (within 3 degrees)? Discuss why the temperature value may not have matched exactly your predicted value.

b. How do you think your results would have been different if you had used more hot water than cold water, instead of equal masses?

4 Making another prediction

Suppose you mix equal masses of cold water and hot metal. Will the final temperature follow the same pattern as the experiment you did in Part 2? Explain your answer.

5 Combining hot metal and cold water

1. Find the mass of the aluminum cube and record in Table 2.
2. Connect the temperature probe to the DataCollector and select meter mode for this experiment.
3. Place the temperature probe in the ice water bath that was left from Part 2 of the experiment.
4. Place the aluminum cube in a foam cup and cover it with very hot tap water. Let the aluminum cube stay in the hot water for several minutes so it gets warm.
5. Measure out a mass of water from the ice water bath that is equal to the mass of the aluminum cube and pour it into a foam cup. Record the mass of the cold water in Table 2. Make sure there is no ice in the foam cup of cold water.
6. Move the temperature probe from the ice water bath to the cup of cold water and record the temperature of the cold water in Table 2.
7. Record the temperature of the hot water and aluminum cube just before putting the cube in the cup of cold water. Record the value in Table 2.
8. Use the tongs to put the aluminum cube in the foam cup containing the cold water.
9. Stir the mixture with the temperature probe.
10. Record the temperature of the cold water and metal cube when the temperature has stabilized. Do not wait longer than 1 minute to measure the temperature. Record this value in Table 2.

Table 2: Temperature data for combining water and metal

Metal mass (g)	Metal temp. before mix (°C)	Cold water mass (g)	Cold water temp. before mix (°C)	Mixture temp. (°C)

6 **Thinking about what you observed**

a. Why didn't the temperature of the water and aluminum mixture come out halfway between the temperature of the cold water and hot aluminum cube, even though you mixed equal masses?

b. Explain what is happening between the aluminum cube and water in terms of temperature and energy.

c. How much energy does it take to raise the temperature of one gram of aluminum by 1°C compared to raising the temperature of one gram of water by 1°C? (Look up this value.) Relate your answer back to your experimental results.

d. Heat and temperature are related, but they are not the same thing. According to your results, what does the concept of heat energy take into account that temperature does not?

11B The Specific Heat of a Metal

How can you use specific heat to identity an unknown metal sample?

If you have ever walked barefoot on a concrete walkway or street during a hot and sunny day, you have felt its warmth on your feet. In fact, the thermal energy transferred to your feet may send you retreating to the grass or even a swimming pool. Why is the temperature of the concrete so different compared to the temperature of the soil or the swimming pool? Even though the sunlight shines on all three surfaces, it is easier to raise the temperature of concrete compared to the water in a swimming pool. A hot summer day may only raise the temperature in a pool by 1 or 2 degrees.

In this investigation, you will use a calorimeter, the specific heat of water, and the law of conservation of energy to determine the specific heat of a sample of copper and two unknown metal samples.

Materials

- CPO DataCollector
- Temperature probe
- Three foam cups (with or without lids)
- Electronic scale (or triple-beam balance)
- Safety goggles
- Lab apron
- Metal samples (from CPO Density Cubes kit): copper and two unknown samples
- Hot water
- Tongs

1 Doing the experiement

1. Place your sample of copper on the balance and record its mass in Table 1.
2. Make a calorimeter by nesting two foam cups.
3. Pour about 150 mL of room-temperature water into the calorimeter. Use the balance to measure and record the mass of the water you add to the calorimeter (dsensity of water = 1g/mL). (*Note*: Make sure there is sufficient water in the calorimeter to submerge your metal samples *completely*.)
4. Fill a styrofoam cup 2/3 with hot water.
5. Place your sample of copper into the cup with hot water. Allow the copper sample to sit in the water for about a minute so it will get warmed by the hot water.
6. Use the temperature probe to measure the temperature of the hot water, and record this temperature once it stabilizes as the initial temperature of the metal in Table 1.
7. Place the temperature probe in the calorimeter. When the temperature stabilizes record it as the initial temperature of water. Leave the temperature probe in the calorimeter.
8. Use the tongs to remove the copper from the hot water and place the copper into the calorimeter. Try to transfer as little hot water as possible into the calorimeter when moving the copper. Go as quickly as possible but do not spill any hot water.
9. Once the temperature stabilizes, record the final temperature in Table 1.
10. Repeat steps 1–9 with each unknown metal provided by your teacher. You may be asked to conduct two trials with your unknown samples, if time allows.

Table 1: Mass and temperature data

	Copper	Unknown Metal #1	Unknown Metal #2
Mass of Metal (g)			
Mass of Water in Calorimeter (g)			
Initial Temperature of Water (°C)			
Initial Temperature of Metal (°C)			
Final Temperature of Mixture (°C)			

2   Processing the data

a. Calculate the temperature change of the water.

b. Calculate the temperature change of the metal.

c. Calculate the heat gained by the water using the equation below.

> **HEAT EQUATION**
>
> $$E = mC_p (T_2 - T_1)$$

Where: E = thermal energy (Joules) lost or gained by the water in the calorimeter
m = original mass of the measured water in the calorimeter
C_p = specific heat of water (4.184 J/g°C)
$T_2 - T_1$ = change in temperature of the water (also referred to as ΔT)

d. The amount of energy released by the metal is equal to the energy absorbed by the water. Knowing the value of E for the metal, calculate the specific heat (C_p) of the metal. (Remember, since the energy is being released by the metal, change the sign of E from answer 3 to use for 4).

e. Identify your unknown metal(s) by comparing your calculated value of its specific heat to known specific heat values of common metals provided by your teacher.

f. Calculate the percent error for your unknown sample(s).

3 Thinking about what you observed

a. What did you determine was the identity of your unknown metal(s)?

b. Looking at your data/class data, were the experimental values too high or too low? Based on the experimental procedure, give an explanation for your observations.

c. How does the law of conservation of energy allows us to make the calculations needed to determine the specific heat of the mystery metal?

d. The second unknown metal sample you tested is an alloy containing up to 80% of one of the other two metals you tested. The specific heat of this alloy should be almost the same as *one* of the other two metals. According to your results, which metal makes up 80% of the second unknown metal?

e. Water has a high specific heat. How does the fact that humans are largely made up of water help us regulate our body temperature?

12A Mystery Material

How do solids and liquids differ?

Review, in your mind, what you know about solids and liquids. You know, for example, that liquids do not keep their shape. They flow. Solids do not flow, they keep their shape. Consider the possibility of a material that is able to act like both a solid and a liquid. Could that be? In this investigation, you will not only consider the possibility, but actually play with such a material.

Materials

- Wax paper or small plastic bowls
- Mystery material

1 Doing the experiment

1. Your teacher will give you a sample of mystery material on a piece of wax paper or in a small plastic bowl.

2. Feel it. Smell it. Look at it. Use your senses to make as many observations as you can. Write down your observations in Table 1.

Table 1: Observations about the mystery material

1.	7.
2.	8.
3.	9.
4.	10.
5.	11.
6.	12.

2 Thinking about what you observed

a. What happens when you squeeze the mystery material and when you release it?

b. How does this material mimic some of the properties of solids and liquids?

c. The mystery material is made of only two ingredients—cornstarch and water. Using your answer from step 1, what do you think is happening to the cornstarch and water when you squeeze it and let go? Or when you hit it quickly or stick your finger slowly into it?

d. A colloidal suspension is a suspension of tiny particles of one substance in a medium of another substance. (The suspension remains intact indefinitely because it is unaffected by gravity.) Based on your observations and the first part of this definition, is the cornstarch and water mixture a colloidal suspension?

3 **Stop and Think**

a. How is the cornstarch and water mixture similar to quicksand?

b. Why does a substance that acts as both a solid and a liquid seem unusual?

c. Can you think of any common material/products that might act as both a solid and a liquid?

12B Buoyancy

Can you make a clay boat?

A solid material will float if it is less dense than the liquid in which it is immersed, and sink if it is denser than the liquid. You may have noticed, however, that ships are often made of steel, which is obviously denser than water. So how does a steel boat float? In this investigation you will experiment with modeling clay to discover how and why boats can be made of materials that are denser than water.

Materials

- Stick of clay (1/2 stick can be used as well)
- Centimeter ruler
- Displacement tank
- 250-mL beaker for overflow
- Water
- Paper towels, sponges
- 100-mL graduated cylinder
- Balance
- Disposable cup to catch displaced water when refilling tank
- Dishpan or shallow bucket for testing clay boats
- Wax paper, for ease of cleanup

1 Measuring your stick of clay

Take your stick of clay and find its density. Use a balance to measure its mass. Use the length × width × height method to calculate its volume. Record your measurements in Table 1.

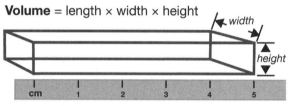

Volume = length × width × height

Table I: Mass, volume, and density of clay stick data

length (cm)		width (cm)		height (cm)		Volume (cm³)
	×		×		=	

Mass (g)		Volume (cm³)		Density (g/cm³)
	÷		=	

a. The density of water is 1g/cm³. How does the density of your clay compare to water?

b. Make a prediction: Will your stick of clay sink or float? Why?

2 Doing the experiment

A. Testing your prediction

1. Prepare the displacement tank for use. Place a cup or beaker under the spout to catch the overflow water. Fill the displacement tank all the way up until it just starts to overflow into the cup or beaker . Once it stops remove the cup or beaker that was catching the overflow water.

2. Place a dry beaker under the spout to catch the overflow water displaced by your clay.

3. Gently put your stick of clay in the water. Did your stick of clay sink or float?

Water level as high as possible without overflowing

Beaker for overflow water

B. Finding the mass and volume of the displaced water

1. Pour the displaced water from the beaker into a 100-mL graduated cylinder. Record the volume in Table 2.

2. Now, calculate the mass of the displaced water using water's density and the volume of displaced water you measured. Record this value in Table 2.

C. Calculating the weight of your clay and the displaced water

Mass and weight measure two different properties of matter. Mass refers to how much matter the object contains. Weight measures the gravitational pull between the object and (in our case) Earth. The gravitational force between a 1-kilogram object and Earth is 9.8 newtons. So a 1-gram object's weight on Earth is 0.0098 newtons.

1. Use the mass of your clay to calculate its weight. Use the formula below and record the mass and weight in Table 2.

mass in grams x (0.0098 N/g) = weight in Newtons

2. Calculate the weight of the displaced water. Use the formula above and record your data in Table 2.

Table 2: Mass and volume of clay and displaced water

	Mass of clay (g)	Weight of clay (N)	Volume of displaced water (mL)	Mass of displaced water (g)	Weight of displaced water (N)
Stick of clay					
Clay boat					

3 Challenge: Can you mold your clay into a shape that floats?

For this part of the investigation, you must use *all* of your clay. Mold it into a shape that you believe will float. Before you do, make a prediction:
How much water will the boat displace compared to the stick of clay?

1. When you are ready to test a shape, lower it into a container of water approximately three-quarters full. If the clay sinks, retrieve it immediately and dry it with a paper towel. Avoid mixing water into your clay, or it will get very slimy. Keep trying until you get a boat that floats.

2. When you have successfully molded a boat that floats, take it out of the water and dry it with a paper towel. Then, prepare your displacement tank just as you did in step 2A.

3. Carefully place your boat into the displacement tank. Avoid making waves. When the water stops flowing, move the beaker away from the displacement tank spout. Safely remove a little water from the displacement tank so it doesn't overflow. Retrieve your boat and set it aside to dry.

4. Pour the displaced water from the beaker into a graduated cylinder. Record its volume in Table 2.

5. Use the density of water to calculate the mass of the displaced water. Calculate its weight using the formula from step C1. Record both the water's mass and weight in Table 2.

6. When your boat is dry, first measure its mass, then calculate its weight using the formula from step C1. Record both the mass and weight in Table 2.

4 Analyzing your data

a. Did the weight of the clay change during the investigation? Give a reason for your answer.

b. Which displaced more water, the stick of clay or the clay boat, and how much more?

c. Which weighed more, the stick of clay or the water it displaced, and how much more?

d. Which weighed more, the clay boat or the water it displaced, and how much more?

5 Why the boat floats

Use your mass and volume data from Table 2 to calculate the apparent density of your clay boat. This value is called the *apparent* density because the total volume of the floating boat is not displaced. The part of your floating boat that is above the surface isn't displacing any water. To find out how much of the boat is below the surface and *is* displacing water, look at the total amount of water you measured that spilled out into the beaker when the boat was floating.

Table 3: Data for boat

Mass of boat (g)	Volume of water displaced by the boat (mL)	Apparent density of the boat (g/mL)

6 Thinking about what you observed

a. Which displaced more water, the stick of clay or the floating clay boat?

b. Assuming the mass of the clay did not change, how do you explain the difference in the volumes displaced by the stick of clay and the clay boat?

c. Look at the boat's apparent density. Why is it different than the density of the stick of clay? What other substance has a density very similar to the boat's apparent density?

d. Out of all the properties you measured and calculated in this investigation, which property tells you the most about weather an object or material will float in water, and how would you use that property to determine weather it will float?

e. Explain why a solid stick of clay sinks but a clay boat can be made to float.

f. What would happen if you added "cargo," like pennies, to your boat? Is there a limit to how much mass you can add before the boat sinks? Does the volume of displaced water increase or decrease when the boat gets heavier? Why? Try the experiment.

13A Boyle's Law

How are pressure and volume of a gas related?

Robert Boyle (1627–1691) conducted a series of experiments to investigate the physical properties of air. It was through these experiments he discovered the relationship between pressure and volume for an enclosed gas. Using a simple experiment, we will measure the pressure of a gas inside a syringe with a gas pressure sensor. You will use your data to derive the mathematical relationship between the pressure and volume of an enclosed gas at constant temperature.

Materials

- Gas Pressure Sensor
- CPO Gas Law kit
- CPO DataCollector

1 Thinking about pressure and volume

a. When you blow up a balloon, what happens to the volume of air inside the balloon?

b. What about the pressure? Does the pressure increase, decrease, or stay the same?

c. Now think about both pressure and volume together. Make a hypothesis about the relationship between pressure and volume of an enclosed gas. (*Hint*: When volume changes, what do you think happens to pressure?)

2 Setting up the experiment

1. Connect the 4-centimeter piece of tubing to the pressure sensor connector as shown.
2. Connect the other end of the tubing to the syringe.
3. Adjust the syringe until the volume of air is 12.0 mL.
4. Screw the pressure sensor connector onto the pressure sensor.

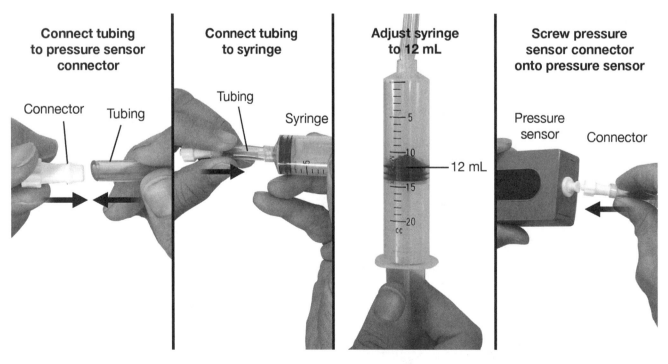

| Connect tubing to pressure sensor connector | Connect tubing to syringe | Adjust syringe to 12 mL | Screw pressure sensor connector onto pressure sensor |

3   Doing the experiment

1. Start the DataCollector in data collection mode. Record the pressure at 12.0 mL (in kPa) in Table 1.
2. Pull the syringe out until it measures 16.0 mL. Hold it until the pressure stabilizes. Again, record the pressure in Table 1.
3. Repeat step 3 for volumes of 18.0 mL and 10.0 mL.
4. Repeat step 3 with a volume of 6.0 mL, however, take the measurement quickly to prevent air from escaping.
5. Stop the DataCollector. Do not disconnect the syringe from the sensor yet!

Table 1: Pressure and volume data

Volume (mL)	Pressure (kPa)	P · V (kPa · mL)	P/V (kPa/mL)
6.0 mL			
10.0 mL			
12.0 mL			
16.0 mL			
18.0 mL			

4   Graphing your data

a. Use your data to make a graph of pressure versus volume.

b. Does the graphical model support your hypothesis? Explain your answer.

c. What happens to the pressure of an enclosed gas when the volume increases?

5   Finding a relationship between pressure and volume

a. Multiply the pressure and volume values for each trial and record the values in the third column of Table 1. Remember to use appropriate numbers of significant figures.

b. Divide the pressure by the volume for each trial and record the values in the last column of Table 1. Again, use the correct number of significant figures.

c. Boyle's law states that there is a mathematical relationship between pressure and volume that always equals a constant value. Based on your calculations, is that relationship $P \times V$ or P/V?

d. According to your data, what is the constant value?

6   Using Boyle's law to make a prediction

a. Using your constant value, calculate what the pressure would be when the volume of the syringe is set to 14.0 mL.

b. Using your graph, what is the pressure that corresponds to 14.0 mL? How does this compare to your calculated value?

c. Test your predicted pressure value for 14.0 mL. How do the values compare?

13B Pressure and Temperature Relationship

How are temperature and pressure of a gas related?

Gas molecules are in constant motion. When the temperature of a gas increases, the molecules move faster. When this happens, the velocity and number of molecular collisions increases. The opposite is true for a gas when the temperature decreases. In this experiment, you will study the relationship between the pressure a gas exerts and the temperature of the gas.

Materials

- Gas pressure sensor
- Single-hole rubber stopper/tube assembly
- Temperature probe
- CPO DataCollector
- 125-mL Erlenmeyer flask
- CPO Displacement Tank
- Cold water
- Hot water
- Safety goggles

1 Thinking about temperature and pressure

a. Car manuals tell you to inflate the tires to a certain pressure when the tires are cold (before driving around on them). Why do you think this is important?

b. Make a hypothesis about the relationship between pressure and temperature of an enclosed gas. (*Hint*: When temperature increases, what do you think happens to the pressure?)

2 Setting up the experiment

1. Fill the displacement tank with ice cold water to the 1,200 mL mark.

2. Place a temperature probe in the water and connect the probe to the DataCollector. The water temperature should be about 10–12°C, but any cold starting temperature is fine.

3. Place the rubber stopper/tube assembly into the 125-mL Erlenmeyer flask. Attach the pressure sensor to the tube.

4. Connect the pressure sensor to the DataCollector.

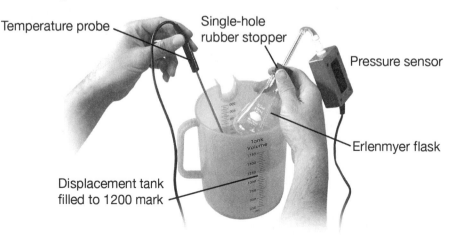

Temperature probe

Single-hole rubber stopper

Pressure sensor

Erlenmyer flask

Displacement tank filled to 1200 mark

3 Doing the experiment

1. Place the flask into the cold water bath and allow it to sit for 2 minutes. Record the temperature and pressure in Table 1 after 2 minutes have passed.
2. Take the flask out of the water. Use a container to remove 400 mL of water from the displacement tank.
3. Get 400 mL of hot water from your teacher and pour it into the displacement tank.
4. Place the flask into this warmer water after it has been in the water for 2 minutes, record the temperature and pressure in Table 1.
5. Repeat steps 2–4 two more times so you have a total of four data points.
6. Convert Celsius temperatures to Kelvin and record in Table 1.

Table 1: Pressure and temperature data

Pressure (kPa)	Temperature (°C)	Temperature (K)	P/T (kPa/K)	P · T (kPa · K)

4 Graphing your data

a. Use your data to make a graph of pressure versus temperature.

b. Does the graphical model support your hypothesis? Explain your answer.

c. What happens to the pressure of an enclosed gas when the temperature increases?

5 Finding a relationship between pressure and temperature

a. Divide the pressure and temperature values for each trial and record the answers in the fourth column of Table 1. Remember to use appropriate numbers of significant figures.

b. Multiply the pressure by the temperature for each trial and record the values in the last column of Table 1. Again, use the correct number of significant figures.

c. There is a mathematical relationship between pressure and temperature that always equals a constant value. Based on your calculations, is that relationship P/T or P × T?

d. According to your data, what is the constant value?

6 Using the pressure-temperature relationship to make a prediction

a. Using your constant value, calculate what the pressure of the air in the flask would be when the temperature is 333 K.

b. Using your graph, what is the pressure that corresponds to 333 K? How does this compare to your calculated value?

c. How would you use the experiment setup to test your predicted pressure value for 333 K?

7 Thinking about what you observed

a. You used a water bath to change the temperature of the air in the flask. Draw a diagram of the experiment setup and use arrows to show the heat transfer that took place when more and more hot water was added to the displacement tank.

b. What two factors in the experiment were constant?

c. Go back to your answer to question 1a. Would you answer the question the same way now? Explain.

14A The Atom

What is inside an atom?

We once believed that atoms were the smallest units of matter. Then it was discovered that there are even smaller particles inside atoms! The structure of the atom explains why nearly all the properties of matter we experience are what they are. This investigation will lead you through some challenging and fun games that illustrate how atoms are built from protons, neutrons, and electrons.

Materials
- CPO Atom Building Game

1 Modeling an atom

In the atom game, colored marbles represent the three kinds of particles. Red or green marbles are protons, blue marbles are neutrons, and yellow marbles are electrons.

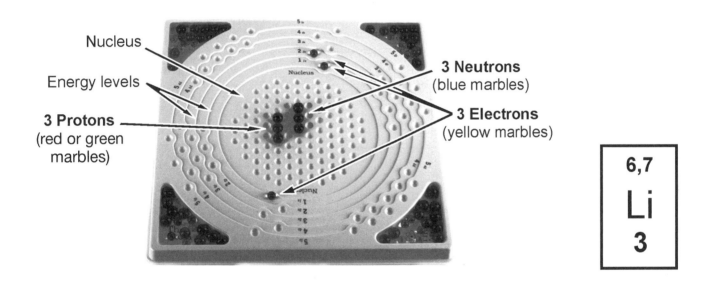

1. Build the atom above using three red or green, three blue, and three yellow marbles.

2 Thinking about the atom

a. What is the number below the element symbol? What does this number tell you about the the atom?

b. What is the number(s) above the element symbol called? What does this number tell you about the atom?

c. Why do some elements have more than one number above the symbol? What are the variations in this number called?

3 Making atoms

Build the six atoms shown on the chart and fill in the missing information Protons and neutrons go in the middle of the board. Electrons go in the outside and fill up the holes from the lowest row to the highest.

	Element	Atomic number	Mass number	Protons	Neutrons	Electrons
3a				●●●●	●●●●●	
3b				●●●●●● ●	●●●●● ●	
3c					●●●●● ●●●	○○○○○ ○
3d		8			●●●●● ●●●	
3e				●●●●●● ●●●●●	●●●●●● ●●●●●	○○○○○ ○○○○○
3f			27	●●●●● ●●●●● ●●●		

4 Stop and think

a. Two of the atoms you made were the same element. What was different about them?

b. One of the atoms had just enough electrons to completely fill the first two rows. Which atom was this? Where on the periodic table is it found?

c. Which atom had an atomic number of 8?

d. Which atom had a mass number of 14?

e. One atom is found in a lightweight, silvery metal used in airplanes. Which atom was it?

f. One atom represents an element that makes up about 21% of the air you breathe. You could not live without this element.

Periodic Table of the Elements 1- 54
(Stable isotopes)

Key

Atomic Number — 42
Element Symbol — Mo
Stable Mass Numbers — 92, 94-100

No.	Sym	Stable Mass Numbers
1	H	1,2
2	He	3,4
3	Li	6,7
4	Be	9
5	B	10,11
6	C	12,13
7	N	14,15
8	O	16-18
9	F	19
10	Ne	20-22
11	Na	23
12	Mg	24-26
13	Al	27
14	Si	28-30
15	P	31
16	S	32-34, 36
17	Cl	35,37
18	Ar	36,38, 40
19	K	39,41
20	Ca	40, 42-44, 46, 48
21	Sc	45
22	Ti	46-50
23	V	51
24	Cr	50, 52-54
25	Mn	55
26	Fe	54,56-58
27	Co	59
28	Ni	58,60-62,64
29	Cu	63,65
30	Zn	64,66-68,70
31	Ga	69,71
32	Ge	70,72-74,76
33	As	75
34	Se	74,76-78,80, 82
35	Br	79,81
36	Kr	78,80,82-84,86
37	Rb	85
38	Sr	84,86-88
39	Y	89
40	Zr	90-92,94,96
41	Nb	93
42	Mo	92,94-100
43	Tc	none
44	Ru	96,98-103,104
45	Rh	103
46	Pd	102,104-106,108,110
47	Ag	107,109
48	Cd	106,108,110-112,114,116
49	In	113
50	Sn	112,114-120,122,124
51	Sb	121
52	Te	120,122,124-126,128,130
53	I	127
54	Xe	124,126,128-132,134,136

14B Atomic Challenge!

How were the elements created?

During the middle ages, people believed you could turn lead into gold if you followed the right procedures. Later, we learned that lead and gold are different elements with different kinds of atoms. You have to change the atoms inside to make lead into gold. Lead atoms have 82 protons in the nucleus. Gold atoms have 79 protons.

Materials

- CPO Atom Building Game

1 Building the elements

About 13 billion years ago, when the universe was much younger, the only atoms in existence were hydrogen, helium, and a small amount of lithium. These are the three lightest elements. Today, we find carbon, oxygen, iron, and even uranium atoms. Where did these heavy atoms come from? All the elements were created in the super-hot cores of stars. Stars get their energy by combining hydrogen atoms together to make other elements, such as helium. Along the way, a few protons get converted to neutrons and electrons, too.

2 Quick review of the atom

In the atom game, colored marbles represent the three kinds of particles. Red or green marbles are protons, blue marbles are neutrons, and yellow marbles are electrons.

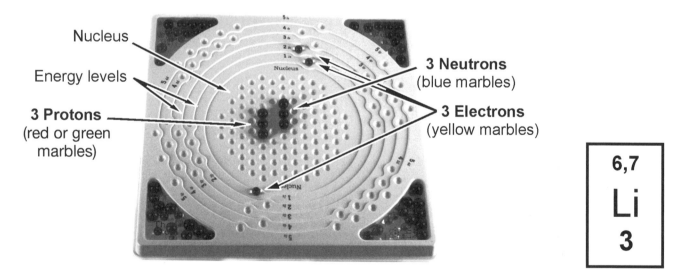

The Three Rules

Rule #1: The number of protons matches the atomic number

Rule #2: The total number of protons and neutrons equals a stable mass number

Rule #3: The number of electrons matches the number of protons

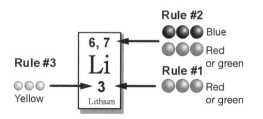

78

3 The game of atomic challenge

This game simulates how the heavy elements were created inside stars. Each player takes a turn adding protons, neutrons, and electrons to the atom to build heavier and heavier elements.

1. The winner of the game is the first player to run completely out of marbles.

2. Each player should start with six blue marbles (neutrons), five red or green marbles (protons), and five yellow marbles (electrons).

3. Each player takes turns adding one to five marbles, but not more than five. The marbles may include any mixture of electrons, protons, and neutrons. *For example*: you can add one blue, one red or green, and one yellow marble in a turn. That makes three total marbles, which is less than five.

4. Marbles played in a turn are added to the marbles already in the atom.

5. Only atoms where the electrons, protons, and neutrons match one of the naturally occurring elements on the table are allowed. If you add marbles that make an atom *not* on the red periodic table you have to take your marbles back and lose your turn.

6. A player can trade marbles with the bank *instead* of taking a turn. The player can take as many marbles, and of as many colors as they need but must take at least as many total marbles as they put in. For example, a player can trade two yellows for one yellow, one blue, and one red or green.

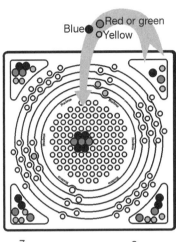

Example of a good move

$Li^7 + p + n + e = Be^9$

4 Stop and think

Atoms which are not on the periodic table shown may exist in nature but they are radioactive and unstable. For example, carbon-14 (C^{14}) is unstable and is not listed, although C^{12} and C^{13} are stable.

a. What four elements make up almost all of the mass in your body?

b. How many stable isotopes does oxygen have?

c. Find one element on the chart that has no stable isotopes.

d. What element has atoms with 26 protons in the nucleus?

e. On most periodic tables, a single atomic mass is listed instead of the mass numbers for all the stable isotopes. How is this mass related to the different isotopes?

15A The Periodic Table

How is the periodic table organized?

Virtually all the matter you see is made up of combinations of elements. Scientists know of 118 different elements, of which about 90 occur naturally. Each element has its own unique kind of atom. The periodic table is a chart that shows all of the elements in order of increasing atomic number.

Materials

- CPO Periodic Table Tiles

1 Building the periodic table

Every element is given a symbol of one or two letters. For example, the symbol for hydrogen is a capital letter *H*. The symbol for lithium is two letters, Li. Each element also has a unique number called the atomic number. The *periodic table* is a chart that shows the elements in an arrangement that helps us recognize groups of elements with similar properties. The picture below shows the shape of the periodic table and the first few elements in sequence from left to right. The elements are arranged from lowest to highest atomic number.

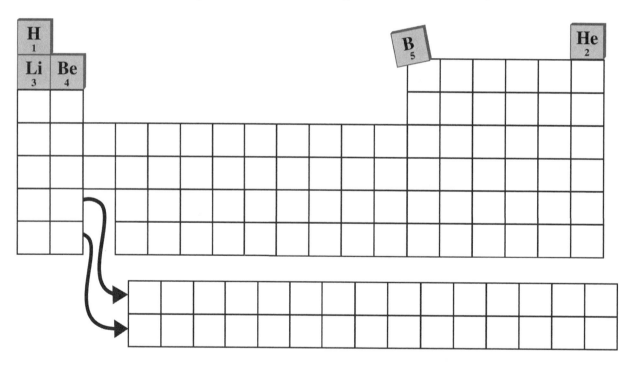

Using the chart as a guide, build the periodic table out of the periodic table tiles. The only tile you should use yellow-side up is the hydrogen tile. The colors will show a pattern when you are finished. There is a tricky part near the bottom of the table. The table breaks off between element 56 (Ba) and element 71 (Lu), and fills in the first of two long rows underneath the main part of the chart.

2 Organization of the periodic table

Look at the periodic table you put together out of the tiles. Use the diagram below, and your model of the periodic table, to answer the questions below.

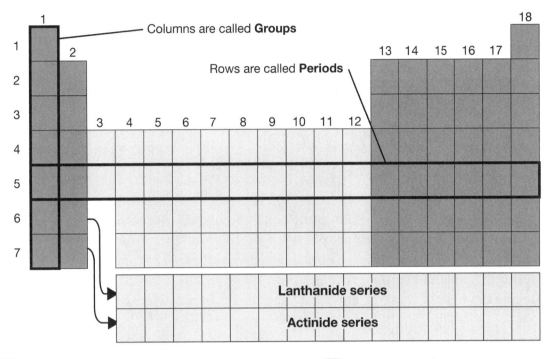

Groups 1-2 and 13-18 are the main group elements ☐ Groups 3-12 are the transition metals

a. Which elements are in group 1?

b. Which elements are in group 8?

c. Name three transition metals.

d. To which group does chlorine belong? What other elements are in that group?

e. Which elements are in the 2nd period?

3 Applying what you have learned

a. Each row (period) of the periodic table contains only a certain number of elements. What does this have to do with the structure of the atom? Research this question in your textbook.

b. Which group of the periodic table above contains the element argon? What characteristic do the elements in this group share?

c. Which group contains the element carbon? What characteristic do the elements in this group share?

15B Periodic Table Challenge

What information can you get from the periodic table?

Each box on the periodic table tells you the element symbol, atomic number, and atomic mass for all the known elements. This is very useful information, but did you know that the arrangement of the elements on the periodic table gives you even more information? Each major column of elements represents a group of elements with similar chemical behavior. Can you see why the arrangement of elements on the periodic table is important?

Materials

- Blank periodic table bingo card sheets; 1 per player
- Caller's clues and checklist; 1 per team
- Copy of the periodic table of elements; 1 per player
- Highlighter or other marker; 1 per player

1 The challenge

Periodic Table Challenge is a bingo-like game that helps you understand how the elements on the periodic table are arranged. Each player will fill out their own five-by-five grid with element symbols, and then the caller will read element clues. The players must interpret the clues and highlight any boxes on the grid that fit the clue. The first player that correctly highlights five boxes across, up-and-down, or diagonally in a row is the winner.

2 Rules of play

1. Designate one member of your group to be the caller. The caller will call out clues and keep track of them on the checklist.

2. Each player will have a sheet of four blank grids. Fill out one of the grids with random element symbols (other grids can be used for additional games). You may choose elements in the atomic number range of 1–54 (hydrogen through xenon). Do not repeat symbols on the card. You will only be able to fit 25 of the possible 54 symbols on the card. You choose which ones to use, and where to place them on the grid.

3. The caller will randomly pick clues from the list, and as a clue is called out, the caller will check off the clue. The answers are only for the caller to check the winner's card!

4. When a clue is called, players check the grid to see if any of the elements fit the clue. Any elements that fit the clue must be highlighted. If no elements fit the clue, then no boxes are highlighted on that turn.

5. When a player has five boxes highlighted in a row up and down, across, or diagonally, play stops. The caller will double check the clue list and answers to see if the clues indeed match the elements. Play continues until a true winner is determined.

3 Caller's clues

Clues can be called in any order. Check off each clue as you use it.

Clue	Possible Answers
A member of the carbon family	C, Si, Ge, Sn
Chemical properties similar to calcium, but not calcium	Be, Mg, Sr
A transition metal that has a "C" in the symbol	Sc, Cr, Co, Cu, Tc, Cd,
A member of the oxygen family	O, S, Se, Te
Chemical properties similar to cesium, but not cesium	H, Li, Na, K, Rb
A member of the noble gas family	He, Ne, Ar, Kr, Xe
A nonmetal in the nitrogen family	N, P
A metal in the boron family	Al, Ga, In
A gas in the oxygen family	O
A solid in the halogen family	I
An element that is liquid at room temperature	Hg, Br
A transition metal with less than 25 protons	Cr, V, Ti, Sc
A transition metal commonly found in jewelry	Ni, Cu, Ag
A metalloid in the carbon family	Si, Ge
Chemical properties similar to aluminum, but not aluminum	B, Ga, In
A transition metal with 39 – 43 protons	Y, Zr, Nb, Mo, Tc
An element symbol with a first letter that is different from the first letter of the name	Na, K, Fe, Ag, Sn, Sb
A member of the nitrogen family with a one-letter symbol	N, P
A transition metal from period 5	Y, Zr, Nb, Mo, Tc, Ru, Rh, Pd, Ag, Cd

4 Periodic table challenge card

Fill in each of the squares with the symbol of an element with atomic number between 1 and 54 (hydrogen–xenon)

You may not use the same element symbol twice.

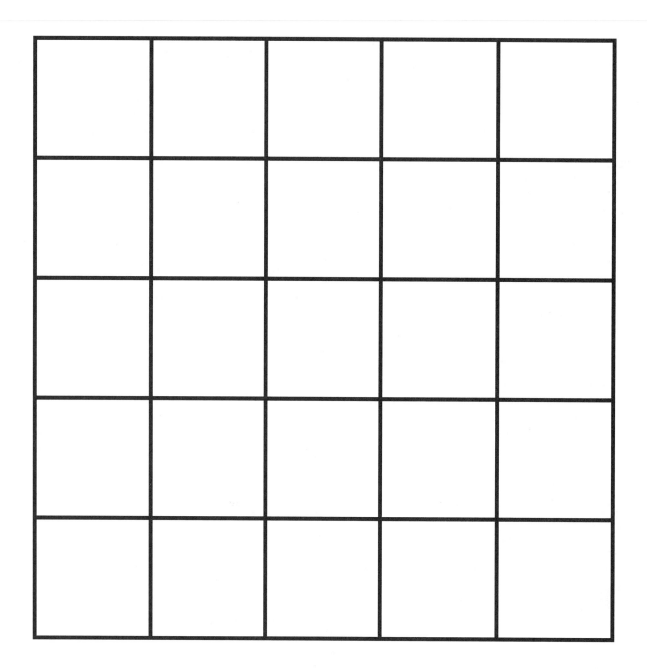

16A Chemical Bonds

Why do atoms form chemical bonds?

Most of the matter on Earth is in the form of compounds. Even when a substance exists as a pure element, it tends eventually to combine with other elements. For example, if you leave an iron nail outside in the rain, it will quickly combine with the oxygen in the air to form iron oxide, better known as rust. In this Investigation you will build models of atoms and discover one of the fundamental ideas in chemistry: how electrons are involved in the formation of chemical bonds.

Materials

- CPO Atom Building Game

 1 **Reviewing atomic structure**

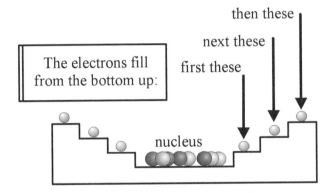

Let's review what you already know about atoms:

- A neutral atom has the same number of electrons and protons.
- The electrons occupy energy levels surrounding the nucleus.
- Since electrons are attracted to the nucleus, they fill the lower energy levels first.

Once a given level is full, electrons start filling the next level.

2 **How many electrons in the outermost level?**

Using the atom building game, build each element in the table. For each element, record the number of electrons in the outermost energy level and the number of unoccupied spaces in the outermost energy level.

element	atomic number	electrons in outermost level	unoccupied spaces in outermost level
hydrogen			
helium			
lithium			
fluorine			
neon			
sodium			
chlorine			
argon			
potassium			

3   What are valence electrons?

Examine the table you just completed and record the answers to the following questions.

  a. Use your textbook to find out about *valence electrons*.

  b. What do lithium, sodium, and potassium have in common?

  c. What do fluorine and chlorine have in common?

  d. What do neon and argon have in common?

4   Modeling a chemical bond

Atoms that have a complete outermost energy level are stable. If there are empty holes, an atom will either gain, lose, or share electrons with another atom in order to complete its outermost level and become stable. When atoms gain, lose, or share electrons with another atom, they form *chemical bonds*.

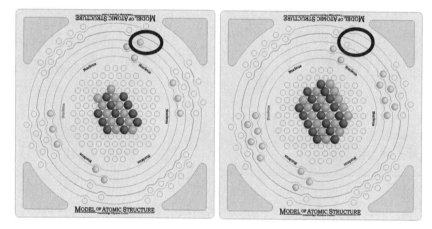

Using two atom building games, build a sodium atom and a chlorine atom. Put them next to each other and answer the questions below.

  a. In order to complete its outermost energy level, do you think sodium will tend to lose its only valence electron, or gain seven? Explain your answer.

  b. In order to complete its outermost energy level, do you think chlorine will tend to lose all of its valence electrons or gain one electron? Explain your answer.

  c. Why might these two atoms bond together to form a molecule? In your answer, describe what you think might happen when sodium and chlorine form a chemical bond.

5 Determining oxidation numbers

An element's *oxidation number* is equal to the charge an atom has when it *ionizes*, that is, gains or loses electrons.

Use your models of sodium and chlorine to answer the questions below.

a. Remove the valence electron from sodium. What has happened to the balance of positive and negative charges? What is sodium's oxidation number?

b. Move the electron you took from sodium into the chlorine. What happens to chlorine's charge when it gains the electron from the sodium atom? What is chlorine's oxidation number?

c. When sodium and chlorine form a chemical bond, what is the overall charge of the molecule? Why do you think sodium and chlorine combine in a 1:1 ratio?

6 Modeling chemical bonds

Use multiple atom boards for this part of the investigation. First, build each atom. Next, move the boards together to model the formation of a chemical bond.

a. one carbon atom and four hydrogen atoms

b. two lithium atoms and one oxygen atom

c. one beryllium atom and two fluorine atoms

7 Applying your knowledge

Read in your textbook about Lewis dot diagrams. Draw a dot diagram for each compound in Part 6.

16B Chemical Formulas

Why do atoms combine in certain ratios?

Chemists have long noticed that groups of elements behave similarly. The periodic table is an arrangement of the elements grouped according to similar behavior. In this investigation you will discover how the arrangement of electrons in atoms is related to groups on the periodic table. You will also learn why atoms form chemical bonds with other atoms in certain ratios.

Materials

- CPO Periodic Table Tiles
- Periodic table with oxidation numbers
- Special Bonds cards

1 Oxidation numbers and ions

An element's *oxidation number* indicates how many electrons are lost or gained when chemical bonding occurs. The oxidation number is equal to the charge an atom has when it *ionizes*, that is, gains or loses electrons to become an *ion*. The partial periodic table below shows the most common oxidation numbers of the elements. The oxidation numbers are written above the group number above each column on the table. The most common oxidation numbers for the main group elements are shown.

Predicting Oxidation Numbers from the Periodic Table

NOTE: Many elements have more than one possible oxidation number.

2 Stop and think

a. How are elements grouped according to the number of valence electrons in their outermost levels?

b. Why do elements in group 2 have an oxidation number of 2+?

c. Why do elements in group 17 have an oxidation number of 1–?

d. Why do the oxidation numbers in the first two groups tend to be positive?

3 Predicting chemical formulas

A *binary compound* is composed of two different elements. Predict the chemical formulas for the binary compounds that are made up of the pairs of elements in the table below. Use the following steps.

1. Using the periodic table on the previous page, determine the ion formed by each element.
2. Figure out how many periodic table tiles of each element will be needed to make the compound electrically neutral.
3. Form the compound with your tiles and write the chemical formula for each compound based on the number of tiles of each element.

Table 1: Writing chemical formulas for binary compounds

element 1	element 2	oxidation no. 1	oxidation no. 2	number of tiles of element 1	number of tiles of element 2	chemical formula
hydrogen	fluorine					
magnesium	sulfur					
calcium	bromine					
aluminum	oxygen					
potassium	chlorine					
lithium	argon					
rubidium	sulfur					

4 Naming compounds

Naming binary ionic compounds is very simple if you follow these rules.

1. Write the name of the element with a positive oxidation number first.
2. Write the root name of the element with a negative oxidation number second. For example, *chlor-* is the root name of chlorine. Subtract the *-ine* ending.
3. Add the ending *-ide* to the root name. *Chlor-* becomes *chloride*.

Using these rules, write the name of each of the compounds in Table 1.

5 Playing Compound Crossword

Now that you understand how elements combine to form compounds, you are ready to play Compound Crossword. In this game, you will score points by forming stable compounds, crossword style. Players use the oxidation numbers of the elements to form correct compounds. Points are determined by adding up the atomic numbers of each atom in the compound.

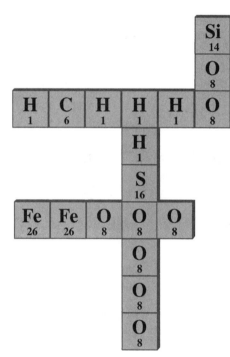

Sample game after four turns:

CH_3OH scores 18 points

Fe_2O_3 scores 76 points

SiO_2 scores 30 points

H_2SO_4 scores 50 points

Starting the game

Each player starts with ten randomly selected tiles. The remaining tiles should be placed in a box or paper bag so that additional tiles may be drawn without being seen. The playing surface can be any flat table (or floor) with minimum dimensions of 75-by-75 centimeters.

Each player draws a tile from the bag; the highest atomic number goes first. Once the starting player has been determined, those tiles are returned to the bag. The play continues to the starting player's right.

Play

1. Players take turns adding a compound to the crossword by using tiles from their set of 10. Either side of a tile may be used.
2. The elements in a compound may be arranged in any order, as long as they are in a single horizontal or vertical row.
3. Each new compound must be shown by the player to have oxidation numbers that add up to zero. Otherwise the player must take back the compound and wait until the next turn.
4. If the compound is correct, the player adds up the atomic numbers of all the atoms in the compound to determine the points and then draws new tiles to restore a set of 10.

5. Play continues until all the tiles in the bag are used and one player is out of tiles, or until all players are unable to make a compound with their remaining tiles.

6. The winner is the player with the highest score at the end of the game.

Determining correct compounds

The oxidation numbers found directly above each element on the periodic table provided are used to determine whether a molecule is correct. The oxidation numbers of all the elements in the compound must add up to zero. In some cases there is more than one oxidation number for an element. Iron (Fe), for example, has oxidation numbers of +2 and +3. The player may choose either oxidation number to add to the total.

The Special Bonds card included with the Periodic Table Tiles gives some additional possibilities for forming compounds.

Examples of correct and incorrect compounds

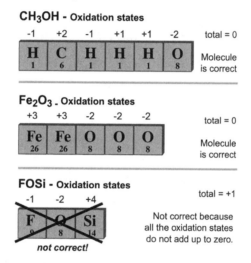

The oxidation number for each element in a compound is counted once for every atom present. The two iron atoms contribute a total of +6, which is balanced by the −6 from the three oxygen atoms.

Note: The Special Bonds card has some extra ways compounds can form when two atoms of the same element bond together, and when hydrogen is involved in unusual ways. The example of CH_3OH (methanol) above uses one of the special bonds that hydrogen can make with carbon.

Miscellaneous rules and strategies

The noble gases do not form bonds, therefore they can't be played. Players may decide at the start of the game to remove these tiles. As another option, players can choose to turn the noble gas tiles over, revealing the + symbol. This symbol could be used as a wildcard in which the player chooses which element the + should represent. The symbol scores no points but allows the player to complete a molecule. Players must agree on the use of the noble gas tiles before the game begins.

17A Chemical Equations

How are atoms conserved in a chemical reaction?

A chemical reaction involves changes in substances that react to form new products. This process involves the breaking of chemical bonds and the formation of new ones. A chemical equation shows the chemical formulas of the substances that react, called reactants, and the chemical formulas of the substances that are produced, called products. The number and type of atoms in the reactants must be exactly equal to the number and type of atoms in the products. How do you write a chemical equation so that the number and type of atoms on the reactants and products sides are balanced?

Materials
- CPO Periodic Table Tiles

1 Writing chemical equations

Magnesium metal reacts with water to produce magnesium hydroxide and hydrogen gas.

The statement above is the word form of a chemical reaction. It tells you the names of the reactants and the products. To write it as a chemical equation, you need to determine the chemical formulas of each of the substances in the reaction.

1. Magnesium metal is an element and exists as an atom. Its chemical formula is Mg.
2. The chemical formula for water is H_2O.
3. Magnesium hydroxide is an ionic compound. To write its chemical formula, you need to find out the charges of each ion it is made out of. The magnesium ion is Mg^{2+}. The hydroxide ion is OH^-. You need 1 Mg^{2+} and 2 OH^- to make a neutral compound so the formula is $Mg(OH)_2$.
4. Pure hydrogen gas always exists as a diatomic molecule so its chemical formula is H_2.

The chemical equation is written as:

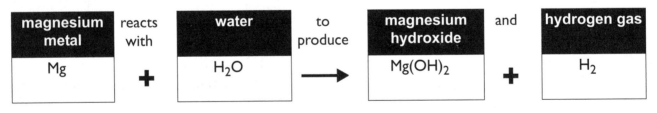

2 Trying out the reaction with periodic table tiles

Use periodic table tiles to make the reactants above.

Rearrange the reactants to make the products. Is there any problem? What are you missing?

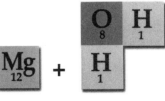

3 Balancing the reaction

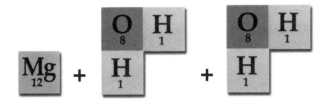

Chemical equations must always balance. This means that you must use all of the atoms you start with and you cannot have any leftover atoms when you are finished. If you need more atoms to make the products, you can only add them in the form of a chemical formula.

You cannot simply add the extra atoms that you need, unless the chemical formula is a single atom—like Mg. Which atoms did you need more of for the reaction you tried? Since you needed more oxygen and hydrogen atoms, you can only add them in the form of another water molecule. Try adding another water molecule to the reactants and rearrange them to form the products again. Did the reaction work this time?

4 Writing balanced chemical equations

To balance the equation for this reaction, you needed to add another water molecule to the reactants side. You ended up with the correct amount of products. Since one magnesium atom reacted with two water molecules to form one magnesium hydroxide molecule and one hydrogen gas, the proper way to write the balanced chemical equation is:

$$Mg + 2H_2O \longrightarrow Mg(OH)_2 + H_2$$

The *2* in front of water is called a coefficient. This number tells you how many water molecules are needed in the reaction. The rest of the reactants and products in the reactants show no coefficients. This is because when the coefficient is *1*, there is no need to write it.

5 Try balancing these chemical equations

The following chemical equations have the proper reactants and products. Try to balance each using the following steps.

1. Assemble the reactants out of the appropriate tiles.
2. Rearrange the reactants to form the products.
3. Figure out the number of each reactant and product required to make the equation balance and write the numbers (the coefficients) in the boxes.

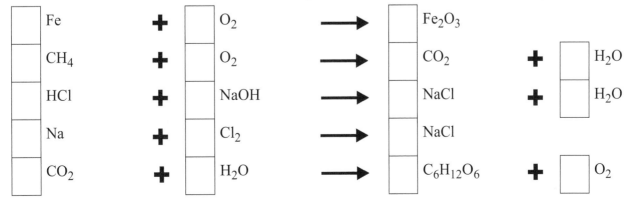

☐ Fe	+	☐ O_2	→	☐ Fe_2O_3				
☐ CH_4	+	☐ O_2	→	☐ CO_2	+	☐ H_2O		
☐ HCl	+	☐ NaOH	→	☐ NaCl	+	☐ H_2O		
☐ Na	+	☐ Cl_2	→	☐ NaCl				
☐ CO_2	+	☐ H_2O	→	☐ $C_6H_{12}O_6$	+	☐ O_2		

6 Challenge! Balancing difficult equations

Use the Periodic Table Tiles to help you balance these harder equations.

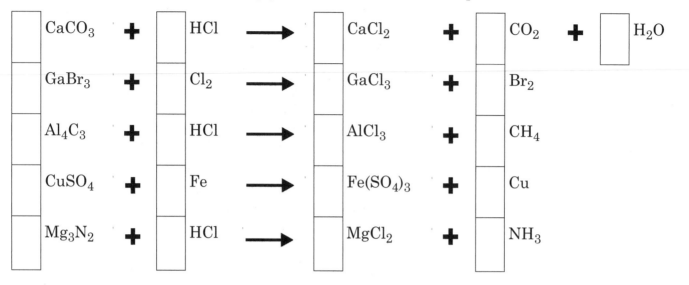

$$CaCO_3 \quad + \quad HCl \quad \longrightarrow \quad CaCl_2 \quad + \quad CO_2 \quad + \quad H_2O$$

$$GaBr_3 \quad + \quad Cl_2 \quad \longrightarrow \quad GaCl_3 \quad + \quad Br_2$$

$$Al_4C_3 \quad + \quad HCl \quad \longrightarrow \quad AlCl_3 \quad + \quad CH_4$$

$$CuSO_4 \quad + \quad Fe \quad \longrightarrow \quad Fe(SO_4)_3 \quad + \quad Cu$$

$$Mg_3N_2 \quad + \quad HCl \quad \longrightarrow \quad MgCl_2 \quad + \quad NH_3$$

Each of these equations has three reactants.

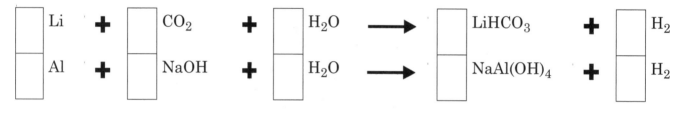

$$Li \quad + \quad CO_2 \quad + \quad H_2O \quad \longrightarrow \quad LiHCO_3 \quad + \quad H_2$$

$$Al \quad + \quad NaOH \quad + \quad H_2O \quad \longrightarrow \quad NaAl(OH)_4 \quad + \quad H_2$$

Can you balance this equation without using the tiles?

$$C_{30}H_{62} \quad + \quad O_2 \quad \longrightarrow \quad CO_2 \quad + \quad H_2O$$

17B Conservation of Mass

How do scientists describe what happens in a chemical reaction?

A French chemist named Antoine Lavoisier was the first to prove the law of conservation of mass. This law says that the total mass of the reactants in a chemical reaction is always equal to the total mass of the products. This is not as easy to see as you might think! As you do this investigation you will discover how tricky it is to show the law of conservation of mass.

Materials

- CPO Periodic Table Tiles
- Effervescent tablet
- Electronic scale (or triple-beam balance)
- Water
- Small paper cup

1 ## Testing the reaction

> **WARNING** — This lab contains chemicals that may be harmful if misused. Read cautions on individual containers carefully. Not to be used by children except under adult supervision.

Step 1:
Tare the balance to zero with the empty cup

Step 2:
Measure the mass of water and tablet

Step 3:
Add tablet to water and observe the reaction

Table I: Conservation of mass data

Step	Data and observations
1. Find the mass of the effervescent tablet.	
2. Put the paper cup on the balance and tare it to zero. Fill the cup about halfway with water. Record the mass.	
3. Put the tablet on the balance beside the cup, but don't put it in the water yet. Record the total starting mass.	
4. Drop the tablet into the cup of water. You can do this while the cup is still on the balance. Record your observations.	
5. Wait for the reaction to stop. Then, tap the cup gently to release as many bubbles as you can. Measure the mass.	
6. Subtract the final mass (5) from the starting mass (3). This is the mass difference between the products and reactants.	

2 Stop and think

a. Does this experiment agree with the law of conservation of mass? Look at the data that you just recorded. Use it to help you to explain why or why not.

b. Explain why you observed a difference in mass. Where did the missing mass go? Did it really disappear?

3 Modeling the reaction

Scientists write chemical reactions like mathematical formulas. The reactants are to the left of the arrow and the products are to the right of the arrow.

Use the tiles to model the chemical reaction

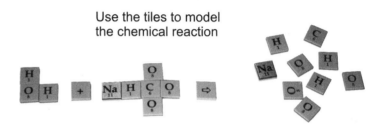

Reactants → Products

The effervescent tablet contains a chemical called sodium bicarbonate. This chemical reacts with water according to the following reaction.

$$H_2O + NaHCO_3 \rightarrow NaOH + CO_2 + H_2O$$

1. Build the reactants side (H_2O + $NaHCO_3$) of the chemical reaction above using the periodic table tiles.
2. Build the products side ($NaOH$ + CO_2 + H_2O) of the chemical reaction using more periodic table tiles.

4 Stop and think

Table 2: Counting atoms of each element

Element	Reactants	Products
Hydrogen		
Carbon		
Oxygen		
Sodium		

a. Fill in Table 2 with the numbers of each type of atom on the reactant side of the equation and on the product side of the equation.

b. How do the numbers of atoms of each element compare on the reactant and product side of the equation? What does this imply for the law of conservation of mass?

c. In what phase are each of the reactants (solid, liquid, or gas)? In what phase are each of the three products (solid, liquid, or gas)?

5 Proving that mass is conserved in a reaction

According to the law of conservation of mass, the mass of the products of the reaction should be exactly equal to the mass of the reactants. Can you design an experiment to prove this is true for the reaction you just observed?

Examine the materials your teacher has given you. These include:

- effervescent tablet
- two beakers
- beaker of water
- two plastic pipettes
- two baggies with zippers
- electronic balance or mass scale

1. Working with your lab partner, devise an experiment that will prove that mass is conserved in the reaction of the tablet and water. You may request additional materials if your teacher has them available.
2. List the materials you will need and their use in the experiment.
3. List the steps you will follow in the experiment.
4. Before you try out your experiment, request approval from your teacher.
5. If your experiment does not work, adjust your procedures and/or materials and try it again.
6. Record your procedures, data, and results.

6 Presenting your results to the class

Prepare a brief presentation for the class about your experiment. Use the following format for your presentation.

a.	**Purpose**	What questions were you trying to answer?
b.	**Materials**	What materials and equipment did you choose and why?
c.	**Procedures**	What were the steps you followed? You may demonstrate your procedures if time and materials allow.
d.	**Data**	What was the data you collected?
e.	**Conclusions**	What does your data prove? If your experiment did not yield satisfactory results, what would you change in your procedures or materials and why?

18A Energy and Chemical Changes

How do chemical changes involve energy?

Atoms come together in compounds by making chemical bonds with other atoms. Chemical bonds are a form of energy. When atoms change their bonds in a chemical reaction, energy can either be used or given off. In this investigation you will make chemical reactions and deduce whether they use energy or give off energy.

Materials

- Temperature probe
- CPO DataCollector
- 5 grams of sodium hydrogen carbonate (baking soda)
- Safety goggles
- Safety apron
- Electronic scale (or triple-beam balance)
- 100-mL graduated cylinder
- 100 mL vinegar
- 2 foam cups
- 4-cm piece of Magnesium ribbon
- 50 mL hydrochloric acid solution
- Paper towels

WARNING — This lab contains chemicals that may be harmful if misused. Read cautions on individual containers carefully. Not to be used by children except under adult supervision.

Special Safety Note: Use extreme caution when handling hydrochloric acid and other chemicals. Wear safety goggles and an apron during the entire investigation.

1 Stop and think

What evidence should you look for that indicates a chemical change (a chemical reaction) is taking place?

2 Reaction #1: Magnesium and hydrochloric acid

In this reaction, you will observe the temperature while adding a 4-centimeter piece of magnesium ribbon to 50 mL of hydrochloric acid solution.

1. Measure 50 mL of hydrochloric acid solution and place it in a pair of nested Styrofoam cups.
2. Place the temperature probe in the solution. Set the DataCollector to record one sample per second (default setting).
3. Measure a 4-centimeter piece of magnesium ribbon with a ruler.
4. When the temperature of the solution has stabilized, press start and drop the magnesium ribbon in the hydrochloric acid solution.
5. Stir the reaction continuously with the temperature probe.
6. Collect data until all the magnesium ribbon has disappeared and the temperature has stabilized.
7. Save the experiment and note the file name.

3 Thinking about what you observed

a. Study the temperature vs. time graph on the DataCollector. Did the temperature go up, down, or stay the same when you did the experiment?

b. Why does a change in temperature indicate a change in energy?

4 Reaction #2: Vinegar and baking soda

In this reaction, you will add 5 grams of baking soda (sodium hydrogen carbonate) to 50 mL of vinegar (acetic acid solution).

1. Rinse the Styrofoam cup with water and dry it with a paper towel.
2. Put 50 mL of vinegar in the pair of nested Styrofoam cups.
3. Place the temperature probe in the vinegar. Select a new experiment on the Data Collector and make sure it is set up to record one sample per second.
4. Measure 5 grams of baking soda with an electronic balance.
5. When the temperature of the vinegar has stabilized, press start and drop the baking soda in the vinegar.
6. Stir the reaction continuously with the temperature probe.
7. Collect data until the temperature stabilizes.
8. Save the experiment and note the file name.

5 Thinking what you observed

a. Study the temperature vs. time graph for the second experiment. Did the temperature go up, down, or stay the same?

b. Look at the graph of each reaction. What is the maximum temperature change in each reaction? What does each graph show about energy changes in each reaction?

c. A reaction that gives off energy is called *exothermic*. Which reaction(s) are exothermic? Support your answer with your data.

d. A reaction that uses energy is called *endothermic*. Which reaction(s) are endothermic? Support your answer with your data.

18B Thermodynamics of Hot Packs/Cold Packs

Can we measure the heat released/energy absorbed by instant hot and cold packs?

All chemical reactions are either exothermic (release energy) or endothermic (absorb energy). However, some physical processes such as dissolution (dissolving) can also release/absorb energy. This is the basis for commercially-available instant hot packs and cold packs. Most hot and cold packs work by breaking a membrane that separates a solid and water. Once the membrane is broken, the solid dissolves in the water. Depending on the nature of the compound, heat is either released (hot pack) or absorbed (cold pack) during the process. In this investigation you will examine the temperature changes of hot and cold packs and determine the energy absorbed or released during the chemical reactions that take place.

Materials

- 2 foam cups
- Temperature probe
- Datacollector
- Safety goggles
- Lab Apron
- Water
- Calcium chloride (from an instant hot pack or ice melt)
- Ammonium nitrate (from an instant cold pack)
- Balance

WARNING — This lab contains chemicals that may be harmful if misused. Read cautions on individual containers carefully. Not to be used by children except under adult supervision.

1 Stop and think

Calcium chloride is used to melt ice on winter roads. Would that process be exothermic or endothermic? Why?

2 Doing the experiment

Part A: Hot pack—record all measurements in Table 1.

1. Use a graduated cylinder to measure 50 mL of water. Record the mass of the water in Table 1. (*Hint*: 1 mL of water = 1 g.)
2. Pour the water into two nested foam cups and place the temperature probe into the water.
3. Use a balance to measure out about 10 g of calcium chloride ($CaCl_2$). Record the mass of the $CaCl_2$ in Table 1.
4. Select new experiment on the DataCollector and press go. Wait for the temperature of the water to stabilize and record that temperature in Table 1 (initial temperature).
5. Pour the $CaCl_2$ into the water and stir with the temperature probe.
6. Watch the graph and the temperature reading as the reaction proceeds.
7. Watch for the highest temperature reading before the temperature starts to go down again. Record that temperature in Table 1 (final temperature).
8. Pour the solution down the drain and then rinse and dry your foam cups.

Table 1: Hot pack mass and temperature data

Mass of water (g)	Mass of CaCl₂ (g)	Initial temp. (°C)	Final temp. (°C)

Part B: Cold pack

1. Use a graduated cylinder to measure 50 mL of water. Record the mass of the water in Table 2. (*Hint*: 1 mL of water = 1 g.)

2. Pour the water into two nested foam cups and place the temperature probe into the water.

3. Use a balance to measure out about 10 grams of ammonium nitrate (NH_4NO_3). Record the mass of the NH_4NO_3 in Table 2.

4. Select new experiment on the DataCollector and press go. Wait for the temperature of the water to stabilize and record that temperature in Table 2 (initial temperature).

5. Pour the NH_4NO_3 into the water and stir with the temperature probe.

6. Watch the graph and the temperature reading as the reaction proceeds.

7. Watch for the lowest temperature reading. Record that temperature in Table 2 (final temperature).

8. Pour the solution down the drain and then rinse and dry your foam cups.

Table 2: Cold pack mass and temperature data

Mass of water (g)	Mass of NH₄NO₃ (g)	Initial temp. (°C)	Final temp. (°C)

3 Analyzing the Data

a. Calculate the temperature change of the CaCl₂ and water reaction.

b. Calculate the heat gained by the solution using the equation below. Assume the specific heat of the solution is equal to the specific heat of water. The specific heat of water is 4.184 J/g°C.

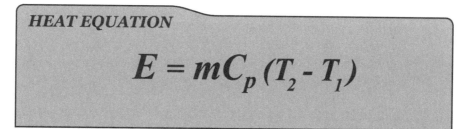

HEAT EQUATION

$$E = mC_p\,(T_2 - T_1)$$

Where: E = heat lost or gained

  m = mass of solution in the calorimeter

  C_p = specific heat of substance

  $T_2 - T_1$ = change in temperature (also referred to as ΔT)

c. Calculate the amount of energy (in joules) released per gram of $CaCl_2$. Remember, Q is the opposite sign of the value you calculate.

d. Calculate the temperature change of the NH_4NO_3 reaction.

e. Calculate the heat lost by the solution using the heat equation. Assume the specific heat of the solution is equal to the specific heat of water.

  Where: E = heat lost or gained

  m = mass of solution in the calorimeter

  C_p = specific heat of substance

  $T_2 - T_1$ = change in temperature (also referred to as ΔT)

f. Calculate the amount of energy (in joules) absorbed per gram of NH_4NO_3. Remember, Q is the opposite sign of the value you calculate.

4 Thinking about what you observed

a. Look at the reactions below. Place the energy value on the appropriate side of the two equations.

$$CaCl_2(s) \rightarrow Ca^{2+}(aq) + 2Cl^-(aq)$$

$$NH_4NO_3(s) \rightarrow NH_4^+(aq) + NO_3^-(aq)$$

b. When $CaCl_2$ dissolves in water the true value for $E = -747$ J/g. When NH_4NO_3 dissolves in water the true value for $E = 326$ J/g. Compare your experimental values by calculating the percent error for each reaction.

c. Describe why your skin feels cool when a cold pack is applied and warm when a hot pack is applied.

19A Solubility Curve of KNO₃

What is a solubility curve?

Solubility refers to the amount of solute that can be dissolved in a certain volume of solvent under certain conditions. In this experiment you will be examining the relationship between temperature and the solubility of potassium nitrate (KNO_3). The solvent will be water. Using class data, you will construct a solubility curve for KNO_3.

> **WARNING** — This lab contains chemicals that may be harmful if misused. Read cautions on individual containers carefully. Not to be used by children except under adult supervision.

Materials

- 5 test tubes
- 400 mL beaker
- Hot plate
- Thermometer
- Test tube holder (a spare 250 mL beaker works well)
- Potassium nitrate (KNO_3)
- 10-mL graduated cylinder
- Water
- Electronic scale (or triple-beam balance)
- 400- or 600-mL beaker
- Ice

1 Stop and think

Based on what you know about dissolving substances in water, do you think the solubility of KNO_3 will increase or decrease with temperature?

2 Doing the experiment

1. Fill a 400-mL beaker ¾ full with water. Place it on a hot plate. Allow it to heat and go on to the next step.

2. Your teacher will assign you a specific amount of KNO_3. Use a balance to obtain the exact mass of potassium nitrate you will be using and put it in a test tube. Record the mass in Table 1.

3. Add 5 mL of water to your test tube containing your KNO_3. Record this volume in Table 1.

4. Place the test tube with the KNO_3 and water into your hot water bath. Allow it to heat until all the KNO_3 dissolves, while stirring. The temperature of the water may need to reach approximately 85°C.

5. Once all solid has dissolved, remove the test tube from the hot water bath and allow it to cool.

6. Place a thermometer in the test tube and watch for the first signs of crystallization. (*Hint*: Stirring occasionally may help you see the small crystals that form.) When you start to see your first crystal gather at the bottom of the test tube, record your temperature in Table 1.

7. If crystals still do not form when the temperature cools down to 30 degrees, place the test tube in a beaker of room temperature water.

8. If the crystals still do not form when the temperature cools down to 25 degrees, take the test tube out of the room temperature water and place it in a beaker of ice water (provided by your teacher).

9. Show your teacher your results. If your teacher gives you permission, place your test tube back in the hot water bath and redissolve the solid. Flush the solution down the drain with plenty of hot water.

10. Rinse and clean all remaining apparatus and put it away.

Table 1: KNO$_3$ crystal formation data

Mass of KNO$_3$ (g)	Volume of water (mL)	Mass of water (g)	Temp. when crystals first appeared (°C)

3 Calculations

a. In the lab you measured out 5.0 mL of water. What is the mass of 5.0 mL of water? Explain.

b. Knowing how many grams of your solid can dissolve in 5.0 g of water, how many grams could dissolve in 100.0 g of water? Report this value to the class. (*Hint*: Set up a ratio.) Record your results and those of the other groups in Table 2.

Table 2:

	Group #1 1 g	Group #2 2 g	Group #3 4 g	Group #4 6 g	Group #5 8 g
Temperature (°C)					
Solubility (g/100g H$_2$O)					

4 Thinking about what you observed

a. Using the class data, construct a solubility curve. Plot the temperature (0°C – 100°C) on the x-axis and the solubility of potassium nitrate (g KNO$_3$/ 100g H$_2$O) on the y-axis. Make sure your graph has a title and the axes are labeled including units. Connect all points with a smooth curve when complete.

b. In your own words, explain how solubility of KNO$_3$ varies with temperature.

c. From your solubility curve, predict the solubility of KNO$_3$ at

1. 65°C
2. 50°C
3. 25°C

d. Is this solubility curve useful for temperature values above 100°C?

e. How many grams of KNO$_3$ can be dissolved in 200.0 mL of water at 35°C?

104

19B Acids, Bases, and pH

What is pH?

Life exists inside a certain range of pH values. A pH value describes whether a solution is acidic, basic (alkaline), or neutral by describing the concentration of hydronium ions in a solution. An acid is a substance that produces hydronium (H_3O^+) ions when dissolved in water, and a base (or alkali) is a substance that produces hydroxide (OH^-) ions when dissolved in water. Neutral solutions have equal numbers of H_3O^+ and OH^- ions.

In this investigation you will learn the pH of several common solutions by making a pH scale using a pH indicator and chemicals of known pH. You will also identify two mystery chemicals with your pH scale.

Materials (per group)

- 2 or 3 well plates, depending on the size (need 12 wells)
- Permanent marker
- Eyedroppers or pipettes
- 5 milliliters of red cabbage juice (a pH indicator)
- 12 each red and blue litmus papers (pH indicators)
- 2 milliliters each of the 12 solutions listed in the data table
- Two 250-mL beakers; one contains warm water for rinsing pipettes, one empty beaker for discarded rinse water

1 Stop and think

Look at the table in the investigation. Using the pH values listed, predict whether the antibacterial soap will be acidic or basic and whether the apple juice will be acidic or basic. Of the solutions in the list, to which are they most closely related?

2 Doing the experiment

A. Make a pH scale using indicators

1. To create your pH scale, you will be using solutions 1 to 7 in the table below. Place the following labels for these solutions in order on a well plate. If you don't have seven wells in a row on one well plate, place two plates side by side. The labels should describe the solution and its pH: Lemon – pH 2, Vinegar – pH 3, Seltzer water – pH 4, Red cabbage juice (the control) – pH 6.5, Baking soda – pH 8.5, Bar soap – pH 10, and Ammonia – pH 11.

2. Using a pipette, place three drops of red cabbage juice in each of the seven labeled wells.

3. Using a pipette, add two drops of each of the solutions to the appropriately labeled well. Use a different eyedropper or pipette for each solution. However, if you must use the same dropper or pipette, thoroughly rinse it in fresh water after each solution before using it for a new solution. Record the color changes in your data table. The color series you see on the plate(s) represents a pH scale. We will refer to it as the pH test plate. You will use it to identify the pH of other solutions.

4. Dip the red litmus paper and the blue litmus paper into each well of the pH test plate. Record the results according to the directions in the data table.

Name of solution	Color when mixed with red cabbage juice	Red litmus paper: if paper turns blue, write "base" or make an "x"	Blue litmus paper: if paper turns red, write "acid" or make an "x"	pH
1. Lemon				2
2. Vinegar				3
3. Seltzer				4
4. Red cabbage juice				6.5
5. Baking soda solution				8.5
6. Bar soap solution				10
7. Ammonia				11
8. Green tea				
9. Antibacterial cleaner				
10. Apple juice				
11. Mystery solution A				
12. Mystery solution B				

B: Using pH indicators to measure unknown pH

1. Repeat steps A2 through A4 for solutions 8 to 12. Use another well plate for these five solutions. The labels should describe the solution. At this point, you do not know the pH of these solutions.

2. Identify the pH of solutions 8 to 12. Compare the color reactions and the litmus paper results for solutions 8 to 12 with the pH test plate.

3 Thinking about what you observed

a. What is the role of a pH indicator? What is the range of pH measured by each of the indicators you used (red cabbage juice, red litmus paper, blue litmus paper)?

b. Which of your solutions has the highest concentration of H_3O^+ ions? Which has the highest concentration of OH^- ions? Explain your reasoning.

c. The red cabbage juice used in the investigation has two roles. It is the pH indicator and, in the series on the pH test plate, it is a control. Why is a control needed on the pH test plate?

d. Mystery solutions A and B are identical to two other solutions you used in this lab. Use your results to identify these solutions. What is the identity of mystery solution A? What is the identity of mystery B? List evidence to support your claims.

e. List the pros and cons of using red cabbage juice and litmus paper as pH indicators.

f. Various professions use pH indicators. For example, photographers traditionally used and still sometimes use stop bath in developing, and swimming pools are maintained using information from pH indicators. Find out how these pH indicators work in these (or other) situations, and what the color changes mean.

20A Electricity

How do you measure voltage and current in electric circuits?

We use electricity every day, nearly every minute! In this Investigation you will build circuits and learn about voltage (volts) and current (amps) which are fundamental quantities that describe the electricity we use.

Materials

- CPO Electric Circuits kit
- 1 "D" battery
- Multimeter with leads
- Metal paper clip, plastic straw, piece of string, rubber band, pen cap or other similar objects

1 Building a circuit

Single bulb circuit

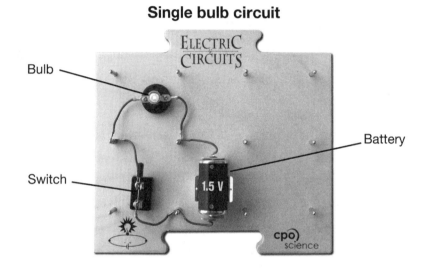

1. Build the circuit shown in the diagram with one battery, a switch, and a bulb.
2. Open and close the switch and see what happens.

2 Thinking about what you observed

a. How can you tell electric current is flowing in the circuit? Can you see the current?

b. Current flows from positive to negative. Trace the flow of current around the circuit with your finger.

c. How does the switch cause the current to stop flowing?

d. Why does the bulb go out when you open the switch?

3 Conductors and insulators

Materials through which electric current flows easily are called *conductors*.
Materials through which current does not flow easily are called *insulators*.

Connect circuit through each object

Paper clip   Plastic straw

String   Rubber band

Pen cap

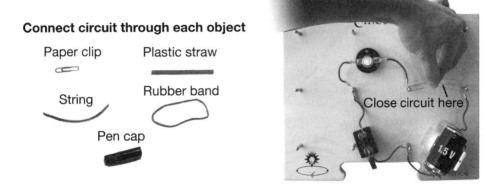

Close circuit here

1.5 V

1. Break one connection in your one-bulb circuit.
2. Complete the circuit by touching different materials between the wire and the post.
3. Which materials allow the bulb to light and which do not?

4 Thinking about what you observed

a. Make a table listing the materials as either conductors or insulators.

b. What characteristics are shared by the conductors you found?

c. What characteristics are shared by the insulators you found?

5 Circuit diagrams

For describing electric circuits we use the language of *circuit diagrams*. In a circuit diagram wires are represented by solid lines. Electrical devices like switches, batteries, and bulbs are represented by symbols.

a. Using these symbols, draw a picture of the circuit you built with one battery, switch, and light bulb.

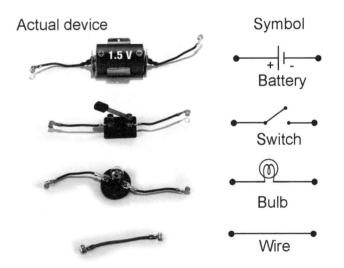

Actual device   Symbol

1.5 V

+   -
Battery

Switch

Bulb

Wire

6 Measuring the voltage of a battery

Turn the dial of your multimeter to DC volts. Red goes to the positive terminal and black to the negative terminal. When you touch two points in a circuit with the leads, the meter reads the voltage between the two points.

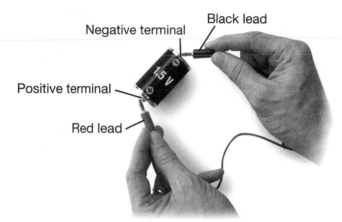

a. Measure the voltage of the battery and record your reading.

b. Take a second battery and connect it to the first by touching the ends together.

c. Measure the voltage for the four possible ways to connect two batteries (+ to –, + to +, – to –, – to +). How do your readings compare to the voltage of just one battery?

7 Measuring current

To measure current, the meter must be connected so the current has to flow through it. This is different from voltage measurement. To measure current you must force the current to flow through the meter by eliminating all other paths the current could go. Follow the instructions below carefully. Too much current can damage the meter.

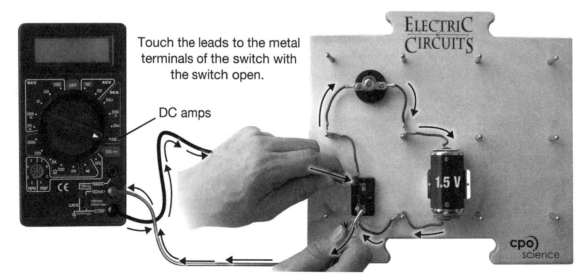

1. Set the multimeter to measure DC amps (current).

2. Open the switch and touch the red lead of the meter to the metal part of the switch closest to the battery's positive terminal (+).

3. Touch the black lead of the meter to the metal part on the other side of the switch.

4. The bulb should light, showing you that current is flowing through the meter. The meter should display the current in amps. This is the total current flowing around the circuit carrying power from the battery to the bulb. Remove the meter.

a. How much current is flowing in the circuit when the bulb is making light?

8 A circuit with a dimmer switch

The potentiometer (or *pot*) is an electrical device that can be used to make a dimmer switch. When the dial on the pot is turned one way the pot acts like a closed switch and current flows freely through it. When the dial is turned the other way the pot resists the flow of current.

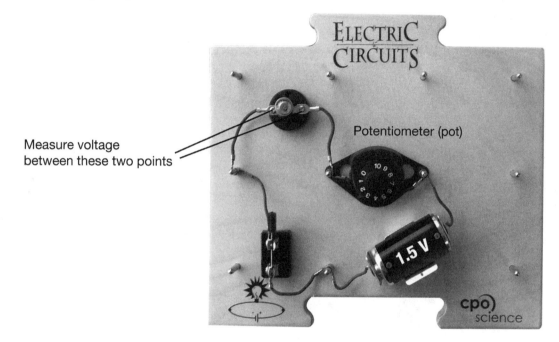

1. Connect the circuit in the diagram using the pot, a battery, wire, and a bulb.

2. Adjust the dial and watch what happens to the bulb.

3. Use the meter to measure the voltage across the bulb for different settings of the pot. Record your data in Table 1.

Table 1: Pot settings and voltage across bulb

Pot dial position	Voltage across bulb (V)	Observed light output of bulb

9 Thinking about what you observed

a. As you changed the settings of the pot, what happened to the voltage across the bulb?

b. Did you observe a relationship between the voltage across the bulb and the light output?

c. Propose a relationship between power and voltage that would explain the light output of the bulb.

20B Resistance and Ohm's Law

What is the relationship between current and voltage in a circuit?

Electrical devices get the energy they use from the current that flows through them. When designing an electrical device or a circuit, it is important for the proper amount of current to flow for the voltage that is available. Resistance is the property of electricity that helps regulate the current in the circuit. You will explore resistance and Ohm's law, the equation that relates voltage, current, and resistance.

Materials

- CPO Electric Circuits kit
- 2 "D" batteries
- Digital multimeter with test leads

1 Mystery resistors

A *resistor* is used in a circuit to provide resistance. You have green, blue, and red resistors in your kit with values of 5 Ω, 10 Ω, and 20 Ω, but you don't know which is which!

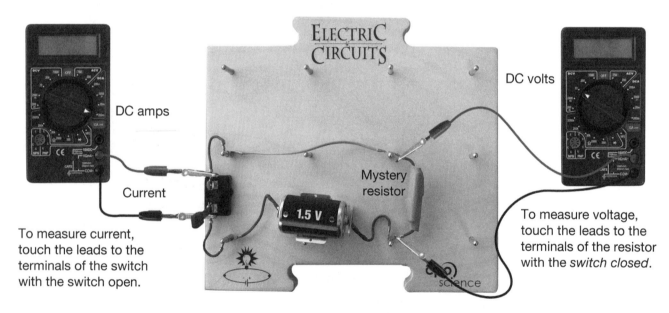

DC amps

Current

To measure current, touch the leads to the terminals of the switch with the switch open.

DC volts

Mystery resistor

1.5 V

To measure voltage, touch the leads to the terminals of the resistor with the *switch closed.*

1. Make a circuit with a switch, battery, and resistor, as pictured above.
2. Set the meter to measure current (DC amps). Open the switch. Measure the current by connecting the meter across the open terminals of the switch.
3. Set the meter to measure voltage (DC volts). Close the switch. Measure the voltage across the mystery resistor as pictured above.
4. Repeat the current and voltage measurements for each of the mystery resistors.

Table 1: Resistor currents

Resistor color	Voltage across resistor (V)	Current (A)

a. Use your knowledge of Ohm's law to determine which resistor is which. The resistance you calculate from Ohm's law will not come out exactly to 5, 10, or 20 because the meter itself has a small resistance.

2 Resistance and potentiometers (pots)

The potentiometer (pot) you used in the previous investigation is really a *variable resistor*. A variable resistor allows you to change its resistance by turning a dial. Many dials you use every day, like dimmer switches, are actually potentiometers.

1. Use the meter to measure the resistance of the pot for different positions of the dial. The pot does not have to be in the circuit; you can just touch the leads across the pot.

2. Take your first reading with the pot turned all the way to the left and take four or five readings until the pot is turned all the way to the right.

Table 2: Pot settings and resistance

Pot dial position	Resistance (Ω)

3 The bulb dimmer circuit

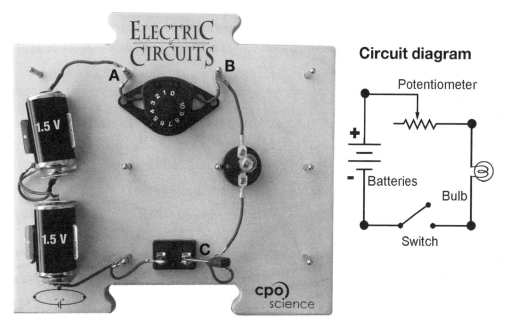

1. Build the dimmer circuit with two batteries, the pot, a switch, and a bulb.

2. Close the switch and observe how the brightness changes as you change the dial on the pot.

a. Use the concept of resistance to explain how the pot controls the brightness of a bulb.

113

4 The voltage drop

The voltage in a circuit is reduced whenever current flows through a device that has a resistance greater than zero. The reduction of voltage is called the *voltage drop*.

DC volts

To measure the voltage drop across the pot, touch the leads to (A) and (B).

Use points (B) and (C) to measure the voltage drop across the bulb.

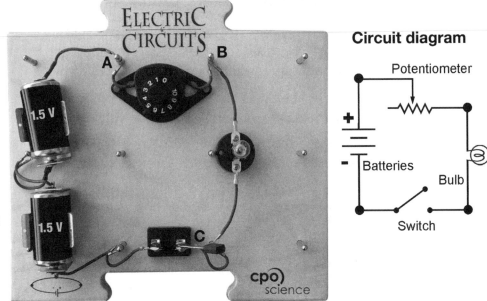

Circuit diagram

1. Connect the dimmer circuit with the pot, switch, two batteries, and a light bulb.
2. The voltage drop is measured by touching the meter leads to the terminals of each device.
3. Measure the voltage drop across the pot and across the bulb for different dial settings of the pot. Record the observed light output at each dial position measured.

Table 3: Pot settings and voltage drops

Pot dial position	Voltage drop across pot (V)	Voltage drop across bulb (V)	Observed light output

a. What is the relationship between the voltage drop across the pot and the voltage drop across the bulb?

b. What does the voltage drop tell you about the electrical energy carried by the current?

c. What relationship do you observe between the measured voltage drops and the battery voltage?

21A Electric Circuits

What are the different types of circuits?

A simple electric circuit contains one electrical device, a battery, and a switch. Flashlights use this type of circuit. However, most electrical systems, such as a stereo, contain many electrical devices connected together in multiple circuits. This investigation introduces two ways to connect multiple devices in a circuit.

Materials

- Electric circuits kit
- Digital multimeter with test leads
- 2 "D" batteries

1 Series circuits

Build this circuit

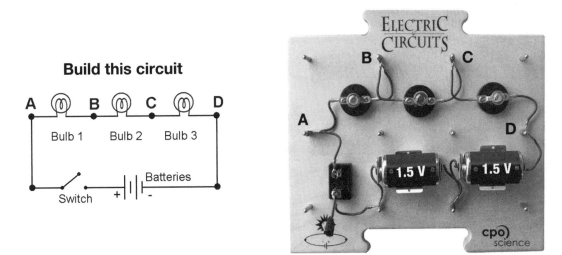

1. Using two batteries, build the simple circuit with three light bulbs and a switch as shown above.
2. Set the meter to DC volts. Close the switch and measure the voltage across the different places by touching the meter's leads to the bulbs' terminals. Record the voltages in Table 1.

Table I: Voltage measurements (volts)

Between A and B (V)	Between B and C (V)	Between C and D (V)	Between A and D (V)

2 Thinking about what you measured

a. What relationships do you see among the voltage measurements in Table 1?

b. What do the voltage measurements tell you about the flow of energy in the circuit?

3 The current in series circuits

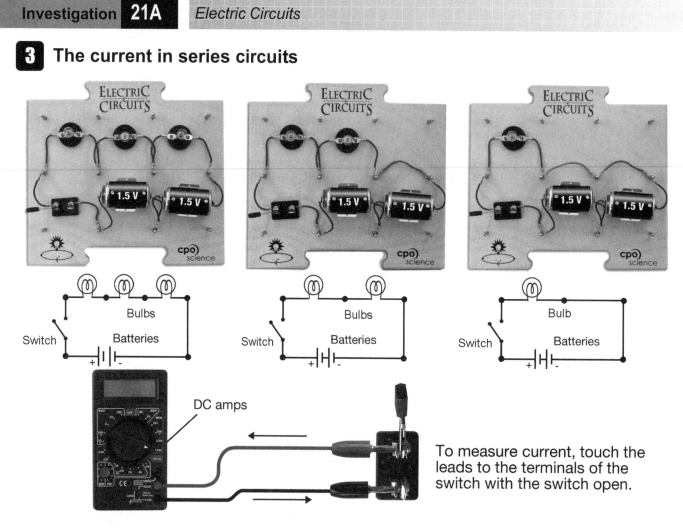

To measure current, touch the leads to the terminals of the switch with the switch open.

1. Set the meter to DC amps. Measure the current by opening the switch and touching the leads of the meter to the terminals of the switch in the three bulb circuit. Record your measurements in Table 2.

2. Remove one bulb and replace it with a wire. Measure and record the current for the two-bulb circuit.

3. Remove a second bulb and replace it with a wire. Measure and record the current again for the one-bulb circuit.

Table 2: Current Measurements (amps)

Three bulbs (A)	Two bulbs (A)	One bulb (A)

4 Thinking about what you observed

a. What happens to the current in the circuit as the number of bulbs is reduced? Explain why this occurs using Ohm's law and the concept of resistance.

b. What happens to the other two bulbs when one bulb is removed from the three-bulb circuit? Try it and explain why the circuit behaves as it does.

5 Short circuits

A short circuit is an easy (but dangerous) shortcut that current can travel through to avoid one or more of the electrical components in the circuit.

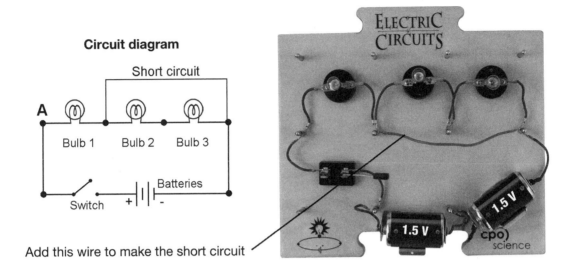

Circuit diagram

Short circuit

A

Bulb 1   Bulb 2   Bulb 3

Switch   + | | | - Batteries

Add this wire to make the short circuit

1. Rebuild your three-bulb circuit with the switch open.
2. Check the current and observe which bulbs light and how bright they are.
3. Add a section of wire that bridges the last two bulbs in the circuit. This wire is the "short circuit."
4. Complete the circuit (with the switch open) using the meter to measure the current. Observe which bulbs light and how bright they are.

6 Thinking about what you observed

Table 3: Short circuit current measurements (amps)

Three bulbs in series (A)	Three bulbs with two short circuited (A)

a. Compare the current in the three-bulb circuit with the current when two bulbs are bypassed by a short circuit. Which is greater? Use Ohm's law and the concept of resistance to explain why.

b. How does the current in the "short circuit" version compare with the current you measured in a one-bulb circuit? Explain why this should be true.

c. How does the resistance of a wire compare to the resistance of a bulb? Measure the resistances to test your answer. *Note*: Most meters cannot measure very low resistance and display "0.00" when the resistance is lower than 0.01 Ω.

d. Why would a short circuit be dangerous? Discuss (as a class) the consequences of very large currents in wires of different sizes.

7 **Parallel circuits**

Build this circuit

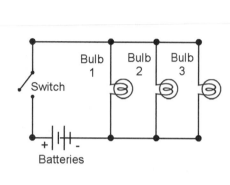

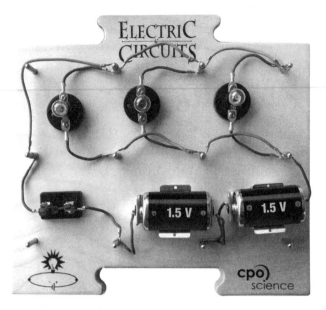

1. Build a circuit with two batteries, a switch, and three bulbs as shown in the diagram.
2. Close the switch and measure the voltage across the battery. All three bulbs are lit.
3. Measure the voltage across each bulb by touching the leads of the meter to the terminals of each bulb separately.
4. Set the meter to DC amps. Measure the total current in the circuit by opening the switch and touching the leads of the meter to the terminals of the switch.

Table 4: Voltage and current in a parallel circuit

	Total circuit	Bulb 1	Bulb 2	Bulb 3
Voltage (*V*)				
Current (*A*)				

8 **Thinking about what you observed**

a. Compare the brightness of the bulbs in the parallel circuit with the brightness in the series circuit.

b. Compare the total current in the single-bulb circuit, the three-bulb series circuit, and the three-bulb parallel circuit. Propose a relationship between the currents that agrees with the brightness of the bulbs.

c. Do the other two bulbs continue to light when the third bulb is removed from the parallel circuit? Try it. How does this differ from what happened with the series circuit?

d. Do you think the electrical outlets in your home are connected in a series or parallel circuit? Give two reasons why one type of circuit has an advantage over the other for connecting outlets.

21B Electrical Energy and Power

How much energy is carried by electricity?

A voltage of 1 volt means 1 amp of current can do 1 joule of work each second. This definition of a volt is really a formula for calculating power from current and voltage. If the voltage and current are multiplied, the result is the power used by the circuit. In this investigation you will explore the relationship between voltage, current, and power.

Materials

- CPO Electric Circuits kit
- 1 "D" battery
- Digital multimeter with test leads
- Capacitor (Super Cap)
- CPO DataCollector

1 Energy and power in an electrical system

Electrical power

Voltage (V)

Power (W) $P = V I$

Current (A)

Voltage x Current = Power

$$\frac{watts}{amp} \times amp = watts\ (W)$$

Circuit diagram

A — Bulb

Switch

+ | - Battery

1. Connect a simple circuit with a single bulb, switch, and battery.
2. Use the meter to measure the voltage and current in the circuit when the bulb is lit.
3. Use the formula above to calculate the power used by the bulb in watts.
4. Repeat the experiment with two batteries connected so the bulb receives 3 V instead of 1.5 V.

Table 1: Power used by a bulb

Voltage (V)	Current (A)	Power (W)

2 Thinking about what you observed

a. How did the power used by the bulb compare at the two different voltages?

b. Was the bulb brighter, dimmer, or about the same at 3 V compared to 1.5 V? Explain any difference you observed using the concept of power.

3 Energy and power from a battery

Circuit diagram

Bulb

Switch

Capacitor
+ | – B
A

+ | –
Battery

Touch this wire here to charge the capacitor. Remove the wire after a few seconds.

ELECTRIC CIRCUITS

A   B

Battery
(use only 1 battery)

Capacitor

cpo) science

Safety Note: The capacitor can be destroyed by connecting positive and negative voltage to the wrong terminals, or by using more than one 1.5 V battery.

Measure the voltage across the terminals of the capacitor.

1. Find the capacitor (labeled *super cap*). This capacitor acts like a battery that charges almost instantly when you touch its terminals to a battery.

2. Make the circuit in the diagram. The positive terminal of the capacitor should meet the red (+) lead of the meter. The meter will probably read 0 volts.

3. Touch the positive wire from the battery to the positive (+) terminal of the capacitor for 5 seconds. Remove the positive battery wire once the capacitor is "charged" up to 1.5 V.

4. Touch the leads of the multimeter across the capacitor and watch what happens to the voltage (DC volts) over time. The bulb should light up then dim and go out as the voltage drops.

4 Thinking about what you observed

a. How was energy flowing when the capacitor was "charging up"? What was the source of the energy and where did it go?

b. How was energy flowing when the bulb was connected and the battery was removed? What was the source of the energy and where did it go?

c. Why did the bulb go out after a few seconds? Explain what you observed in terms of the ideas of energy and power.

5 Energy and power

You are going to use the CPO Timer mode to measure how long the capacitor can keep one or more bulbs lit.

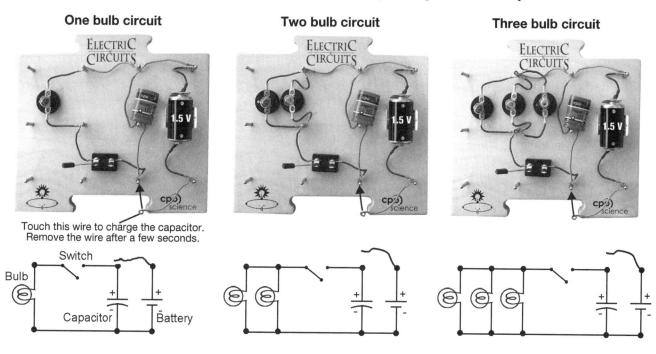

1. Set up the three circuits above, one at a time.
2. For each circuit, charge the capacitor for 5 seconds then use the DataCollector to measure how long the bulb produces light. Start the DataCollector when you close the switch to light the bulb. Stop the DataCollector when you can no longer see any light. Use stopwatch mode.
3. Repeat the test three times and take the average. Use Table 2 to record your data.

Table 2: Energy and power data at 1.5 V

Starting voltage (V)	Number of bulbs	Time until bulb goes out (s)			Average of 3 trials (s)

6 Thinking about what you observed

a. What is the total power used by one, two, and three bulbs connected in parallel? In a parallel circuit each device draws current as if it were the only device in the circuit. (*Hint*: Look back at your data from Part 1.)

b. What relationship do you observe between the time the bulbs stay lit and the total power used?

c. Since power is energy ÷ time, the formula can be rearranged to give energy = power × time. For example, if you use 10 watts for 10 seconds, you have used a total of 100 joules of energy (100 J = 10 W × 10 s.). Use your data to estimate how many joules of energy are stored in the capacitor at 1.5 V.

22A Magnetism

How do magnets and compasses work?

Magnets are used in almost all electrical and electronic machines from motors to computers. How far does magnetic force reach? How can you use a compass to detect magnetic forces? In this investigation you will use magnets and a compass to answer these and other questions about magnetism.

Materials

- 2 magnets (from kit)
- Compass (from kit)
- Metric ruler

1 How far does magnetic force reach?

How far does the magnetic force of a magnet reach? This is an important question concerning machines such as motors and generators that use magnets.

How far does the magnetic force reach?

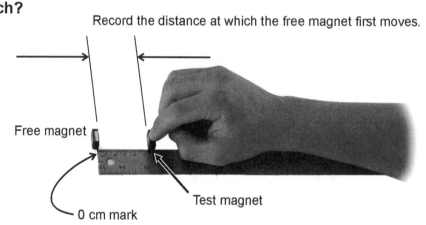

Record the distance at which the free magnet first moves.

Free magnet

Test magnet

0 cm mark

1. Place one magnet at the 0 cm mark of the ruler and slide a second magnet closer and closer until the first magnet moves. Practice the technique several times before recording data.
2. Record the distance between the magnets when you first see movement.
3. Try each of the combinations of poles—north-north, south-south, and north-south.
4. For each combination, complete three trials, and average your three distances.

Table 1: Magnetic forces between two magnets

	North-South	South-South	North-North
Distance 1 (mm)			
Distance 2 (mm)			
Distance 3 (mm)			
Average distance (mm)			
Average estimated error (mm)			

2 Thinking about what you observed

a. What is the average estimated error for each magnet combination? Subtract each individual distance for the north-south magnet combination from the average of the three distances. Drop any negative signs. Once you have found these three differences, average them and record in Table 1. Repeat for the other two magnet combinations.

b. Are the attract and repel distances *significantly* different? Your answer should include a comparison between average estimated errors and the differences between magnet combination average distances.

3 Using a compass to detect magnetic forces

The needle of a compass is a permanent magnet. Earth is magnetic, so a compass needle is attracted to north in the absence of other (stronger) magnets.

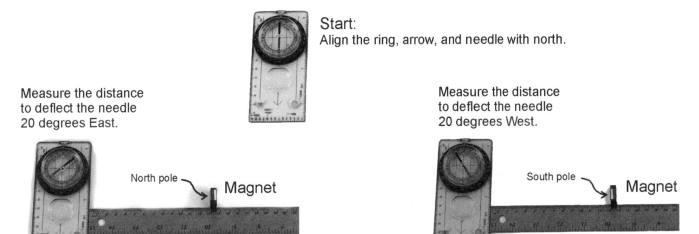

Start:
Align the ring, arrow, and needle with north.

Measure the distance
to deflect the needle
20 degrees East.

North pole — Magnet

Measure the distance
to deflect the needle
20 degrees West.

South pole — Magnet

1. Set a compass on your table far from any magnets. Rotate the compass so the needle, dial, and arrow are all aligned with north.

2. Place a metric ruler to the side of the compass and line it up perpendicularly with the north pole of the compass. Move a small magnet near the compass and note the distance at which the needle moves 20 degrees from north.

3. Reverse the pole of the small magnet and note the distance at which the needle moves 20 degrees in the opposite direction.

4 Thinking about what you observed

a. At a distance of 10 cm, which is stronger: the magnetic force from Earth or the magnetic force from the small magnet? How is your answer supported by your observations?

b. Is the end of the compass needle a magnetic north or a magnetic south pole? How is your answer supported by your observations?

c. Is the geographic north pole of the planet Earth a magnetic north or a magnetic south pole? How is your answer supported by your observations?

22B Electromagnets

How are electricity and magnetism related?

Almost every electrical device that creates motion, such as a motor, uses magnets. Permanent magnets are not the only type of magnets used in these devices. Often, electromagnets are used. Electromagnets create magnetic forces through electric currents. This investigation will explore the properties of electromagnets.

Materials

- CPO Electric Circuits kit
- Electromagnet coil (in kit)
- 1 permanent magnet (in kit)
- compass (in kit)
- 1 "D" battery

1   Electromagnets

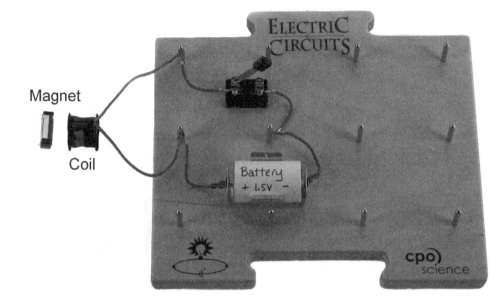

1. Attach the coil, battery, and switch in the circuit shown above. Leave the switch open so no current flows.

2. Place a permanent magnet about 1 centimeter away from the coil. Stand the magnet up on its end.

3. Close the switch and watch what happens to the magnet. *Don't* leave current running or the coil will overheat. Open the switch after each trial.

4. Turn the permanent magnet around so its other pole faces the coil. Close the switch and see what happens now.

5. Reverse the wires connecting the battery to the circuit. This makes the electric current flow the other way. Repeat steps 3 and 4 of experiment with the magnet.

2   Thinking about what you observed

a. Write two to three sentences that explain what you saw when the switch was closed.

b. Propose an explanation for why the magnet moved.

c. When the magnet was reversed, did the force between it and the coil change direction? How did the force change?

d. When the coil wires were switched, did the force from the coil change direction? How do you know?

e. How is a current-carrying coil like a magnet? How is it different? Explain how this shows that electricity and magnetism are related.

3 Comparing the electromagnet to a permanent magnet

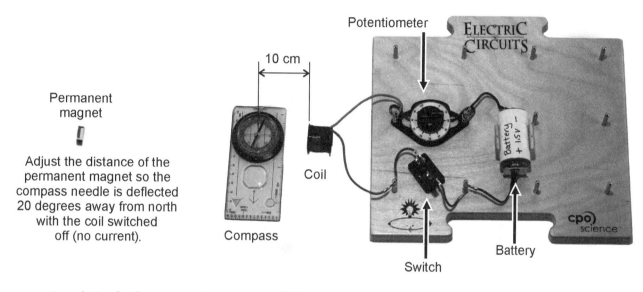

Permanent magnet

Adjust the distance of the permanent magnet so the compass needle is deflected 20 degrees away from north with the coil switched off (no current).

10 cm

Compass

Coil

Potentiometer

Battery

Switch

1. Attach the potentiometer, coil, battery, and switch in the circuit shown in the diagram. Leave the switch open so no current flows.
2. Set the compass so the needle, ring, and arrow are all aligned with north. Put the coil about 10 cm from the center of the compass.
3. Place a permanent magnet on the side of the compass opposite the coil. Bring the magnet close enough to deflect the needle 20 degrees away from north.
4. Close the switch and adjust the potentiometer so the needle returns to north. The coil should deflect the compass needle back toward north. Reverse the permanent magnet if the needle moves the wrong way. *Don't* leave current running or the coil will overheat. Open the switch after each trial.
5. Try moving the permanent magnet to different distances and using the potentiometer to return the compass needle to north with force from the electromagnet.

4 Stop and think

a. The permanent magnet is pulling the compass needle to the left. The electromagnet is pulling the needle in the opposite direction to the right. When the needle returns to north what can you say about the magnetic forces from the permanent magnet and electromagnet?

5 Iron and electromagnets

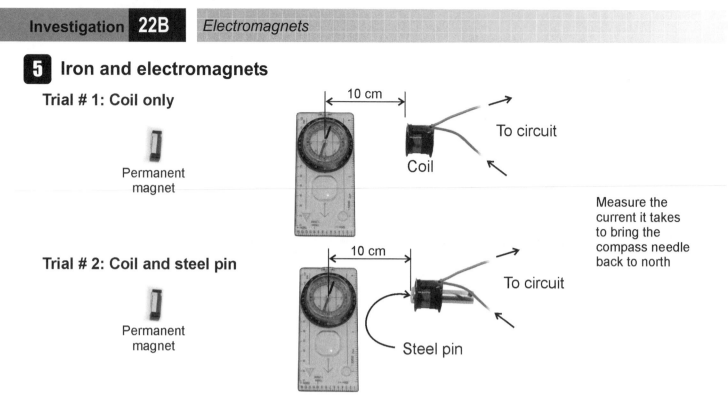

Trial # 1: Coil only

Permanent magnet

10 cm

To circuit

Coil

Measure the current it takes to bring the compass needle back to north

Trial # 2: Coil and steel pin

Permanent magnet

10 cm

To circuit

Steel pin

1. Use the same circuit as for part 3 with one battery, switch, coil, and potentiometer.

2. Rotate the compass until the needle and dial are aligned with north. *There should be no magnets nearby, and no current in the coil for this step.*

3. Move a permanent magnet close enough to deflect the needle 20 degrees from north.

4. The coil should be 10 cm from the center of the compass (see diagram above). Close the switch, then use a multimeter to measure and record how much current it takes for the coil to bring the needle back to north. Adjust the current with the potentiometer. Once you have recorded the measurement in Table 1, open the switch to stop the current.

5. Put the steel pin in the coil so its head is against the coil and 10 cm from the center of the compass.

6. Adjust the distance of the permanent magnet so the compass needle is deflected 20 degrees from north, like you did in step 3. *There should be no current in the coil for this step.*

7. Close the switch, then use a multimeter to measure and record the current it takes to return the needle to north with the steel pin in the coil.

Table 1: Electromagnet current with and without the steel pin

Current with bare coil	Current with steel pin	Difference in current	Percent difference

6 Thinking about what you observed

a. How did the steel pin affect the magnetic force created by the coil? Was the magnetic force reduced, increased, or did it stay about the same? Use your observations to support your answer.

23A Harmonic Motion

How do we describe the back-and-forth motion of a pendulum?

Harmonic motion is motion that repeats in cycles. Many important systems in nature and many useful inventions rely on harmonic motion. For example, the phases of the moon and the seasons are caused by Earth's harmonic motion. This Investigation will explore harmonic motion using a pendulum. The concepts you learn with the pendulum will also apply to other examples of harmonic motion.

Materials

- CPO DataCollector and 1 photogate
- CPO Physics Stand
- CPO Pendulum
- Graph paper

1 Setting up the pendulum

Attach the pendulum to one of the top holes in the stand.

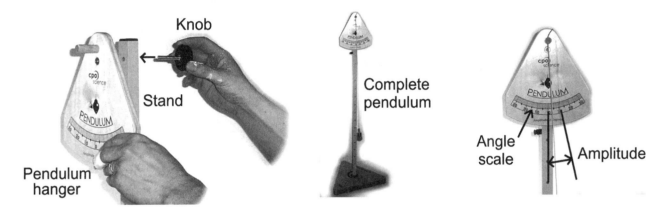

Start the pendulum swinging and watch it for a minute. Think about how to describe the motion.

a. Write one sentence about the motion using the word *cycle*.

b. The <u>*amplitude*</u> is the maximum amount the pendulum swings away from its resting position. The resting position is straight down. One way to measure amplitude is the angle the pendulum moves away from center. Write one sentence describing the motion of your pendulum using the word *amplitude*.

c. Draw a sequence of sketches that describe one complete cycle using arrows to indicate the direction the pendulum is going at that point in the cycle.

2 Oscillators and period

a. Use the stopwatch mode of the DataCollector to measure the period of your pendulum. Time 10 cycles. Do three trials and use Table 1 to record your data.

b. Divide the average time for 10 cycles by 10 to get the period.

c. Write a one-sentence description of how you measured the period.

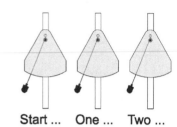

Count 10 cycles

Start ...   One ...   Two ...

Divide time by 10

example
period = 15.20 sec ÷ 10
= 1.52 seconds

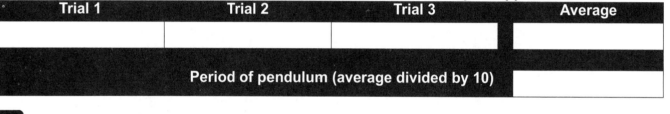

Table 1: Pendulum period data: Time for 10 cycles (s)

Trial 1	Trial 2	Trial 3	Average
Period of pendulum (average divided by 10)			

3 Measuring period with a photogate

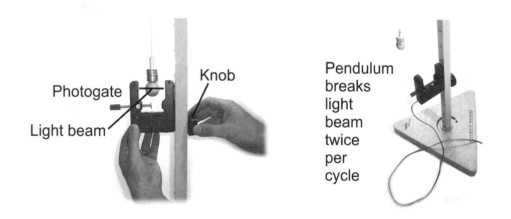

Photogate

Light beam

Knob

Pendulum breaks light beam twice per cycle

1. Attach the photogate as shown in the diagram. The pendulum breaks the light beam when it swings through the photogate. Try to keep the string length close to the length you used in part 2 and try to release the pendulum bob straight so that it swings evenly through the photogate.

2. Put the DataCollector on the period function and let the pendulum swing through the light beam.

3. A hold value can be displayed by pressing the memory (m) button on the lower right of the screen. The value is displayed to the right of the active value, which is always displayed.

4 Thinking about what you observed

a. Write down the time measurement you get from the DataCollector.

b. Is the time you get from the DataCollector the period of the pendulum? Explain why the time is or is not the period of the pendulum. (*Hint*: Compare to your results from Part 2.)

c. Explain how the time measured by the DataCollector is related to the period of the pendulum.

5 What variables affect the period of a pendulum?

In this experiment, the period of the pendulum is the only dependent variable. There are three independent variables: the mass of the bob, the amplitude of the swing, and the length of the string.

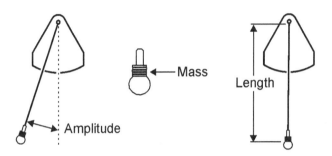

1. The amplitude can be changed by varying the angle that the pendulum swings.
2. There are washers that you can use to change the mass of the bob.
3. The length of the string can be changed by sliding it through the slot in the peg. Measure the length of the string from the bottom of the string peg to the bottom of the washers.

Design an experiment to determine which of the three variables has the largest effect on the period of the pendulum. Your experiment should provide enough data to show that one of the three variables has much more of an effect that the other two. Be sure to use a consistent technique that gives you consistent results.

a. Think of three experiments you can do to see what variables affect the period of the pendulum. Write down one sentence describing each experiment.

b. Do the three experiments and record the measurements you make to assess the effect of changing each variable.

6 Analyzing the data

a. Of the three things you can change (amplitude, mass, and string length), which one has the biggest effect on the pendulum and why? In your answer you should consider how gravity accelerates objects of different mass.

b. Split up your data so that you can look at the effect of each of the three variables by making a separate graph showing how each one affects the period. To make comparison easier, make sure all the graphs have the same scale on the *y*-axis (period). The graphs should be labeled like the example below.

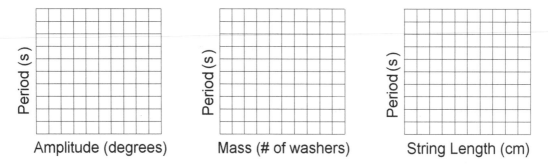

7 Applying what you know

Pendulum clocks were once among the most common ways to keep time. It is still possible to find beautifully-made pendulum clocks for sale today. To make a pendulum clock accurate, the period must be set so a certain number of periods equals a convenient measure of time. For example, you could design a clock with a pendulum that has a period of 1 second. The gears in the clock mechanism would then have to turn the second hand 1/60th of a turn per swing of the pendulum.

a. Using your data, design and construct a pendulum that you can use to accurately measure a time interval of 30 seconds. Test your pendulum clock against the electronic stopwatch.

b. Mark on your graph the period you chose for your pendulum.

c. How many cycles did your pendulum complete in 30 seconds?

d. If mass does not affect the period, why is it important that the pendulum in a clock is heavy?

e. Calculate the percent error in your prediction of time from your pendulum clock. The percent error is 100 times the difference between your prediction and 30 seconds, divided by 30 seconds.

f. You notice in a magazine that a watch manufacturer advertises that its quartz watch loses no more than 5 seconds per month. Assume that the watch loses the maximum amount (5 seconds) in 31 days. Calculate the percent error of the quartz watch by comparing 5 seconds to the number of seconds in a month.

Gears of clockworks

Pendulum

23B Natural Frequency and Resonance

What is resonance and why is it important?

The pendulum oscillated at only one frequency for each string length. The frequency at which objects vibrate is called the natural frequency. Almost everything has a natural frequency, and most things have more than one. We use natural frequency to create all kinds of waves, from microwaves to the musical sounds from a guitar. In this investigation you will explore the connection between frequency of a wave and its wavelength.

Materials

- CPO DataCollector
- Sound & Waves Machine
- Fiddlehead
- Wiggler
- CPO Physics Stand

1 Setting up the experiment

Connect the DataCollector to the Sound & Waves console as shown in the diagram. The telephone cord connects the DataCollector and Sound & Waves console. The stereo cord goes between the Sound & Waves console and the Wiggler.

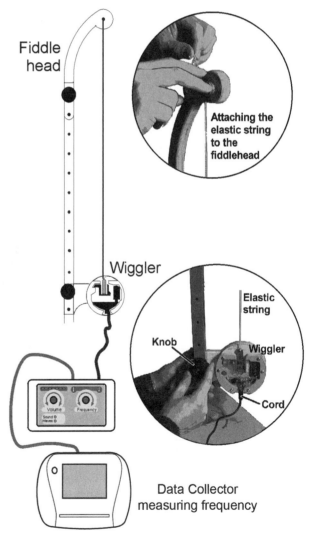

Fiddle head

Attaching the elastic string to the fiddlehead

Wiggler

Elastic string

Knob

Wiggler

Cord

Data Collector measuring frequency

1. Attach the fiddle head to the top of the stand, as high as it goes.

2. Attach the Wiggler to the bottom of the stand, as low as it goes.

3. Stretch the elastic string a little (5–10 centimeters) and attach the free end to the fiddle head. Loosen the knob until you can slide the string between any two of the washers. *Gently* tighten the knob just enough to hold the string.

4. Turn on the DataCollector and be sure to plug in the AC adapter.

5. Set the Sound & Waves console to waves using the button. The Wiggler should start to wiggle back and forth, shaking the string.

6. Set the DataCollector to timer mode in the frequency window. You should get a reading of about 10 Hz, which means the Wiggler is oscillating back and forth 10 times per second.

7. Try adjusting the frequency of the wiggler with the frequency control on the Sound & Waves console. If you watch the string, you will find that interesting patterns form at certain frequencies.

2 Resonances of a vibrating string

At certain frequencies the vibrating string will form wave patterns like those shown in the picture. Each of the patterns occurs at a *resonance* of the string. The resonances are called harmonics and they are described by the number of "bumps" seen on the vibrating string.

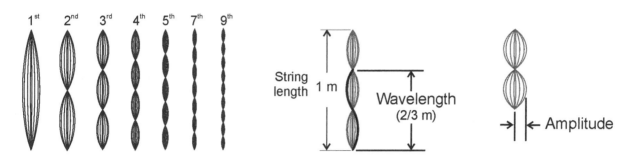

The wavelength of each harmonic is the length of one complete wave. One complete wave is two "bumps." Therefore, the wavelength is the length of two bumps. The string is 1 meter long. If you have a pattern of three bumps, the wavelength is 2/3 meters, since three bumps equal 1 meter and a whole wave is two of the three bumps.

3 Finding the standing waves

You noticed that the standing waves only occur at certain special frequencies. The wiggler applies a periodic force to the string. When the periodic force matches the natural frequency of the string, a large response develops (resonance).

1. Use the frequency control to find the first through the eighth harmonics of the string (at least).

2. Record the frequency and wavelength for each harmonic in Table 1. You should fine-tune the frequency to get the largest amplitude wave before recording the data. Look for harmonics two to six before looking for the first one. The first harmonic, also called the *fundamental*, is hard to find with exactness. Once you have the frequencies for the others, they provide a clue for finding the frequency of the first harmonic.

Table 1: Frequency, harmonic, and wavelength data

Harmonic #	Frequency (Hz)	Wavelength (m)	Frequency times wavelength
1			
2			
3			
4			
5			
6			

4 Thinking about what you observed

a. In one or two sentences, describe how the frequencies of the different harmonic patterns are related.

b. Why is the word *fundamental* chosen as another name for the first harmonic?

c. Give an equation relating frequency (*f*) and wavelength (λ) that best describes your observations.

d. If the frequency increases by a factor of two, what happens to the wavelength?

e. Propose a meaning for the number you get by multiplying frequency and wavelength.

5 Frequency and energy

Waves are useful because they carry energy from one place to another. The energy of a wave can also carry information such as a voice signal from a cell phone or a TV picture.

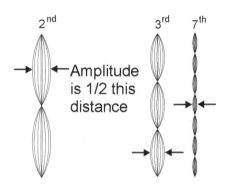

1. Set up several wave patterns and measure the amplitude for each harmonic.
2. Measure at least five different harmonics, including the 6th or higher.

Table 2: Frequency vs. amplitude data

Harmonic #	Frequency (Hz)	Amplitude (cm)

6 Thinking about what you observed

a. What happens to the amplitude of the waves as their frequency increases?

b. How does the energy of a wave depend on its frequency if the amplitude stays constant? How is your answer supported by your observations of the vibrating string?

7 Resonance

The diagram shows a useful way to think about pushing a swing. The person pushing applies a periodic force to the swing, just like the wiggler does to the vibrating string. Like the string, a swing is a system in harmonic motion. If the push is applied at the swing's natural frequency, the amplitude grows large, like the standing wave on the string. The response of a swing to a periodic push is an example of *resonance*. The harmonics on the vibrating string are another example of resonance. Resonance happens when the force applied to a system matches its natural frequency. We use resonance to create waves with specific frequencies, such as in a musical instrument, cell phone, or microwave oven.

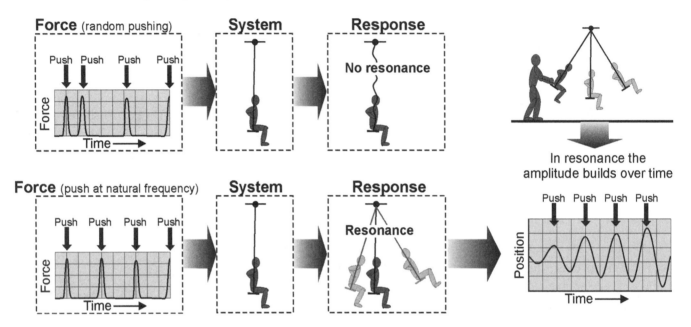

24A Properties of Sound

Does sound behave like other waves?

Sound is one of the most important of our senses. We use sounds to express the whole range of human emotion. Scientifically, sound is one of the simplest and most common kinds of waves. Sound is a rich and beautiful palette from which musicians create works of joy, excitement, and drama. In this investigation you will listen to beats and show how they can be explained if sound is a wave, create interference of sound waves, and demonstrate resonance.

Materials

- CPO DataCollector
- Sound & Waves Machine
- Fiddlehead
- Wiggler
- Tuning forks

1 Beats, consonance, and dissonance

How do we know sound is a wave? What experimental evidence proves sound is a wave? Suppose two sounds reach your ear at the same time. Interference occurs when more than one wave is present at the same time, in the same place.

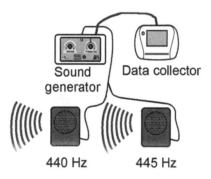

1. The teacher will set up two sound waves generated by one machine set to operate in "beat" mode. One sound wave will be at 440 Hz and the other will be at 445 Hz.
2. Listen to the 440 Hz sound by itself.
3. Listen to the 445 Hz sound by itself.
4. Listen to the combination of 440 Hz and 445 Hz together.
5. The teacher will keep one sound at 445 Hz and adjust the frequency of the other one between 444 and 430 Hz. Listen to the combination.

2 Thinking about what you observed

The oscillations of loud and soft you hear from the two sound waves are called *beats*. Beats are caused by small differences in frequency between multiple sounds heard at the same time.

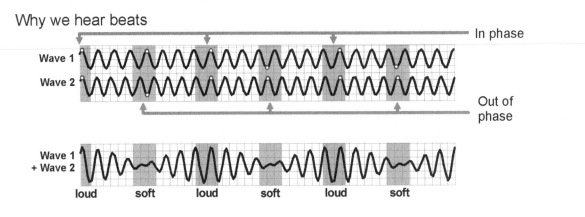

Why we hear beats

Conduct experiments that can answer the following questions about beats.

a. What makes the beats get faster or slower? In your answer you should describe what you do to the frequencies to make the beats faster or slower.

b. Is the sound of beats pleasant to listen to or unpleasant? The word *consonant* is used by musicians to describe sounds that fit smoothly together. The opposite of consonant is *dissonant*. Dissonant sounds tend to make people anxious and irritable. Describe the relationship between consonance, dissonance, and beats.

c. How could you use beats to match one frequency to another frequency? This is done every day when musicians in an orchestra tune their instruments.

d. How much different do the two frequencies have to be before you do not hear any beats?

3 Interference

Beats are only one way sound waves interact with each other. Suppose you have two identical sound waves and you are standing where you can hear them both. For certain positions, one sound wave reaches your ear in the opposite phase with the other wave and the sound gets softer, like in beats. Move over a little and the two sound waves add up to get louder. These effects are called interference and are easy to demonstrate.

1. Set up one sound generator with two speakers. Place one speaker about 1/2 meter behind the other.

2. Set the frequency between 400 Hz and 800 Hz.

3. Stand 3 or 4 meters in front of one speaker and have your lab partner slowly move one of the

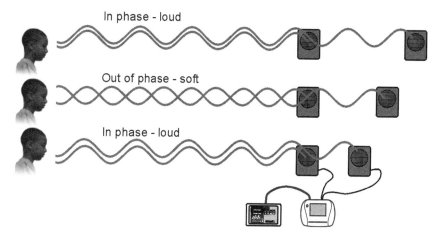

two speakers away. You will hear the sound get loud and soft and loud again when the distance between speakers has changed by one wavelength.

When two speakers are connected to the same sound generator they both make the exact same sound wave. If you move around a room you will hear places of loud and soft whenever your distance from each speaker differs by one wavelength.

4 Thinking about what you observed

a. Try to make an approximate measurement of the wavelength of sound by changing the separation of the two speakers. The speakers have been moved one wavelength when the sound heard by the observer has gone from loudest, to softest, and back to loudest again. For this to work you need to keep the observer and both speakers in the same line.

b. Why do we not usually hear interference from stereos even though they have two speakers?

5 Resonance

Many objects that can create sound also demonstrate resonance. When struck, played, or rubbed, these objects produce a characteristic sound at their natural frequency. A tuning fork is a good example.

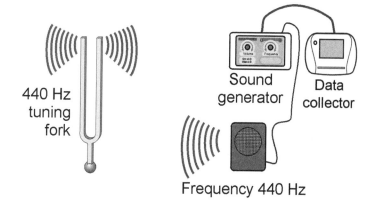

137

1. Select a tuning fork and tap it on your knee or another firm (but not hard) surface.

2. Listen to the sound. Does it change in frequency or do you hear a single frequency that does not change?

3. Use the sound generator and DataCollector to measure the frequency of the resonance by matching the frequency of the sound generator with the sound you hear from the tuning fork. The match is perfect when you no longer hear any beats.

4. Try several different size tuning forks and use the chart below to record the resonant frequency for each one.

Table 1: Resonant frequencies for tuning forks

Tuning fork description	Measured resonant frequency (Hz)	Labeled resonant frequency (if any)

6 Thinking about what you observed

a. Did you observe any relationship between the size (or shape) of the tuning fork and the frequency at which it was resonant?

b. What range of frequencies did you hear that seemed to match the frequency of the tuning fork? Give your answer in the form of a range written like 429 Hz–451 Hz.

c. Strike the tuning fork and hold the bottom end against a hard, thin surface, like a window. Does the sound get louder, softer, or remain unchanged? Explain what you hear by describing what might be happening between the tuning fork and the surface you touched.

24B Resonance in Other Systems

How can resonance be controled to make the sounds we want?

Almost all objects show some kind of resonance. A good example is a wine glass. If you take a wine glass and rub a moistened finger around the rim you can hear a resonant sound. Music is a combination of sound and rhythm that we find pleasant. Some people like music with a heavy beat and strong rhythm. Other people like music where the notes rise and fall in beautiful melodies. In this investigation you will create musical notes by choosing frequencies of sound, make a simple musical instrument called a straw kazoo, and learn the foundations of musical harmony.

Materials

- CPO Sound & Waves Machine
- CPO DataCollector
- Wine glasses
- Glass bottles
- Scissors
- Ruler
- Straw

1 Resonance in other systems

A - Wine Glass

1. Obtain a good-quality wine glass, like the ones shown in the diagram.

2. Hold the glass firmly from its base and rub the rim with a a moistened finger to hear the resonance.

3. Use the sound generator and DataCollector to match the frequency as close as you can to the sound of the glass.

4. Fill the glass to different heights with water and use the same technique to find the resonant frequency for each different height.

5. Use the table below to record the height of water and the resonant frequency you found for each different height.

Use different heights of liquid.

Table 1: Resonant frequencies of glass of water

Trial #	Water height	Frequency (Hz)

B - Tall Glass Bottle

1. Use a tall glass bottle, like the one in the diagram.
2. You can make a resonant sound by blowing over the open mouth of the bottle, as shown. This is a little tricky and you have to find the right angle for blowing air over the mouth of the bottle.
3. Fill the bottle to different heights of water and see how the sound changes.
4. Use the sound generator and DataCollector to estimate the frequency of the sound you get at different heights and write the results in the table below.

Blow over the mouth of the bottle to make the sound.

Table 2: Resonant frequencies of bottle of water

Trial #	Water height	Frequency (Hz)

2 Thinking about what you observed

What was the relationship between the frequencies and the heights? In coming up with your answer, remember the waves on the vibrating string and how the frequency and wavelength were related. Do you see similar behavior with the sounds and heights from the glass and bottle? For each case, what might be the vibrating element that would explain your observed changes in frequency?

3 Making notes

Musical notes are different frequencies of sound. Over thousands of years people have found combinations of frequencies that sound good together. The frequencies are different enough to not make beats but not so different that they cannot make musical melodies that flow.

1. Set up your sound generator and DataCollector.
2. Turn down the volume so you cannot hear the sound but you can still read the frequency from the DataCollector.
3. Each group in the class will be given a different frequency to tune to. Tune your frequency using the DataCollector until you are within 1 Hz of the frequency you were given.

Your teacher will tell you to turn up and down different frequencies so they can be heard together. Don't change the frequency, just adjust the volume up and down when you are asked.

a. Describe the sound of the three frequencies—264 Hz, 330 Hz, and 396 Hz—when you hear them together. Which three notes are these? (Look at the diagram below.)

b. Describe the sound of the three frequencies—264 Hz, 315 Hz, and 396 Hz—when you hear them together.

c. Contrast the two sounds. Does one sound more happy or sad compared with the other? Does one sound spookier than the other? Which combination reminds you more of spring, which of fall?

d. Describe the effect of adding a frequency of 528 Hz to each group of frequencies.

C major Scale								
Note	C	D	E	F	G	A	B	C
Frequency (Hz)	264	297	330	352	396	440	495	528
Ratio to C-264	$\frac{1}{1}$ $\left(\frac{264}{264}\right)$	$\frac{9}{8}$ $\left(\frac{297}{264}\right)$	$\frac{5}{4}$ $\left(\frac{330}{264}\right)$	$\frac{4}{3}$ $\left(\frac{352}{264}\right)$	$\frac{3}{2}$ $\left(\frac{396}{264}\right)$	$\frac{5}{3}$ $\left(\frac{440}{264}\right)$	$\frac{15}{8}$ $\left(\frac{495}{264}\right)$	$\frac{2}{1}$ $\left(\frac{528}{264}\right)$

4 Controlling frequency and wavelength

Most musical instruments use resonance. This means that when instruments are played the sounds they make are based on their natural frequencies. How do musical instruments make so many notes at different frequencies? Why does a guitar player use frets and a flute player use different fingerings?

These players are controlling the frequencies of their instruments by changing the wavelength of the vibrating string or column of air. If the wavelength is shorter, the frequency goes up. If the wavelength is longer, the frequency goes down. The chart on the previous page shows the ratios of frequency to make a musical scale. If the frequency goes up, the wavelength must go down proportionally. That means to double the frequency, the wavelength is reduced by half. To make the frequency 3/2 higher (to get the note E), the wavelength must be 2/3 because $2/3 \times 3/2 = 1$.

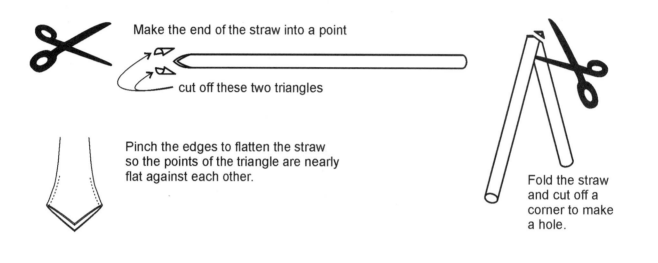

Make the end of the straw into a point

cut off these two triangles

Pinch the edges to flatten the straw so the points of the triangle are nearly flat against each other.

Fold the straw and cut off a corner to make a hole.

a. Make a straw kazoo and make some sound with it. Take a pair of scissors and cut off the end of the kazoo. What happens to the frequency of the sound it makes?

b. Take the scissors and cut a small hole exactly in the middle of your kazoo. Cover the hole with your finger. Blow through the kazoo and lift your finger to cover and uncover the hole. What happens to the sound? (*Hint*: What is vibrating in the straw is a length of air.)

c. Identify at least three musical instruments that use vibrating objects of different lengths.

25A Color

What happens when you mix different colors of light?

All the colors of visible light can be created artificially using a combination of three primary colors: red, blue, and green. In this investigation you will use a white light source and color filters to discover what happens when you mix different colors of light. You will also learn how the filters work.

Materials

- CPO Optics with Light & Color kit
- Colred pencils

1 Sources of light

a. Compare the light from a light bulb with the light from the same bulb when seen in a mirror. In both cases, describe the path of the light from the source to your eyes.

b. Look at your clothes. Does the light reaching your eye from your clothes originate in your clothes? Or does the light originate somewhere else?

c. Turn off all the lights, and shade the windows so it is completely dark. Can you see your clothes in the dark? What does this experiment tell you about whether your clothes give off their own light or reflect light from somewhere else?

d. Turn on a television or computer screen in a dark room. Can you see the TV or computer screen in the dark? What does this experiment tell you about whether the TV or computer screen give off their own light or reflect light from somewhere else?

2 Making colors

1. Slide all three flashlights into their own light holder.
2. Connect the red and green flashlights by sliding their stands together using the rail and slot connectors on the side.

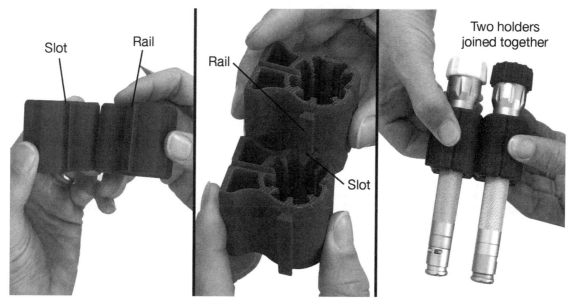

Slot   Rail   Rail   Slot   Two holders joined together

3. Place the blue flashlight on top of the red and green lights, making a small pyramid stack. Set the blue light on top of the other two with the holder on its side, so that the rail on the stand fits in the small groove created between the holders of the red and green lights. Turn the lights on.

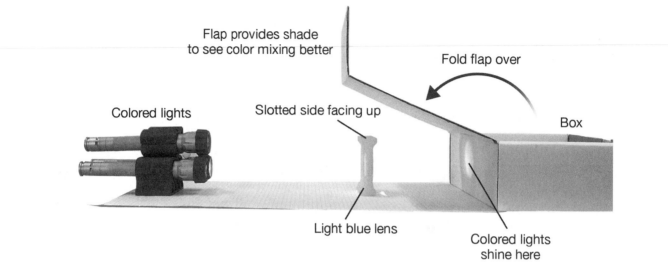

Flap provides shade
to see color mixing better

Fold flap over

Colored lights

Slotted side facing up

Box

Light blue lens

Colored lights
shine here

4. Set the light blue lens just in front of the lights so they shine through it. Place the lens so the slotted side is facing up.

Rail on blue
light holder

Groove
between
red and
green lights

5. Set the white box that the Optics with Light & Color kit comes in on the opposite side of the paper from the lights. Fold the top of the box over to shade the area where the three colored lights are shining on the box.

6. Slowly move the lens away from the lights and toward the box until you see the three spots of color (red-green-blue) overlap on the screen.

3 Thinking about what you observed

a. What color do you see when red and green light mix?

b. What color do you see when red and blue light mix?

c. What color do you see when blue and green light mix?

d. What color is produced when all three colors of light equally mix?

Table 1: Mixing primary colors of light

Color combination	Color you see
Red + Green	
Green + Blue	
Blue + Red	
Red + Green + Blue	

e. Research and explain the following terms from the diagram below: cone cells, rod cells, retina.

f. Research and explain how the eye sees white light in terms of the photoreceptors in the eye.

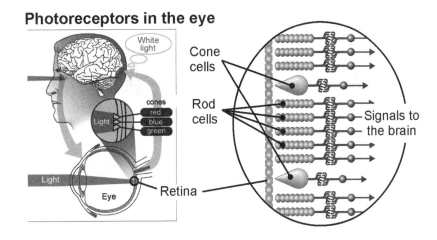

Photoreceptors in the eye

4 How does a color filter work?

A red laser can produce a single pure color of red which can be useful in some applications. For example, making three-dimensional images, called holograms, requires a very pure source of light which a laser can provide.

In the Optics with Light & Color kit, you have three different sources of colored light; but just how "pure" are these colors? In this part of the Investigation you will examine the light produced by each colored light, and learn how a *color filter* works. You will use the diffraction glasses to make your observations.

1. Examine the red light with the diffraction glasses.
2. Using colored pencils, sketch what you see in the appropriate column of table 2.
3. Repeat steps 1 and 2 for the green and blue lights.
4. Remove one of the color filter from one of the color lights. Examine the light produced by the white LED and record your observations in the table.

Table 2: Examining colors

Red light	Green light	Blue light
White light		

 Drawing conclusions

a. Compare the colors in the red light to those in the green light. What are the similarities and differences in the range of colors?

b. Compare the colors in the green light to those in the blue light. What are the similarities and differences in the range of colors?

c. How do the colors in the white light compare to the red, green, and blue lights combined?

d. The red light consists of a white LED covered with a red filter. What does the red filter do?

e. What do color filters do?

f. If you wanted to get yellow light, what part of the spectrum would the color filter have to absorb?

25B Reflection and Refraction

How does light behave when its path is changed?

Looking in a mirror we see a twin of ourselves reversed left-to-right. A fish underwater appears in a different place from where the fish really is. Both of these illusions are caused by the bending of light rays. This investigation explores reflection and refraction, two processes that bend light rays. You will also use refraction to calculate the focal point of a lens.

Materials
- CPO Optics with Light & Color kit
- Protractor and metric ruler
- Index card
- Pencil
- Graph paper (2 pieces)
- Sheet of blank white paper

1 Observing the law of reflection

How to trace the beam of the laser

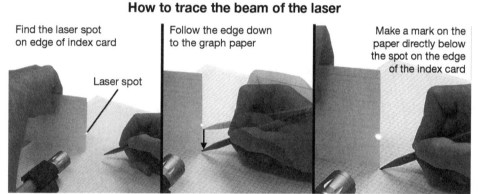

Find the laser spot on edge of index card — Laser spot

Follow the edge down to the graph paper

Make a mark on the paper directly below the spot on the edge of the index card

1. Set a sheet of graph paper on your lab table.
2. Slide the laser into a holder, turn the laser on, and put it on the graph paper.
3. Align the laser so the beam follows one horizontal line across the paper.
4. To line up the beam with the horizontal line on the graph paper, place an index card on its side onto the paper. Keep its long side flat on the graph paper and slowly slide the card over until you can just start to see the beam on the very edge of the card. Follow the vertical edge of the index card down and make a mark on the paper. The mark tells you where the beam is, and you can use this method to trace the path of the beam in all the Optics with Light & Color activities.
5. Follow the beam as it moves across the graph paper and make sure it lines up with one of the horizontal lines on the paper.
6. Set the mirror on the graph paper so the light beam from the laser hits its shiny front at an angle. The mirror should be placed so its long side is down on the paper.
7. Draw a line on the graph paper marking the front face of the mirror.

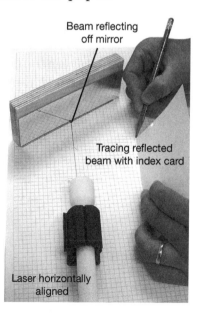

Beam reflecting off mirror

Tracing reflected beam with index card

Laser horizontally aligned

8. Use a pencil and the index card to trace the light rays going toward and away from the mirror. Label it ray #1.

9. Draw small arrows every couple of inches indicating the direction the beam is traveling.

2 Thinking about what you observed

a. A diagram showing how light rays travel is called a *ray diagram*. Lines and arrows on a ray diagram represent rays of light.

Drawing the ray diagram

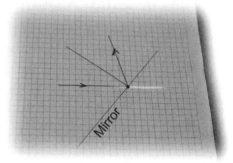

b. Look at your ray diagram showing the surface of the mirror and the light rays before and after the mirror.

c. Which is the incident ray? Label it on your ray diagram.

d. Which is the reflected ray? Label it on your ray diagram.

3 The law of reflection

a. Move the laser and the mirror to a new location on the graph paper. Make sure the beam hits the mirror at a slightly different angle and repeat steps 7–10. Be sure to label each ray. Continue shining and tracing the beam from a total of 4 different locations. Label the rays 1–4.

b. For each ray diagram, draw a line perpendicular to the mirror surface at the point where the rays hit. This line is called the *normal line*.

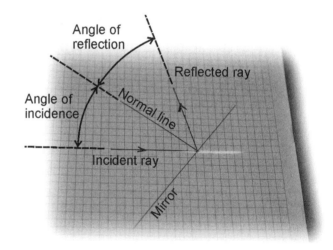

c. Use a protractor to measure the angle between the normal and the incident and reflected rays. Record your measurements in Table 1.

d. Write down your own statement of the law of reflection, describing the relationship between the angles you measured.

e. A laser shines at a mirror at an angle of incidence of 75 degrees. Predict its angle of reflection. After predicting, test your prediction. Were you right?

Table 1: Angles of incidence and reflection

	Diagram #1	Diagram #2	Diagram #3	Diagram #4
Angle of incidence				
Angle of reflection				

4 Light rays going through a prism

A prism is a solid piece of glass with polished surfaces. Prisms are useful for investigating how light bends when it crosses from one material into another, such as from air into glass or glass into air.

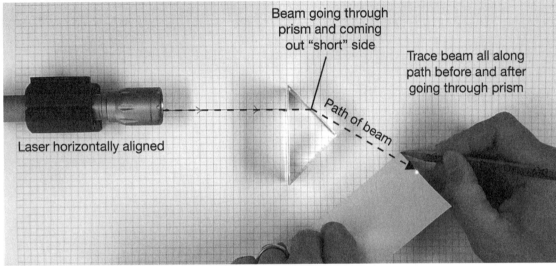

1. Flip your graph paper over and set the laser on the left side of the paper. Turn the laser on. Face the laser so it is shining horizontally across the paper.

2. Place the prism in the middle of the paper into the laser beam so the beam comes out the opposite short side.

3. Rotate the prism in the beam and observe where the beam comes out.

4. Keep rotating the prism until you can see the beam refracted and reflected at the same time.

5 Sketching what you observed

a. Draw at least one ray diagram showing a laser beam that is refracted after passing through the prism. The *refracted ray* is the ray that comes out of the prism at a different angle than it entered.

b. Draw a ray diagram showing a laser beam that is reflected.

c. Draw a ray diagram showing a laser beam that is both refracted and reflected.

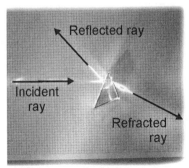

6 Seeing reflection and refraction at the same time

Both refraction and reflection often occur when light hits a boundary between materials such as the boundary between glass and air. The amount of light reflected or refracted depends on the angle at which you are looking relative to the surface.

Fold a paper card marked with A and B

The image in the prism changes as you move you head!

1. Take a piece of graph paper about the size of a business card and draw a line about 5 centimeters from one edge, dividing the rectangle in half. Draw the letter A on one side of the line and the letter B on the other side.

2. Fold the paper on the line and wrap it around one of the corners of the prism that is not a right angle.

3. Move your head up and down to change the angle at which you look into the prism.

7 Thinking about what you observed

a. Draw a diagram showing the path of the light when you see the letter A.

b. Draw a diagram showing the path of the light when you see the letter B.

c. Is the image in the prism always reflected or refracted or can there be both reflection and refraction at the same time?

8 Refracting light through a lens

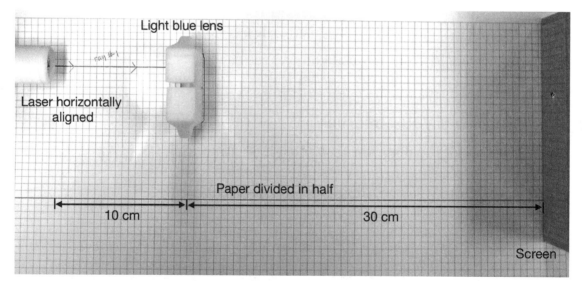

1. Divide a new sheet of graph paper in half horizontally. For the first part of this activity use the top half of the new sheet of graph paper. Place the laser on the edge of the paper and shine the laser so it follows a horizontal grid line across the paper.

150

2. Place the light blue lens 10 centimeters to the right of the laser with the slot facing up. Line the lens up vertically using the grid lines on the graph paper. It is important that the beam is perpendicular to the lens. Make sure the beam of the laser is lined up with the middle of the lens. There are lines on the side of each lens indicating the middle of the lens.

3. Trace around the base of the lens so it can be removed and put back in place in case you need to move it to complete ray tracing.

4. Shine the laser through the lens so the beam passes off-center, almost at the very outer edge of the lens. Set the block with the mirror about 30 centimeters on the right side of the lens so the beam hits it after passing through the lens. Use the side of the block with the graph paper on it so you can clearly see where the beam hits the block.

5. Trace the laser beam before and after it passes through the lens. Be sure to always carefully mark the points that the beam exits the laser, enters the lens, exits the lens, and then hits the block. Connect all these points to see the path of the beam.

6. Realign the laser with a different horizontal grid line parallel to the original beam and closer to the center of the lens. Again, trace the path of the beam before and after it passes through the lens.

7. Realign the beam so it passes directly through the center and trace the beam again.

8. Trace two more beams passing through the lens on the other side of the center of the lens for a total of five beams. Label the beams 1–5 on both sides of the lens.

9. Repeat steps 1–8 with the dark blue lens using the bottom half of your graph paper.

9 Thinking about what you observed

a. Feel the glass surface with your fingers and note the shape of the lenses. How are they different?

b. Draw a quick sketck of the shape of each lens itself with no stand from a side view. Label each lens.

c. Describe the paths of the rays before and after they traveled through the light blue lens. Include the words *refract*, *converge*, and *diverge* in your description.

d. What is the focal point of a lens? Mark the focal point on the first ray diagram.

e. What is the focal length of the lens? Measure the focal length of the light blue lens.

f. Describe the paths of the rays before and after they traveled through the dark blue lens. Include the words *refract*, *converge*, and *diverge* in your description.

g. How are the two lenses different?

h. One lens is referred to as a diverging lens, and the other a converging lens. They are also sometimes referred to as convex or concave. Research these terms and explain which is which.

10 Making an image with a lens

Certain types of lenses can make an image of a distant light source. The image forms about one focal length away from a lens when the object is far away.

1. Find a wall at least 5 meters away from a lamp or sunlit window. Tape a piece of white paper to the wall to create a screen for seeing the image.

2. Get the light blue lens. Hold the lens at different distances parallel to your screen and window or light source. Try distances between 15 and 25 centimeters.

3. Move the lens until you see a sharp image of the lamp or window on the screen. An image is produced when your lens is about one focal length away from the screen.

4. Measure the distance from the lens to the wall and record in Table 2. Use this technique to determine the focal lengths for both lenses.

Table 2: Focal lengths of lenses

	Focal length (cm)
Light blue Lens	
Dark blue lens	

Images can be smaller or larger than the object that created them. Images can also be right side up or inverted.

a. Was the image created by the light blue lens smaller or larger than the object?

b. Was the image right side up or was it inverted?

11 Projecting an image with a lens

You can think about a lens as collecting a cone of light from each point on an object. For a perfect lens all the light in the cone is bent so it comes together at a point again to make the image. This is how movie projectors take an image on film and project it onto a screen.

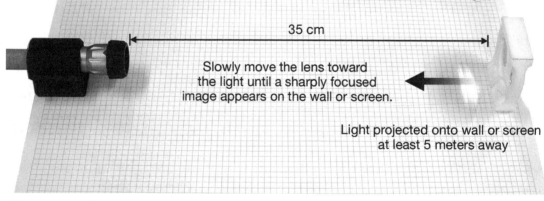

35 cm

Slowly move the lens toward the light until a sharply focused image appears on the wall or screen.

Light projected onto wall or screen at least 5 meters away

1. Place one of the lights near the edge of the graph paper. Put the "F" filter on the light. Shine it horizontally.

2. Take the light blue lens and set it on the graph paper 35 centimeters away from the light.

3. Shine the light at a distant light colored wall at least 5 meters away. If one is not available, affix a piece of paper to the wall as your projection screen. Slowly move the lens toward the light until you see a sharp image of the "F" on the wall or screen. Have one group member check the projected image closely while the lens is slowly moved to find the exact place the lens needs to be to make it come into focus.

   At what distance from the light does the lens produce a sharply focused image?

4. Take a paper card and use it to block some of the light from the lens. The card should be 2 to 3 centimeters from the lens and on the same side as the light.

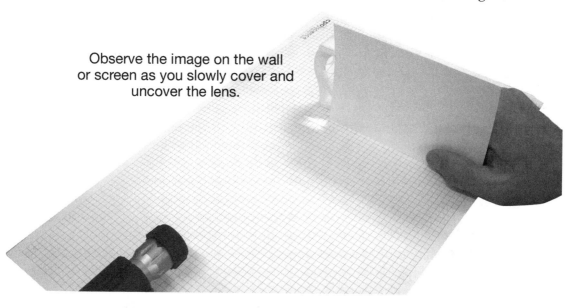

Observe the image on the wall
or screen as you slowly cover and
uncover the lens.

12 Thinking about what you observed

a. Describe the characteristics of the image formed by the lens. Characteristics include whether the image is right-side-up, inverted, larger, or smaller.

b. Discuss with your class why blocking part of the lens makes the image dimmer, even though you still see the entire image.

c. *Challenge*: The thin lens formula is used to calculate the exact focal length of a lens. Calculate the focal length of your light blue lens using the thin lens formula. The distance of the object from the lens is 35 centimeters. You will need to measure the distance from the lens to your projection screen or wall where the image

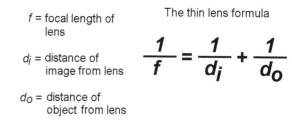

The thin lens formula

f = focal length of lens

d_i = distance of image from lens

d_o = distance of object from lens

$$\frac{1}{f} = \frac{1}{d_i} + \frac{1}{d_o}$$

became sharply in focus. How does it compare with the other two focal lengths of the light blue lens you observed? Was the method from section 8 or 10 more accurate compared to the focal length you just calculated using the thin lens formula?

Optional Investigations

The investigations in this section are designated as C Level. They are not required as part of the course but may be used to further explore and extend the concepts in the chapter.

1C Significant Digits

How do we make precise measurements?

We commonly make distance measurements in everyday life, whether to find the height of a person, the length of a rug, or the width of a doorway. In this investigation you will learn how to make precise measurements and to record your measurements using the correct number of significant digits.

Materials

- Meterstick
- Small ruler
- Pencil
- Paper clip
- Two thick books

1 Significant digits and measuring length

Precise measurements are often required in science and engineering. A measurement that is a millimeter off could cause serious problems if you were designing parts for a computer, car engine, or space shuttle. Being careful when making measurements is important if you wish to be precise, but having the right tool for the job is also a key factor. Suppose you wanted to measure the mass of a quarter. Would you use a scale designed for people or a small digital scale?

When recording a measurement, you are only allowed to record the meaningful, or significant digits.

Significant digits are those that you are certain of plus one additional estimated digit.

Consider the length measurement shown to the right. The pencil looks to be a bit more than 7.5 centimeters long. Should it be recorded as 7 centimeters? 7.5 centimeters? 7.9 centimeters? 7.90 centimeters?

When the tip of the pencil is lined up with the ruler, you can definitely tell that the pencil is between 7.9 centimeters and 8.0 centimeters. You can therefore be sure of the 7 and 9 in your measurement, so these are both significant digits.

You can make the measurement more precise by estimating the last digit. The pencil tip may look like it's on the 7.9-centimeter mark or right on the 8.0-centimeter mark, so the length falls between 7.90 and 8.00 centimeters. You might estimate the length to be 7.95 centimeters. It's impossible to tell this last digit exactly, and someone else might record the length as 7.90 centimeters. However, you could *not* record the length as 7.950 centimeters because both the five and the zero would be estimated.

2 Making measurements

Use either a meterstick or small ruler to make the following measurements in centimeters using the correct number of significant digits.

a. The length of a sharpened pencil

b. The diameter of a pencil eraser

  c. The length of a paper clip

  d. The height of your desk or table

  e. The length of your classroom

3 Analyzing the data

  a. For which measurements did you use the meterstick? Why?

  b. Which measurement was the most precise?

  c. Which measurement was the least precise?

  d. Describe two ways you could have made more precise measurements. You may include the use of tools you used other than the ruler and meterstick.

  e. The distances you measured were relatively small. How could you measure a larger distance such as the length of a football field or the distance from your school to your house?

4 Another way to measure

Sometimes it is possible to use the tools we have to make measurements in a creative way to increase precision. You will need two different thick books such as textbooks or novels.

  a. Suppose you wanted to measure the thickness of a single sheet of paper in each of the books. Can you do this with a ruler? Try it, and record your measurements using the correct number of significant digits.

  b. According to your measurements, are the thicknesses significantly different from each other?

  c. Discuss a better way to measure the thickness of a sheet of paper with your group members. Describe the steps you follow to make your measurements. Record your data and show any calculations you make. Use the correct number of significant digits to express your answers.

  d. How many significant digits do your thickness measurements have now? How does this compare to the number of significant digits in your measurements from question a?

  e. According to your measurements using your more precise method, are the thicknesses significantly different?

  f. Describe another measurement you could make using a similar method to the one you used in step c.

2C Thickness of Aluminum Foil

What is the thickness of aluminum foil?

In this investigation you will be challenged to determine the thickness of aluminum foil. It is obviously much too thin to measure its thickness with a ruler, so how will you achieve your goal? You will use your knowledge of density, volume, and area to arrive at a value and compare it to the findings of your classmates.

Materials

- Aluminum cylinder
- Aluminum foil
- Electronic scale (or triple-beam balance)
- Ruler
- 50 mL graduated cylinder
- Scissors
- Water

1 Doing the experiment

1. Obtain an aluminum cylinder from your teacher and record its mass in Table 1.
2. Measure 20 mL of water in the graduated cylinder and record the volume in Table 1.
3. Carefully place the aluminum cylinder in the graduated cylinder and record the combined volume in Table 1.
4. Cut out a 20-centimeter-by-20-centimeter piece of aluminum foil and record its mass in Table 1.

2 Stop and think

Is the density of the aluminum cylinder and the aluminum foil the same?

Table I: Aluminum data

Mass of aluminum cylinder (g)	Volume of water (mL)	Volume of water and aluminum (mL)	Mass of aluminum foil (g)	Dimensions of aluminum foil (cm x cm)

3 Analyzing your data

a. What is the volume of the aluminum cylinder as calculated by water displacement?

b. What is the density of the aluminum cylinder?

c. Using the density of the aluminum cylinder calculated above, and the mass of the aluminum foil, what is the volume of the foil in mL?

d. What is the volume of foil in cm^3 (1 mL = 1cm^3)?

e. What is the area of the aluminum foil (cm^2)?

f. Calculate the thickness of the aluminum foil by dividing the volume by the area.

4 Thinking about what you observed

a. How does your answer compare your with those of other students in the class?

b. Research aluminum foil. Is it pure aluminum? Be sure to cite your sources.

c. Do you think it is reasonable to use the density for the aluminum cylinder for your aluminum foil calculation?

d. A very thin layer of gold plating was placed on a metal tray that measured 25.22 centimeters by 13.22 centimeters. The gold plating increased the mass of the tray by 0.0512 grams. Find the thickness of the plating. The density of gold is 19.3 g/cm^3.

3C Looking for Significant Differences

Do you really need photogates to study the motion of the Energy Car, or is a stopwatch good enough?

People often ask if electronic timing is really necessary when conducting classroom motion experiments. Isn't a stopwatch good enough? To explore this question, you will compare travel times for the Energy Car with and without a homemade "sail." You will collect time data with photogates and with a simple stopwatch. Keep in mind that *significant differences* are differences that are much larger than the estimated uncertainty (or error) in the results. That means two results are "the same" *unless* their difference is much greater than the estimated error.

Materials

- CPO DataCollector and 2 photogates
- CPO Energy Car and track
- CPO Physics Stand
- 1 steel marble
- Tongue depressor
- Large paper plate
- Tape

1 Predicting

You will compare travel times for the Energy Car as it rolls down a gentle slope with and without a "sail." You will collect travel times using photogates and a stopwatch.

a. Write your hypothesis for how the sail will affect the travel time of the car.

b. Write your hypothesis for how the photogate times will compare to the stopwatch times for the same types of trials.

2 Setting up the experiment

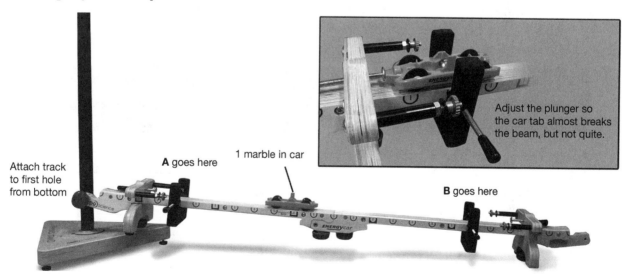

Attach track to first hole from bottom

A goes here

1 marble in car

Adjust the plunger so the car tab almost breaks the beam, but not quite.

B goes here

1. Assemble a straight track and attach it to the first hole from the bottom of the stand.
2. Place one stop at the top of the track and one at the bottom; place a lump of clay on the plunger at the end of the track (so the car won't bounce back through the photogate).
3. Attach the photogates as shown. Put photogate A at the top of the ramp.

159

4. Put one steel marble in the center of the Energy Car.

5. Place the Energy Car at the top of the track so it rests against the stop's plunger. Adjust the plunger so the light beam is just about to be broken by the tab sticking straight up on the car; as you change the plunger position, the tab on the car will move in and out of the beam. Watch the photogate's green/red light indicator. The light should be green, but about to become red as soon as you release the car.

3 Doing the experiment

1. Run the car down the track five times and record the time from A to B (t_{AB}) for each trial in Table 1.

2. Use the DataCollector in stopwatch mode to time the car from when it is released until the tab passes through the second photogate. It is a good idea for the person operating the stopwatch to call out "1, 2, 3, GO!", and start the stopwatch as he or she says "go." The car operator should release the car on "go." Then, the stopwatch operator should look straight on at photogate B and stop the stopwatch when the car's tab passes through the second photogate. Record times for five different trials in Table 1.

3. Tape a tongue depressor to the flag on the side of the car. Tape a paper plate to the tongue depressor. Use enough tape to make sure it is securely attached. You may need to slightly adjust photogate A so it isn't blocked by the tongue depressor which is just a little wider than the car's tab.

4. Repeat steps 1 and 2 and record the times in Table 1.

5. Find the average times and record in Table 1.

Table I: Car travel times

Trial	Without Sail photogate time A to B (s)	Without Sail stopwatch time A to B (s)	With Sail photogate time A to B (s)	With Sail stopwatch time A to B (s)
1				
2				
3				
4				
5				
average				

4 Thinking about the results

a. Can you tell from the average times whether the sail had a significant effect on the car's motion? Why or why not?

b. How do your average times compare to your hypotheses from Part 1?

5 Analyzing the data

1. To find the estimated error in your measurements find the difference between the average photogate time for the car without the sail and each of the individual trial times. Record absolute values (drop negative signs) in Table 2.

2. Calculate the average estimated error.

3. Repeat steps 1 and 2 for the stopwatch times for the car without the sail, and the times from the photogates and stopwatch for the car with the sail.

Table 2: Analyzing time data

Trial	Without Sail		With Sail	
	Estimated Error photogate	Estimated Error stopwatch	Estimated Error photogate	Estimated Error stopwatch
1				
2				
3				
4				
5				
average estimated error				

Now you can compare estimated error with average times to see if the sail had a significant effect.

a. Find the difference between the average photogate times for the car with and without the sail. Compare this difference to the average estimated error for the photogate times with and without the sail. If the time difference is at least three times greater than the estimated error, you can conclude that the sail did change the motion of the car significantly. Did the sail change the motion of your car significantly, according to photogate times?

b. Find the difference between the average stopwatch times for the car with and without the sail. Compare this difference to the average estimated error for the stopwatch times with and without the sail. Is the time difference at least three times greater than the estimated error? Did the sail change the motion of your car significantly, according to stopwatch times?

6 Drawing conclusions

a. Re-read the key question for this lab. Answer the key question and refer to evidence you collected in this lab to justify your answer.

b. Describe at least one way you could improve this experiment so you can be even more sure that the change in the car's motion is due to air friction from the sail, and not some other effect.

4C Studying Two-part Motion

What happens to the Energy Car as it travels down a hill and across a flat section of track?

In the previous Chapter 3 investigations, you explored the motion of the car on a flat track and again on a hill. This time, you will put the track together so it has both a hill and a flat section. What will the speed vs. time graph look like? You will soon find out!

Materials

- CPO Data Collector and 2 photogates
- CPO Energy Car and Track
- CPO Physics Stand
- 1 steel marble

■ Predicting

You will set up the track so it has a steep incline and a flat section joined. What will the speed vs. time graph look like?

a. Draw a sketch of what you think the speed vs. time graph will look like. Put *time* on the *x*-axis and *speed* on the *y*-axis.

■ Setting up the experiment

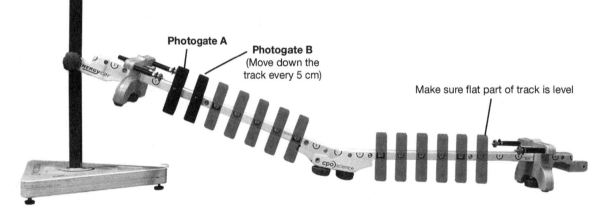

1. Join the steeper hill with the flat track and attach it to the fourth hole from the bottom.
2. Place a stop at the top of the track with the plunger all the way back so the end is flush with the stop.
3. Place the other stop at the bottom of the track; put a lump of clay on the plunger so the car won't bounce back through photogate B when it is near the end.
4. Attach photogate A as shown in the photo, and leave it there.
5. Photogate B will be placed every 5 centimeters, as shown in the photo.
6. *Make sure the flat part of the track is level.* Use the leveling feet on the physics stand base and on the bottom stop.
7. Place the Energy Car at the top of the track so it rests against the stop's plunger. Put one marble in the center of the car. Photogate B should be 5 centimeters from photogate A.

3 Doing the experiment

1. Release the car and record the time through A, the time through B, the time from A to B, and the distance traveled in Table 1.

2. Move the photogate to the next 5-centimeter mark and repeat step 1. Do this all along the track until you reach the last mark possible. You will not be able to take time measurements at 35, 40, or 45 centimeters away from photogate A.

Table 1: Energy car data

Distance A to B (cm)	Time A (s)	Time B (s)	Time AB (s)	Speed A (cm/s)	Speed B (cm/s)
5					
10					
15					
20					
25					
30					
50					
55					
60					
65					
70					
75					

4 Finding the speeds

a. Find the speed at A and speed at B for each trial and record in Table 1. Remember, to find the speed of the car, use the width of the flag (1.00 centimeters) for the distance, and the time through the photogate for the time ($s = d/t$).

b. Look at the A speeds. What does this data tell you in general about the experiment?

c. Look at the B speeds. What does this data tell you in general about the motion of the car as it moved down and across the track?

5 Graphing the data

a. Create a speed vs. time graph for the data. Put *time AB* (s) on the *x*-axis and *speed at B* (cm/s) on the *y*-axis. Draw a best fit line.

b. How does the graph compare to your prediction? Explain.

6 Thinking about what you observed

a. Where is the car accelerating? Justify your answer with evidence from the experiment.

b. Where is the car moving at a constant speed? Justify your answer with evidence.

5C Gravity and Falling Objects

How does gravity affect the motion of falling objects?

Gravity causes objects to accelerate as they fall. An object is in *free fall* if it is moving under the influence of only gravity. For example, when you drop a ball, it is in free fall from the time it leaves your hand until it hits the ground. In this investigation you will compare the motion of objects with different masses that are in free fall.

Materials

- CPO DataCollector and 2 photogates
- CPO Physics Stand
- Plastic ball and steel marbles
- Piece of string
- Tape

1 Setting up the experiment

1. This investigation should be done with the Physics Stand on the floor and with the pole as perfectly vertical as you can make it. Tape the steel marble to a piece of string to make a plumb bob. Hold the string at the top of the Physics Stand and adjust the leveling feet until the string hangs down the center of the pole.

2. Attach photogate A near the top of the stand. The bottom of the "U" of the photogate should be against the pole.

3. Attach photogate B so it is 50 centimeters (10 holes) below photogate A.

4. Plug both photogates into the DataCollector, then remove the tape and string from the steel marble.

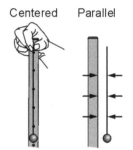

Centered   Parallel

When the pole is vertical, the string is centered and parallel

2 Collecting data

1. Examine the photogates and find the two small rectangular openings where the infrared light beam is emitted and detected. Hold the steel marble so it is above the top photogate, centered just above the openings.

2. Carefully drop the marble without giving it a push. Allow it to fall to the bottom of the stand where one group member should catch it. The marble should fall straight through the center of the two photogates. This may take some practice.

3. Put the DataCollector in CPO timer mode and select the interval function. Record the time through photogate A (t_A), the time through photogate B (t_B), and the time from A to B (t_{AB}) in Table 1.

4. Repeat for a total of three trials with the steel marble.

5. Repeat with the plastic marble.

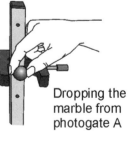

Dropping the marble from photogate A

Table 1: Photogate data

Marble	t_A (s)	t_B (s)	t_{AB} (s)
steel			
steel			
steel			
plastic			
plastic			
plastic			

3 Calculating acceleration

1. Calculate the speed of the marble through each photogate. The distance a marble moves when passing through the photogate is its diameter, 0.019 meters.

2. Use the two speeds and the time A to B to calculate the acceleration for each trial.

Table 2: Speed and acceleration data

Marble	speed through A (m/s)	speed through B (m/s)	acceleration (m/s^2)
steel			
steel			
steel			
plastic			
plastic			
plastic			

4 Analyzing the data

a. Calculate the average acceleration for your three trials for the steel marble. Use the average from each group in your class to find the class average for the steel marble's acceleration.

b. Calculate your average and the class average for the plastic marble's acceleration.

c. How do the accelerations compare? Are they about the same, or are they very different?

d. Which marble has the greater weight, and is therefore pulled on by a stronger force of gravity?

e. Suppose you wanted to move the steel and plastic marbles across the floor with the same acceleration. Which would require more force to accelerate?

f. Use your answers from questions d and e to explain why the accelerations of the two marbles in free fall compared as they did.

g. Why was it important to drop the marbles straight through the center of the photogate beam?

6C Collisions

Why do things bounce back when they collide?

Newton's third law tells us that when two objects collide, they exert equal and opposite forces on each other. However, the effect of the force is not always the same. What happens when you collide two Energy Cars that have unequal masses?

Materials

- CPO Energy Car and track
- CPO DataCollector and 2 photogates
- Thick rubber band
- Electronic scale (or triple-beam balance)

1 Making a collision

Launching the car

Rest your palm on the wood and pull the car against the screw with your finger on the tab nearest the far end of the car.

Moving car →   Target car

1. Set up the long straight track with a rubber band on one end and a clay ball on the other end. Use the bubble level to set the track level.
2. Place one steel marble in each car.
3. Wrap the thick rubber band around the moving car. Place both cars on the track so their noses are pointed toward the rubber band launcher.
4. Place the target car near the center of the track. Use the screw to launch the car using the same deflection of the rubber band each time. This means the same force is applied to each launch. You will use this car to create the collision.
5. To make a collision, release the moving car from the rubber band launcher. It will speed down the track, and hit the target car. This is an efficient way to produce collisions on the track.

a. Does the *moving* car bounce back after the collision?

b. Does the *moving* car keep going forward after the collision?

c. Does the *moving* car stop at the collision?

d. How does the target car behave?

2 Thinking about what you observed

a. Describe in words the motion of the two cars before and after the collision.

b. The target car must exert a force on the moving car to stop it. How strong is this force relative to the force the moving car exerts on the target car to get it moving? How could you use the photogates to provide evidence for your answer?

3 Gathering evidence

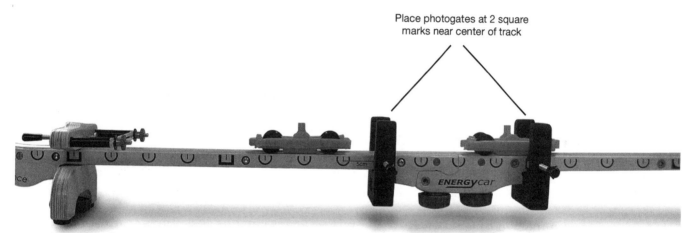

Place photogates at 2 square marks near center of track

1. Try the experiment again, but now use two photogates to collect time data.
2. Place two photogates on the square marks near the middle of the track.
3. Put the target car on the track so it is near photogate beam B.
4. Release the moving car from the rubber band launcher as before and make a collision.
5. Repeat several times and record trial times in Table 1.

Table 1: Collision times

Collision Trial	Time for moving car to pass through A before collision (s)	Time for target car to pass through B after collision (s)
1		
2		
3		
4		
5		

a. Newton's third law tells us that when the moving car exerts a force on the target car, the target car exerts an equal and opposite force on the moving car. Does your data provide evidence for this? Explain.

b. You can compare times through A and B for each individual trial. How can using these times show there are equal and opposite forces at work?

4 Changing the masses

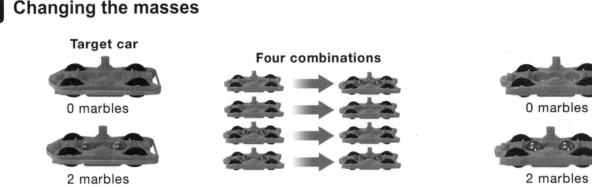

Target car

0 marbles

2 marbles

Four combinations

0 marbles

2 marbles

1. Try the experiment with the four combinations of mass shown above. You do not need to use photogates for this part of the investigation. If you want to use photogates, you will have to use the memory button for several of the collisions. This is explained in the teacher's guide, and your teacher can provide guidance.

5 Applying what you have learned

a. Describe the motion of the two cars when the target car has more mass than the moving car.

b. Describe the motion of the two cars when the target car has less mass than the moving car.

c. Explain how your observations support the idea that there are action and reaction forces.

d. If the action and reaction forces are equal in strength, why does one car move at a different speed after the collision than the other car when the masses are unequal? (*Hint*: The answer involves the Newton's second law.)

7C Energy and Efficiency

How well is energy changed from one form to another?

All processes that involve energy exchanges lose small amounts of energy to friction and heat. Efficiency is a measure of how well energy is transformed from one kind to another or transferred from one object to another. A process that is 100% efficient is one in which no energy is "lost," or converted to forms such as heat or sound.

Materials

- CPO DataCollector and two photogates
- CPO Energy Car and track
- Two rubber bands
- Three steel marbles
- Electronic scale (or triple-beam balance)

 Setting up the experiment

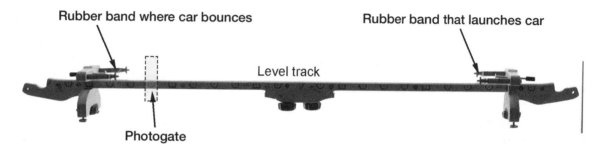

Rubber band where car bounces

Rubber band that launches car

Level track

Photogate

1. Set up the long straight track so it is level with rubber bands on both ends. The rubber bands should be twisted so they make an *X* in the middle.
2. Measure the mass of the empty car in kilograms and record it in the first row of Table 1.
3. Place the car so it is at one end of the track, just touching the rubber band. Position a photogate so the car's flag will break the light beam right after the car moves away from the rubber band.
4. Place the car at the opposite end of the track from the photogate. Use the rubber band to launch the car toward the photogate. Measure the time the car takes to pass through the photogate before and after the car bounces off the rubber band. You will need to use the memory button to display the "before" time. Catch the car after the bounce.
5. Perform a couple of practice launches until you get consistent times. Record the before and after times and calculate the average speeds before and after hitting the rubber bands.
6. Change the mass of the car by adding a marble and repeat the procedure for a total of four trials.

Table 1: Bounce data for different masses

Mass of the car (including any marbles) (kg)	Time before bounce (s)	Speed before bounce (m/s)	Time after bounce (s)	Speed after bounce (m/s)

2 Thinking about what you observed

a. Describe the energy flows that occur from when the car is launched until after it bounces off the rubber band.

b. If the transformation of energy were perfect (100% efficiency) what would you expect the speed of the car to be before and after the bounce with the rubber band?

c. Calculate the kinetic energy of the car before and after bouncing off the rubber band for each trial. Record your answers in Table 2.

> **Useful relationships**
>
> Kinetic energy = $\frac{1}{2}mv^2$
>
> Efficiency = $\dfrac{\text{Final energy}}{\text{Initial energy}}$

d. Calculate the efficiency of the process of bouncing the car off a rubber band for each trial. Record your answers in Table 2.

e. Did the efficiency change when mass was added to the car?

Table 2: Energy and efficiency data

Mass of car (kg)	Kinetic energy before bounce (J)	Kinetic energy after bounce (J)	Efficiency (%)

3 Changing a different variable

In the first part of the experiment, you investigated the effect of changing the car's mass on the efficiency. However, changing the mass also had the effect of changing the car's launch speed. In this part of the experiment, you will keep the mass constant and only change the car's speed.

1. Adjust the thumb screw so the rubber band only stretches back a small amount before touching the metal stopper. This will cause the car to launch at a slow speed. Launch the empty car and record its time before and after the bounce with the rubber band at the other end of the track.

2. Twist the thumb screw so the rubber band will stretch back a slightly greater distance. You will be doing four more launches, so adjust the screw so the stopper moves approximately 1/4 of the way back toward the wooden bumper. Launch the car and measure the times. Record your readings in Table 3.

3. Continue until you have a total of five launches at different speeds. Use the recorded time data to calculate the speeds of the car and record your calculations in Table 3.

Table 3: Bounce data for different speeds

Mass of the car (kg)	Time before bounce (s)	Speed before bounce (m/s)	Time after bounce (s)	Speed after bounce (m/s)

4 Thinking about what you observed

a. Calculate the kinetic energy and efficiency of the rubber band for the different speeds you tested. Record the values in Table 4.

Table 4: Energy and efficiency data

Speed before bounce (m/s)	Speed after bounce (m/s)	Kinetic energy before bounce (J)	Kinetic energy after bounce (J)	Efficiency (%)

b. Plot a graph showing the efficiency on the vertical (*y*) axis and the speed before the bounce on the horizontal (*x*) axis. Does the speed of the car affect the efficiency?

171

8C People Power

What's your work and power as you climb a flight of stairs?

When you walk up a flight of stairs, you do work to lift your body against the force of gravity. If you know your weight and the vertical distance you climb, you can calculate the work you do. Measuring the time it takes to climb the stairs allows you to also calculate your power.

Materials

- CPO DataCollector or simple stopwatch
- Meter stick
- Bathroom scale

1 Collecting the data

1. You will be doing this activity as a class. Choose several students as volunteers who will be climbing a flight of stairs as other students measure the time.

2. Use a bathroom scale to measure the weight of each volunteer. Convert each weight to newtons using the conversion factor: 1 pound = 4.448 newtons. Record each person's weight and name in Table 1.

Table 1: Stair climbing data

Name	Weight (N)	Stair height (m)	Time 1 (s)	Time 2 (s)	Time 3 (s)	Average time (s)

3. Choose three students who will be timekeepers and two students who will be stair height measurers. These should not be the same students who are climbing the stairs.

4. Locate an empty stairwell with one or two flights of stairs. The stair height measurers should measure the total vertical distance a person climbs when going from the top to the bottom. The easiest way to do this is to measure the height of one stair, count the number of stairs, and multiply.

5. Have each person listed in Table 1 climb the stairs once as the three timekeepers measure the time. Record all of the times in Table 1. Calculate the average time for each person.

2 Calculating work and power

1. Calculate the work done by each person. The force for each person is his or her weight. Record the work in Table 2.

2. Use each person's average time to calculate the power. Record each power in Table 2.

Table 2: Work and power

Name	Work (J)	Power (W)

3 Analyzing the data

a. Who did the most work? What do you notice about this person's weight?

b. Who did the least work? What do you notice about this person's weight?

c. Who had the greatest power? Must this be the person with the fastest time?

d. Who had the least power? Must this be the person with the slowest time?

e. Calculate the average work for the students.

f. The Calorie is also a unit of work. One Calorie equals 4,186 joules. Calculate the average number of calories of work done by the students. You may be surprised at how small the answer is!

g. Calculate the average power of the students.

h. A typical bright light bulb has a power of 100 watts. How does this compare to the average power of the students?

i. Imagine that two people of equal weights climb the same flight of stairs. One runs, and the other walks. Do they burn the same number of calories? Do they have the same power? Explain.

j. Juan's weight is twice the weight of his little sister Anna. They climb the same set of stairs and find that they have the same power. Explain how this can be possible.

9C Mechanical Advantage

What is mechanical advantage, and how do ropes and pulleys give you mechanical advantage?

Ropes and pulleys create large output forces from small input forces—but how large can the output forces be? What is the trade-off? In this investigation you will explore the mechanical advantage of different rope and pulley setups. You will soon discover a quick and easy way to determine the mechanical advantage of any rope and pulley system.

Materials

- Top and bottom pulley block
- CPO Physics Stand
- Weights (4)
- Spring scale (0–10 N)
- Yellow string with brass clip and cord stops
- Knobs (1 threaded, 1 regular)

1 Setting up the experiment

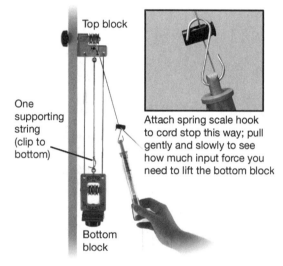

Top block

One supporting string (clip to bottom)

Attach spring scale hook to cord stop this way; pull gently and slowly to see how much input force you need to lift the bottom block

Bottom block

1. Attach four weights to the bottom block. Use a spring scale to measure the weight (N) of the bottom block and record it in Table 1 as the *output force*.

2. Attach the top block near the top of the Physics Stand.

3. Thread the yellow string over one or more of the pulleys of the top and bottom pulley blocks. The yellow string can be clipped to either the top block or the bottom block.

4. Build combinations with 1, 2, 3, 4, 5, and 6 strands directly supporting the bottom block, so you always pull down on the string to raise the block. (*Hint*: 1, 3, and 5 have the string clipped to the bottom block; 2, 4, and 6 have the string clipped to the top block.)

5. Attach the spring scale to the cord stop as shown in the photo. This way of sliding the spring scale hook over the cord stop on the string will give the best force measurement. If you insert the hook into the hole of the cord stop, you will have some friction interfering with the measurement.

6. Use a force scale to measure the force needed to slowly lift the bottom block for different combinations of supporting strings.

Safety Tip: Don't pull sideways, or you can tip the stand over!

Table 1: Rope and pulley force data

Number of supporting strings	Input force (N)	Output force (N)	Output force ÷ Input force
1			
2			
3			
4			
5			
6			

2 Mechanical advantage

a. Mechanical advantage refers to the number of times effort force is multiplied in a simple machine like ropes and pulleys. The ratio of output force to input force equals the mechanical advantage, so divide output force by input force for each trial and record in Table 2. *Mechanical advantage has no unit; it is a ratio.*

b. What is the relationship between number of supporting strands and mechanical advantage?

c. The mechanical advantage for your first trial is 1. Since any number multiplied by 1 equals the same number, your effort force is not multiplied. What, then, could the advantage be for using one supporting strand? (*Hint*: This arrangement is often used to raise a flag on a flagpole.)

d. A windjammer is a large sailing ship that was popular in the 1700s and 1800s. Now, tourists enjoy sailing on reproductions like the one in the photo. Rope and pulley systems (called block and tackle) are used to lift the sails, which can require a lot of force in a strong wind! What is the mechanical advantage of a windjammer's rope and pulley system for one of its sails if there are five supporting lines?

3 Input and output distances

Rope and pulley systems with a mechanical advantage greater than 1 will reduce the amount of force you have to put into the machine to make it work. However, this multiplied effort force comes at a "cost." What is the trade-off?

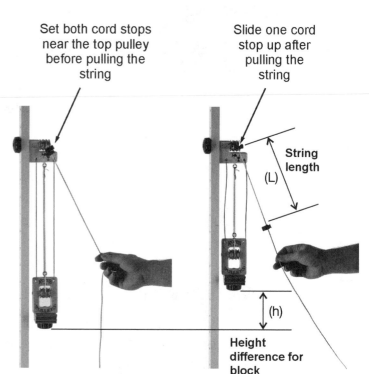

Set both cord stops near the top pulley before pulling the string

Slide one cord stop up after pulling the string

String length (L)

Height difference for block (h)

Measuring string length and height difference

1. Use the marker stop (cord stop) to mark where the string leaves the top pulley.

2. Choose a distance that you will lift the bottom pulley during each trial of the experiment. This is the *output distance.* Your output distance should be at least 20 centimeters.

3. Pull the yellow string to lift the block your chosen distance.

4. Measure how much string length you had to pull to lift the block. This is the *input distance.*

5. Measure the input and output distances for each of the different configurations (1, 2, 3, 4, 5, and 6). The table only shows two of the data rows.

Table 2: Rope and pulley distance data

Mechanical advantage	Input distance (cm)	Output distance (cm)
1		
2		

a. Study the data in Table 2. What is the "cost" for having mechanical advantages greater than 1?

b. You can calculate mechanical advantage using the input and output distances instead of forces. Study the data in Table 2 and figure out a new way to calculate the mechanical advantage of a rope and pulley system.

c. Windjammers usually have two or more masts with sails. Suppose one sail weighs 3,000 N, and it is rigged with a rope and pulley system that has five supporting lines. The sail must be raised 35 meters. How much line will be needed to make this system work?

10C Freezing Point of a Stable Mixture

What is the freezing point of a unique ice cream topping?

Have you ever put "shell" topping on a frozen desert like ice cream? The topping is a liquid in the plastic bottle, but when you put it on ice cream, it hardens very quickly to form a shell or crust over the desert. The ice cream topping contains lecithin, a substance that stabilizes the mixture, so it acts like a pure substance when heated or cooled. In this investigation, you will compare the freezing points of different shell topping brands.

Materials

- Shell ice cream topping
- Foam cup (large)
- 1 large glass or plastic test tube
- CPO DataCollector
- Temperature probe
- Ice water

1 Doing the experiment

1. Fill a foam cup about 3/4 full with ice water.
2. Shake the bottle of ice cream topping well, and pour about 15 mL into the test tube. This step might already have been completed for you.
3. Place the temperature probe in the test tube.
4. Connect the temperature probe to the DataCollector and set up a new experiment. Choose a sample rate of 5 seconds per sample (5 s/sample). This means temperature data will be taken and placed in the table every 5 seconds.
5. Start the DataCollector. Place the test tube into the ice water bath. Use the temperature probe to gently stir the mixture while the temperature data is collected. Continue until the topping is a solid, and you can't move the thermometer any more. When the topping is a solid, continue collecting data until the temperature reaches 4 or 5°C (the temperature of the ice water bath).
6. Save the DataCollector experiment and make a note of the file name.
7. Follow your teacher's instructions for cleanup.

2 Analyzing the data

Go to the graph screen on your DataCollector. The graph should show temperature on the *y*-axis and time on the *x*-axis. If this is not the case, select the correct variable for each axis. Study the graph and answer the questions below.

a. As you cooled the mixture, what happened to the temperature at first?

b. At some point in the cooling process, you will see that the line on the graph is relatively flat (this is called a plateau). What does this tell you about the temperature during this time period?

c. What is happening to the ice cream topping during this point in the cooling process?

177

d. Did the temperature drop again after the plateau? Discuss. On a piece of graph paper, make a sketch of the graph you have on the DataCollector. You do not have to use numbers, but you should label each axis with the correct variable. On your sketch, label the area of the graph where freezing occurred, and make a note of the average temperature (freezing point). Or, you can download the data to a spreadsheet and create a graph to print and place in your lab notebook.

3 Thinking about what you observed

Different brands of shell ice cream topping have similar ingredients, but they are not all identical mixtures. Are their compositions different enough to affect the freezing point? You will compare results with other groups to find out.

a. Based on your data analysis, at what temperature did your brand or type of ice cream shell topping freeze?

b. Compare your freezing point with other groups that used the same brand. Is the temperature similar? Discuss.

c. Compare your freezing point with other groups that used a different brand or type of topping. Is the temperature similar? Discuss.

d. Based on your observations, if your teacher gave you an unknown brand of shell topping, would you be able to identify the brand or type by finding its freezing point? Explain your answer.

4 Applying your knowledge

a. When the topping was in the ice water bath, thermal energy was transferred away from the topping. At first, the temperature dropped rapidly, and then the temperature stalled. Why?

b. What would shell topping be like if the freezing point was 20°C?

c. What would shell topping be like if the freezing point was 0°C?

d. Pure substances have unique freezing/melting points, but mixtures generally do not. Shell ice cream topping is a mixture that *does* freeze and melt at a certain temperature range. Why does the ice cream topping act like a pure substance?

11C Mass Determination Without a Balance

Can the mass of an object be determined without the use of a balance?

The mass of an object is the amount of matter in that object. This physical property can easily be measured with the use of a common piece of laboratory equipment: a balance. How could you determine the mass of a pure substance if the lab balance was out of order?

Materials

- 1 Styrofoam cup
- Metal sample
- Hot plate
- Tongs
- Safety goggles
- Balance
- 100-mL graduated cylinder

- CPO DataCollector
- Temperature probe
- ~600 mL water
- Lab apron
- 1 400-mL beaker
- Heat mitt

The following table of specific heat values will be useful:

Name of Substance	Specific Heat, J/g°C
Aluminum	0.899
Brass	0.38
Copper	0.38
Nickel	0.443
Iron	0.46
Steel	0.46
Water	4.18
Zinc	0.388

1 Stop and think

a. When choosing a material to serve as an insulator, should a material with a high specific heat or a low specific heat be chosen? Explain your answer.

2 Doing the experiment

1. Heat 200 mL of water in the beaker using the hot plate until the water boils. Gently lower the metal sample into the beaker using the tongs. Allow the sample to settle in the boiling water for 2 to 3 minutes so its temperature will be equal to that of the boiling water.

2. While the metal is warming up in the boiling water, begin to set up the calorimeter.

3. Measure exactly 100.0 mL of room temperature water in a graduated cylinder and pour the water into the Styrofoam cup. Record this volume in the Table 1.

179

4. Measure and record the stabilized temperature of the water in Table 1.

5. After 2 to 3 minutes have passed, measure the temperature of the boiling water with the temperature probe and record this value in Table 1.

6. Using the tongs, carefully remove the metal from the boiling water and quickly transfer it to the calorimeter.

7. Stir the water in the calorimeter carefully with the temperature probe.

8. Watch the temperature reading as you stir. When the temperature reaches a plateau (no longer increases), record the temperature of the metal-water system in Table 1, stop stirring, and remove the metal.

9. Repeat the procedure for trial 2, replacing the water in the calorimeter with fresh water.

Table I: Determining mass data

	Trial 1	Trial 2
V_{H2O} in calorimeter (mL)		
T_i of H_2O in calorimeter (°C)		
T_i of metal in hot water (°C)		
T_f of system (°C)		
Mass of metal (g)		

3 Analyzing the data

A. Calculate the heat absorbed by the water.

1. Find the mass (m_1) of the original volume of water using V_{H2O} and density

2. Find the change in temperature of the water using $\Delta T = T_f - T_i$

3. Find the energy (E) absorbed by the water using $Q_{H2O} = mC_p\Delta T$

B. Calculate the mass of the metal.

1. Find the change in temperature of the metal using $\Delta T = T_f - T_i$

2. Find the heat released by the metal (Q_{metal}) using $-Q_{metal} = Q_{H2O}$

3. Find the mass of the metal (m) using $Q_{metal} = mC_p\Delta T$

4. Perform all calculations up to this point for both trial 1 and trial 2, then average your two mass predictions and use your average value for the calculation in step 6.

5. Use the balance to measure the mass of your metal sample.

6. Percent error, where % error $= \dfrac{experimental - real}{real} \times 100$

4 **Thinking about what you observed**

a. A sample of nickel is found to absorb 4.25 kJ as it is heated from 15.0°C to 37.5°C. What is the mass of this piece of nickel?

b. Predict how your results would differ if you allowed your metal to stay in the boiling water for only 2 minutes. Explain.

c. Name two possible sources of error for this experiment. How would they affect your data? How would they affect your results?

12C Density of Fluids

What is the maximum load a boat can hold before sinking? How is the maximum load affected by the density of the water in which the boat floats?

In Investigation 12B, you designed and created clay boats that floated in water. You learned that the density of the boat should be equal or less than the water in order to float. You also saw that altering the shape of the clay changed its ability to float. In this investigation you will work to see what element of boat design increases the maximum load that your boat can handle before sinking and how this is all related to the density of water.

Materials

- Modeling clay (same amount as from Inv. 12B)
- Metal washers or pennies
- Water
- Shallow pan or bucket
- Displacement tank
- 100 mL graduated cylinder
- 250 mL beaker for overflow
- Electronic scale (or triple-beam balance)
- Salt
- Paper towels, sponges
- Disposable cup to catch displaced water when filling up tank

1 Stop and think

a. What element of design do you think will affect the ability of your boat to hold more or less weight without sinking? Explain.

2 Finding the apparent density of your clay boat

1. Form your clay into a floating boat like the one you used for Investigation 12B.

2. Find the total volume of the clay boat. This means the sum of the volume of the clay itself and the empty air space of the boat. Record your values in Table 1.

   a. Measure the volume of your clay boat by displacement.

   b. Measure the volume of empty air space of your boat. Start by filling a 100-mL graduated cylinder with water up to the 100 mL line. Pour water from the cylinder into your boat until it completely fills up. Once it is full, see how much water is left in the graduated cylinder. Subtract that amount from the 100 mL you started with to determine the volume of air space of your boat.

   c. Calculate the total volume of the clay boat.

Step B

Start with 100 mL

Fill your boat with water

Calculate the difference between 100 mL and what is left in the cyliner

3. Measure the mass of the boat.

4. Calculate the apparent density of your clay boat (mass/total volume).

Table 1: Volume, mass, and density data

Volume of clay used in boat (mL)	Volume of empty space (mL)	Total volume of clay boat (mL)	Mass of boat (g)	Apparent density of your boat (g/mL)

3 Predicting the maximum load of the boat

The boat will sink once it becomes denser than the water. You are going to predict what the maximum load should be for your boat based on the data you collected in Table 1. To do this, you will come up with a mathematical relationship that enables you to solve for the maximum load. Start by looking at your boat's apparent density, and the density it must remain less than to stay afloat.

a. What was the mass of your boat?

b. What was the total volume of your boat?

c. What was your boat's apparent density?

d. What is the maximun apparent density your boat can attain and still remain afloat?

e. Where would the additional mass of the load your boat carries enter into the apparent density calculation for your boat?

f. Write an equation to calculate the apparent density of your boat when carrying a load.

g. Solve your equation for maximum load. What is your calculated maximum load?

4 Testing the theoretical value

1. Place your boat in the water.

2. Record your calculated maximum load in Table 2.

3. Add one washer at a time to your boat. Once the boat starts to sink, stop adding washers and measure the total mass of all the washers your boat successfully carried. Record this value in Table 2.

4. Find the percent error and record this value in Table 2.

5. Who in the class was able to achieve the largest load? Look at his/her design and others. What design characteristics do the most successful boats share?

Table 2: Maximum load data for fresh water

Calculated maximum load (g)	Measured maximum load (g)	Percent error of calculated maximum load

5 Changing the density of the liquid

The Dead Sea is located in the Middle East, between Jordan on its east bank and Israel, and the West Bank on its west. It is known for its dense salt water. Would your boat have the same capacity for a maximum load if it were in very salty water with a much higher density than the fresh water you've used so far?

1. You will need to find the density of the salt water. Find the mass of 100 mL of the salt water solution by using a graduated cylinder. Record the mass in Table 3.
2. Calculate the density of the salt water sample. Record the density in Table 3.
3. Use your equation from part 3 to calculate the maximum load for your boat in the saltwater solution.Record this value in Table 3.
4. Test the maximum load in the salt water solution. Record the value in Table 3.
5. Find the percent error and record in Table 3.

Table 3: Maximun load data for salt water solution

Mass of salt water sample (g)	Density of salt water sample (g/mL)	Calculated maximum load (g)	Measured maximum load (g)	Percent error of calculated maximum load

6 Thinking about what you observed

a. In order to load more on a boat, what element of the design needs to be changed? Explain.

b. With a greater water density, can the boat hold fewer or more weights? Why?

c. For both the freshwater and saltwater, explain why you think the percent errors were as you found.

d. In an estuary, salt water from the ocean and fresh water from a river meet. What would you expect to happen in the estuary itself with these waters? Would there be any stratification?

e. Find out what the average density is of a typical sample of ocean water. How does its density compare to fresh water and to the sample you used that modeled the Dead Sea? Would your boat hold more or less washers in fresh water and typical ocean water compared to the Dead Sea water?

13C Charles's Law

What is the relationship between the volume and temperature of a gas?

Jacques Charles (1746–1823) determined the relationship between temperature and volume for an enclosed gas. In this simple investigation you will measure the volume of air in a balloon, heat the system, and observe and collect temperature and volume data as the system cools. From this data, you will be able to derive Charles's law.

Materials

- Balloon
- Plunger assembly
- Displacement tank
- Tray or dish pan
- Ice
- Temperature probe
- CPO DataCollector
- Styrofoam cup

1 Thinking about temperature and volume

a. If you inflate a balloon and leave it on a sunny windowsill, what do you think will happen to the balloon?

b. Make a hypothesis about the relationship between volume and temperature of an enclosed gas. (*Hint*: When temperature increases, what do you think happens to the volume?)

2 Setting up the experiment

1. To begin making the plunger assembly, use the weights base that comes with the equipment kit. Remove all the steel weights (you won't need them).

2. Cut a Styrofoam cup so that it is 12 centimeters high and then make a small hole in the side of the cup.

3. Poke a hole in the bottom of the cup using one of the posts and leave the cup attached to the weights base as shown in the photo. You will use this plunger assembly to submerge the balloon in the displacement tank.

4. Blow up a balloon but don't tie it. Allow it to deflate. Repeat this process three times. This will stretch the balloon so it is easier to use in experiment.

5. Blow up the balloon with enough air that it will fit easily in the displacement tank. It should *not* fit snugly (approximately 12 centimeters in diameter).

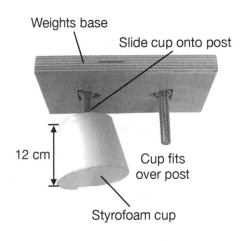

Weights base

Slide cup onto post

12 cm

Cup fits over post

Styrofoam cup

185

3 Doing the experiment

1. Place the displacement tank on a tray or dish pan. Add 1,250 mL of ice water to the displacement tank.

2. Submerge the balloon by pushing down on it with the plunger assembly. Be sure that it is completely submerged. Water will flow out of the tank. If it does not, add water until some runs out of the spout into the pan.

3. Place the temperature probe in the displacement tank. Wait 1 minute. If the water level has decreased and is no longer on the verge of overflowing, fill the tank with the same temperature water as used in that trial until it just starts to overflow.

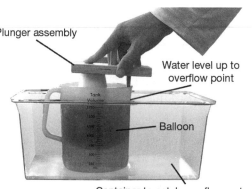

Plunger assembly

Water level up to overflow point

Balloon

Container to catch overflow water

4. Remove the weights base/styrofoam cup assembly and balloon.

5. Record the displaced volume of water. There is a measured scale down the side of the displacement tank labeled "Displaced Volume." Record the values in Table 1.

6. Empty the displacement tank until the water level reads 750 mL. Then add warm water until the level again reaches 1,250 mL.

7. Check the temperature of the tank water. It should be about 10–15 degrees warmer. Adjust the water temperature if necessary by adding ice or warm water.

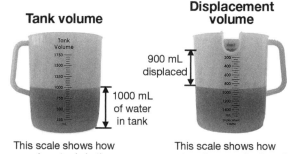

Tank volume

1000 mL of water in tank

This scale shows how much water is in the displacement tank.

Displacement volume

900 mL displaced

This scale shows how much water was displaced.

8. Repeat steps 2–7, until you have at least four data points.

9. Find the volume of the balloon for each trial by subtracting the tank volume from 1,900 mL (which is the total tank volume). Record in Table 1.

10. Convert Celsius temperatures to Kelvin temperatures and record in Table 1.

Table 1: Volume and temperature data

Tank volume (mL)	Volume of the balloon and plunger as read from tank (mL)	Temperature (°C)	Temperature (Kelvin)	V*T (mL*K)	V/T (mL/K)

4 Graphing the data

Use your data to make a graph of volume versus temperature.

a. Does the graphical model support your hypothesis? Explain your answer.

b. What happens to the volume of an enclosed gas when the temperature increases?

5 Finding a relationship between volume and temperature

a. Divide the volume and temperature values for each trial and record the answers in Table 1. Remember to use appropriate numbers of significant figures.

b. Multiply the volume by the temperature for each trial and record the values in Table 1. Again, use the correct number of significant figures.

c. There is a mathematical relationship between volume and temperature that always equals a constant value. Based on your calculations, is that relationship V/T or $V \times T$?

d. According to your data, what is the constant value? (You can record an average.)

6 Using Charles's law to make a prediction

a. Using your constant value, calculate what the volume of the balloon and plunger assembly would be when the temperature is 290 K. (Or a similar temperature if this is already one of your data points.)

b. Using your graph, what is the volume that corresponds to 290 K? How does this compare to your calculated value?

c. How would you use the experiment setup to test your predicted volume value for 290 K?

7 Thinking about what you observed

a. If you do this experiment with much hotter water (such as 60°C), the balloon/plunger volume measurements should increase, but they don't. Why do you think this happens? (*Hint*: Think about the way the experiment is set up.)

b. Go back to your answer to question 1a. Would you answer the question the same way now? Explain.

14C Energy and the Quantum Theory

How do atoms absorb and emit light energy?

The electrons in an atom are organized into energy levels. You can think of energy levels like a staircase where the electrons can be on one step or another but cannot exist in-between steps. When an electron changes levels, the atom absorbs or emits energy, often in the form of light. This investigation will teach you a challenging and fun game that simulates how atoms exchange energy through light. The process is fundamentally how a laser works.

Materials

- CPO Atom Building Game

1 The neon atom

1. Build a neon atom with 10 each of protons (red or green marbles), neutrons (blue marbles) and electrons (yellow marbles).

2. Set the electrons in the lowest spaces possible.

3. Find the following cards in the Photons and Lasers can
    Pump 1 (red)
    Pump 2 (yellow)
    Laser 1 (red)

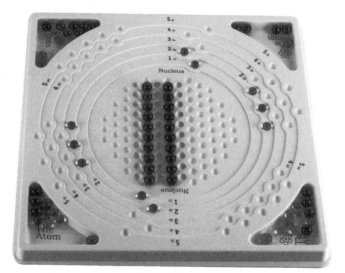

Neon-20 (Ne^{20})

10 protons, 10 neutrons, 10 electrons

2 How atoms exchange energy

a. Explain the meaning of the term "ground state" when applied to an atom.

b. Can the second energy level of neon hold any more electrons? How does this affect neon's chemical properties and position on the periodic table?

c. Take the red pump 1 card from your hand and put it on the atom board. Move one electron from level 2 to level 3. Explain what this sequence of actions represents in a real atom.

d. Take the yellow pump 2 card from your hand and put it on the atom board. Move any one electron up 2 levels. Explain what this sequence of actions represents in a real atom.

e. Take the red laser 1 card from your hand and put it on the atom board. Move any one electron down one level. Explain what this sequence of actions represents in a real atom.

3 The photons and lasers game

Photons and lasers card deck

Pump cards
Add energy to the atom and advance electrons up levels

Laser cards
Release energy from the atom and drop electrons down levels

1. The first player to reach 10 points wins the game.

2. Each player starts with five cards and plays one per turn. Draw a new card to maintain a hand of five.

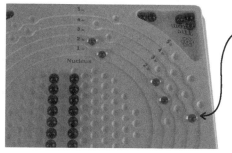

A **Laser-2** card can drop this electron 2 levels scoring 2 points

3. Playing a pump card allows the player to advance one electron up by the number of levels shown on the card (1–4). No points are scored by playing pump cards.

4. Playing a laser card allows the player to drop electrons from one level to a lower level. The player scores one point per electron per level. For example, moving two electrons down two levels scores four points.

5. Rules for playing laser cards:
   Electrons can only be moved down if there are empty states for then to move to.
   Electrons can only be moved from one level in a turn.
   If the card says "laser 2" then each electron must move two levels.

4 Thinking about what you learned

a. What does the term "excited state" mean with respect to energy and atoms?

b. What physical principle prevents two electrons from moving into the same state?

c. In order of increasing energy, arrange the following colors of light: blue, red, green, yellow.

d. Could an atom emit one photon of blue light after absorbing only one photon of red light? Explain why or why not.

e. Suppose a real atom had energy levels just like the game. Could this atom make blue-green light with an energy in between blue and green? Explain what colors this atom could make.

15C Activity Series of Metals

How reactive are different metals?

An activity series is a list of elements arranged from most reactive to least reactive. When you place a solid piece of metal in contact with a solution, there may or may not be a reaction. In order for a reaction to proceed, the solid metal that is touching the solution must be more reactive than the metal that is part of the ionic compound (solute) dissolved in the water. In this investigation you will examine several metals and rank them from most to least active based on how many reactions take place for each metal.

Materials

- Well plate (5x5) or overhead (lead acetate sheet)
- Copper solid
- Magnesium solid
- Zinc solid
- Lead solid
- Forceps
- Eyedroppers
- Goggles
- Apron

- $Mg(NO_3)_2$ solution
- $Zn(NO_3)_2$ solution
- $Pb(NO_3)_2$ solution
- $AgNO_3$ solution
- $Cu(NO_3)_2$ solution

1 Stop and think

Based on the metals given in the materials list, which do you think will be the most reactive?

2 Doing the experiment

1. You will need a 5-by-5 well plate. It will be arranged similar to the layout of Table 1. With an eyedropper, place seven drops of each solution into each of four wells. For example, place seven drops of $Cu(NO_3)_2$ solution in each of four wells across the top of the well plate

2. If you are using a clear plastic well plate, place a sheet of white paper underneath the it. It will allow you to see evidence of a potential chemical reaction more easily.

3. Place one sample of each metal into each solution. For example, place one sample of copper in the first well of the row containing the $Cu(NO_3)_2$ solution. Then place a sample of copper into the first well of the row containing $Zn(NO_3)_2$, and so on until the first well in each row has a sample of copper in it. Repeat this process with one sample of zinc placed in each of the second wells in each row, lead in the third, and magnesium in the fourth.

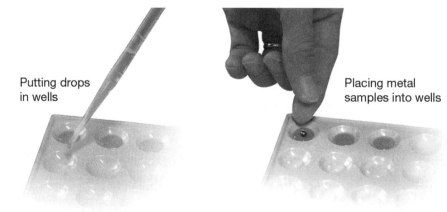

Putting drops in wells

Placing metal samples into wells

4.   After 15 minutes, use forceps to examine each metal. Be sure to turn the metal over and look at the underside for evidence of a chemical reaction.

5.   Place an *X* in any square of the data table where a reaction occurs.

6.   Clean up according to your instructor's directions and be sure to wash your hands.

7.   Add up the number of *X*s for each metal and write the total in the second data table.

Table 1: Reactivity data

	Cu	Zn	Pb	Mg
Cu(NO₃)₂				
Zn(NO₃)₂				
Pb(NO₃)₂				
Mg(NO₃)₂				
AgNO₃				

Metal	Cu	Zn	Pb	Mg
Number of Reactions				

3 Thinking about what you observed

a.   What evidence did you observe to indicate a chemical reaction had taken place in this experiment?

b.   Rank the solid metals used in the experiment from most reactive to least reactive.

c.   Even though silver solid was not used in this experiment, make a judgement as to where it would rank compared to the other metals. Explain.

d.   Compare the activity series you just constructed with one provided by your teacher. How do they compare?

16C Carbon and its Chemistry

What are some common molecules that contain carbon?

Living organisms are made up of a great variety of molecules, but the number of different elements involved is very small. Organic chemistry is the science of molecules that contain carbon and these are the ones most important to living organisms. This investigation will introduce you to some small organic molecules.

Materials
- CPO Periodic Table Tiles
- Reference book of organic compounds

1 The chemistry of carbon

Carbon is the central element in the chemistry of living things. This is because carbon can make complex molecules. Each carbon atom can make four bonds because carbon has four electrons in the outer energy level, which can hold a total of eight. Carbon can also form double and triple bonds by sharing two or three electrons with a single atom. Because of carbon's flexible bonding ability, many molecular structures are possible.

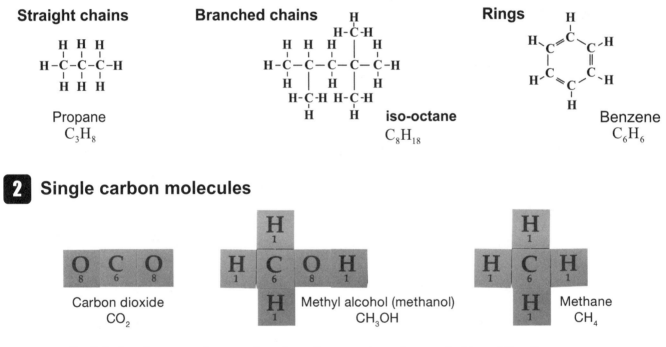

Straight chains

Propane
C_3H_8

Branched chains

iso-octane
C_8H_{18}

Rings

Benzene
C_6H_6

2 Single carbon molecules

Carbon dioxide
CO_2

Methyl alcohol (methanol)
CH_3OH

Methane
CH_4

1. Build the three carbon molecules above using the periodic table tiles.
2. Build a model of carbonic acid: H_2CO_3.

3 Stop and think

a. Research and describe at least one use of methyl alcohol.

b. Research and describe the use and production of methane.

4 Molecules with two carbon atoms

Once there are two carbon atoms, the structures get more complicated. The carbon atoms may share a single, double, or triple bond between them.

Acetic acid
CH_3COOH

Ethane
C_2H_6

1. Build the two-carbon molecules above using the periodic table tiles.
2. Build a model of ethyl alcohol (ethanol): C_2H_5OH. (*Hint*: Each carbon atom makes four bonds and the oxygen atom makes two bonds.)
3. Build a model of acetylene: C_2H_2. (*Hint*: There is a triple bond between the two carbon atoms.)

5 Stop and think

a. Research and describe where acetic acid is found.

b. Research and describe at least one use of ethyl alcohol.

6 Biological molecules

Living organisms are constructed mainly of proteins, which are very large carbon-based molecules, such as hemoglobin (right). A single protein may contain 10,000 or more atoms. Proteins themselves are constructed of simpler units called amino acids. For example, the hemoglobin molecule contains 584 amino acids.

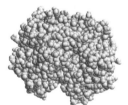

Hemoglobin molecule

Use the periodic table tiles to build models of the three smallest amino acids.

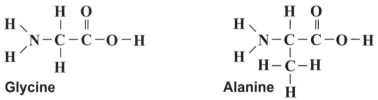

Glycine   **Alanine**   **Serine**

7 Stop and think

a. What is similar about all three amino acids?

b. Is the chemical in the diagram on the right an amino acid? Explain why you think your answer is correct.

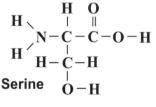

Is this an amino acid?

17C Classifying Chemical Reactions

How can you predict the products of a chemical reaction?

In a previous investigation, you learned to balance chemical equations. You may have noticed some patterns in those reactions. For example, you balanced some reactions in which a carbon compound reacted with oxygen gas to produce carbon dioxide and water. In this investigation you will explore patterns like these and learn how they can help you predict the products of a chemical reaction.

Materials
- CPO Periodic Table Tiles

1 Addition reactions

When two substances combine to form one new substance, we call the reaction an *addition reaction*. The general formula for an addition reaction looks like this: $A + B \rightarrow AB$. The sodium-chlorine addition reaction built using the Periodic Table Tiles looks like this:

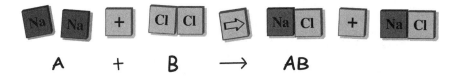

2 Decomposition reactions

In other chemical reactions, you may find one substance is broken down into two substances. This is called a *decomposition reaction*. Water, for example, can be broken down into the elements hydrogen and oxygen: $2H_2O \rightarrow 2H_2 + O_2$. The general formula for a decomposition reaction is $AB \rightarrow A + B$.

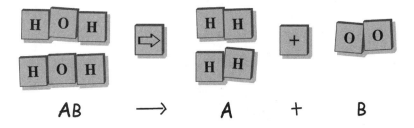

3 Single-displacement reactions

A third type of reaction, called a *single-displacement reaction*, occurs when one element replaces a similar element in a compound. If you put an iron nail into a beaker of copper chloride, you will see reddish copper forming on the nail.

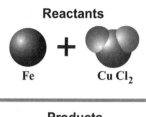
Reactants

Fe   Cu Cl$_2$

Iron replaces copper in the solution, and copper falls out of the solution as a metal: $CuCl_2 + Fe \rightarrow FeCl_2 + Cu$. The general formula for a single-displacement reaction is $AX + B \rightarrow BX + A$.

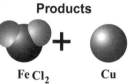
Products

Fe Cl$_2$ Cu

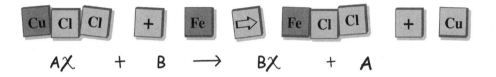

4 Double-displacement reactions

A *double-displacement* reaction occurs when ions from two compounds in a solution switch places to form two new compounds. This happens in the reaction between hydrochloric acid and sodium hydroxide: $HCl + NaOH \rightarrow NaCl + H_2O$. The general formula for a double-displacement reaction is $AB + CD \rightarrow AD + CB$.

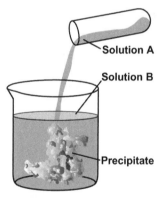
Solution A
Solution B
Precipitate

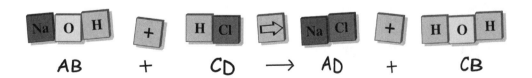

195

5 Combustion reactions

A fifth type of chemical reaction occurs when something burns. We call these reactions *combustion reactions*. You are probably familiar with combustion reactions in which a carbon compound is burned to produce carbon dioxide and water.

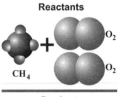

For example, methane (natural gas) is burned to heat homes: $CH_4 + 2O_2 \rightarrow CO_2 + 2H_2O$. The general formula for a carbon combustion reaction is: carbon compound $+ O_2 \rightarrow CO_2 + H_2O$.

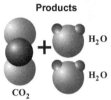

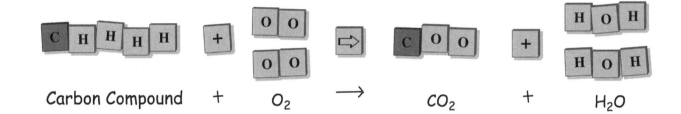

Carbon Compound $+$ O_2 $\longrightarrow$ CO_2 $+$ H_2O

6 Summary of types of reactions

Type	General Equation	Example
addition	A + B → AB	2Na + Cl$_2$ → 2NaCl
decomposition	AB → A + B	2H$_2$O → 2H$_2$ + O$_2$
single-displacement	AX + B → BX + A	CuCl$_2$ + Fe → FeCl$_2$ + Cu
double-displacement	AB + CD → AD +CB	HCl + NaOH → NaCl + H$_2$O
combustion	carb cpd + O$_2$ → CO$_2$ +H$_2$O	CH$_4$ + 2O$_2$ → CO$_2$ + 2H$_2$O

7 Predicting the products of a chemical reaction

Using the table above, predict the products of these chemical reactions:

a. The addition of magnesium and iodine: $Mg + I_2 \rightarrow$?

b. The decomposition of mercury oxide: $HgO \rightarrow$?

c. In potassium nitrate, the potassium is replaced by lead: $KNO_3 + Pb \rightarrow$?

d. The reaction between hydrochloric acid and potassium hydroxide: $HCl + KOH \rightarrow$?

e. The combustion of liquid hexane: $C_6H_{14} + O_2 \rightarrow$?

8 **Balancing equations given only the reactants**

Use the periodic table tiles to help you complete and balance the following chemical equations:

a. $Al + Br_2 \rightarrow$

b. $KBr + Cl_2 \rightarrow$

c. $HCl + K_2SO_3 \rightarrow$

d. $C_2H_6 + O_2 \rightarrow$

e. $Al_2O_3 \rightarrow$

f. $ZnSO_4 + SrCl_2 \rightarrow$

g. $Mg + HCl \rightarrow$

h. $CaCl_2 \rightarrow$

i. $C_5H_{12} + O_2 \rightarrow$

j. $Sb + I_2 \rightarrow$

18C Nuclear Reactions

How do we model nuclear reactions?

You would be very surprised to see a bus spontaneously transform into three cars and a motorcycle. But radioactive atoms do something very similar. If left alone, a radioactive atom eventually turns into another kind of atom, with completely different properties. This investigation looks at some basic concepts behind radioactivity.

Materials

- CPO Atom Building Game
- 50 pennies
- Cup
- Graph paper

1 Radioactivity

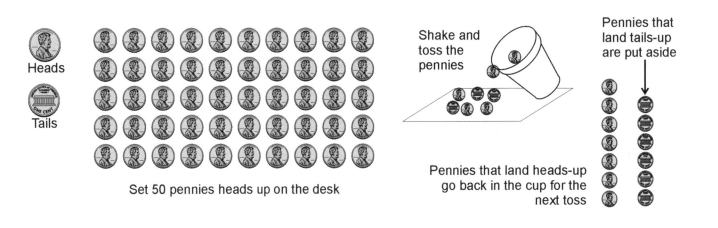

Heads

Tails

Set 50 pennies heads up on the desk

Shake and toss the pennies

Pennies that land tails-up are put aside

Pennies that land heads-up go back in the cup for the next toss

1. Place 50 pennies in a paper cup, shake them and dump them on the table. Each penny represents an atom of carbon-14.

2. Separate the pennies that land tails-up. Count the heads-up pennies and tails-up pennies and record the number of each in Table 1 in the row for the first toss.

3. Put *only the pennies that landed heads-up* back in the cup. Put the tails-up pennies aside. Shake the cup again and dump the pennies on the table.

4. Record the number of heads-up pennies in the row for the second toss.

5. Repeat the experiment using only the pennies that landed heads-up until you have one or no pennies left.

Table 1: Coin toss decay simulation

Heads	Heads-up pennies	Tails-up pennies
Start	50	0
First toss		
Second toss		
Third toss		

2 Thinking about what you observed

a. Make a graph showing the number of heads-up pennies on the *y*-axis and the number of tosses on the *x*-axis (0, 1, 2, 3, etc.).

b. On average, what percentage of pennies are lost on each toss? "Lost" means they came up tails and were removed.

c. How does the concept of half-life relate to the experiment with pennies? What does one half-life correspond to?

3 Build a radioactive atom

Carbon - 14

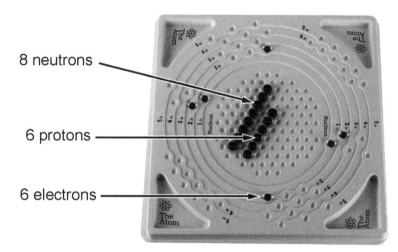

8 neutrons

6 protons

6 electrons

1. Build a carbon-14 atom (C^{14}). This isotope of carbon is radioactive.
2. Take one neutron out and replace it with a proton and an electron. This is what happens in radioactive decay of C^{14}.

4 Thinking about what you did

a. Research what happens to C^{14} when it decays. What element does it become? What particles are given off?

b. What is the average time it takes for 50 percent of the C^{14} atoms in a sample to decay?

c. Suppose you have 50 atoms of C^{14} and you watch them for a very long time. How do the results of your penny-flipping experiment describe the number of C^{14} atoms?

d. We actually find C^{14} in the environment. Research where it comes from.

e. Describe two other types of radioactivity and give an example of each.

f. *Challenge*: You cannot predict when any one atom will decay, just as you cannot predict whether a penny will come up heads or tails. Why can you predict that 50 percent of the C^{14} atoms will decay every half-life?

5 Introduction to Nuclear Reactions

If you were to add one, two or four extra neutrons to lithium-7 you would have created lithium-8, lithium-9, and lithium-11, respectively. Each of these isotopes of lithium is *radioactive*. These means that the atomic force in the nucleus (called *strong nuclear force*) is not strong enough to hold these atoms together. The nuclei of these atoms fly apart.

The goal of Nuclear Reactions is to earn points by creating atoms that are stable (not radioactive) and neutrally charged (not ions). Remember that *ions* are atoms that have different numbers of protons and electrons so they have a charge.

Each player starts with eight protons, eight electrons, and eught neutrons in their pocket of the Atomic Building Game board. The game will last for about a half-hour. The first player to 20 points wins.

6 Playing Nuclear Reactions

To begin play, each player is dealt five cards from the deck of Nuclear Reactions cards. These are held and not shown to anyone else.

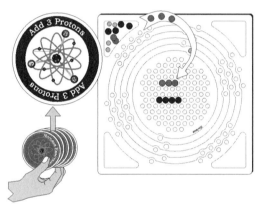

Players take turns, choosing which card to play each turn, and adding or subtracting particles from the atom as instructed on the card. For example, playing an "Add 2 Electrons" card would mean you place two yellow marbles in the atom.

Sub-atomic particles that are added or subtracted from the atom must come from, or be placed in your own pocket. You may not play a card for which you do not have the right marbles. For example, a player with only two protons left cannot play an "Add 3 Protons" card.

Each time you play a card, draw a new card from the deck so you always have five cards. Played cards can be shuffled and reused as needed.

7 Scoring points

The number of points scored depends how many of the conditions below are satisfied by the atom you create. You can use the periodic table to determine strategy and points. In particular it is useful to know which cards to play to get to stable isotopes, neutral atoms, or stable and neutral atoms.

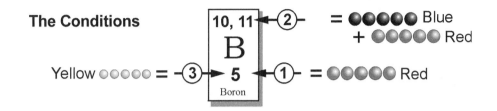

> **Condition #1:** The number of protons (red or green marbles) matches the atomic number.

> **Condition #2:** The number of protons (red or green marbles) plus the number of neutrons (blue marbles) equals one of the correct mass numbers for the element of Rule #1. This creates a stable nucleus.

> **Condition #3:** The number of electrons (yellow marbles) equals the number of protons (red or green marbles). This creates a neutral atom.

1. You score one point if your move creates or leaves a stable nucleus. For example, you score one point by adding a neutron to a nucleus with six protons and five neutrons. Adding a neutron makes a carbon 12 nucleus, which is stable. The next player can also score a point by adding another neutron, making carbon 13. Points cannot be scored for making a stable nucleus by adding or subtracting electrons, because electrons do not live in the nucleus! To get the nucleus right you need to satisfy conditions #1 and #2.

2. You score one point for adding or taking electrons or protons from the atom if your move creates or leaves a neutral atom. A neutral atom has the same number of electrons and protons. Getting the electrons and protons to balance satisfies condition #3.

3. You score three points (the best move) when you add or take particles from the atom and your move creates a perfect, stable and neutral atom. Both adding and subtracting can leave stable, neutral atoms. For example, taking a neutron from a stable, neutral carbon 13 atom leaves a stable, neutral carbon 12 atom, scoring three points. You get three points if your turn makes an atom that meets all three conditions.

201

8 Miscellaneous rules

Taking a turn

When it is your turn you must either

1. play a card and add or subtract marbles from the atom, or

2. trade in your cards for a new set of five.

Trading in cards

You may trade in all your cards at any time by forfeiting a turn. You have to trade all your cards in at once. Shuffle the deck before taking new cards.

Using the periodic table

All players should be allowed to use the special periodic table of the elements in the course of the game.

The marble bank

You may choose to play two versions of the marble bank.

Version 1: Players may take marbles from the bank at any time so they have enough to play the game.

Version 2: Players must lose a turn to draw marbles from the bank, and may draw no more than five total marbles (of any colors) in one turn.

9 Applying what you learned

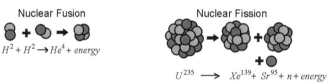

Nuclear Fusion
$$H^2 + H^2 \rightarrow He^4 + energy$$

Nuclear Fission
$$U^{235} \longrightarrow Xe^{139} + Sr^{95} + n + energy$$

a. There are two basic kinds of nuclear reactions, fission and fusion. Fission splits heavy elements up into lighter elements. Fusion combines lighter elements to make heavier elements. Both can release energy, depending on which elements are involved. What element do you get when you fuse lithium 6 and boron 11 together? It is stable or radioactive?

b. Write down a nuclear reaction using only two elements that would allow you to build fluorine 19 starting with boron 10.

c. Suppose you split a uranium 238 atom. If you have to break it into two pieces, name two elements that could be formed. Be sure that your two elements use up all the neutrons and protons in the uranium. Are either of your two elements stable or is one (or both) radioactive?

19C Solubility of CO$_2$

How is the solubility of a gas affected by temperature?

The carbonation from a soda is carbon dioxide gas that is dissolved in solution. The can is pressurized with carbon dioxide gas in order to maximize the amount of the gas dissolved in the beverage. As you have probably experienced, once you open the can, the carbon dioxide begins to escape and eventually the soda will taste "flat." The purpose of this investigation is to examine the solubility of carbon dioxide gas in solution.

Materials
- CPO DataCollector with temperature probe
- 2 cans of soda
- 600-mL beaker
- 1 thermometer
- Centigram balance
- Paper towels
- Heat-resistant gloves or hot mitts
- Hot plate

1 Stop and think

Based on what you know about carbonated drinks, how will the mass of carbon dioxide dissolved in solution change over time? When heated?

2 Doing the experiment

Part A: Solubility of Carbon Dioxide versus Time

1. Dry the outside of a room temperature unopened can of soda.
2. Carefully open the can and place it on the balance immediately. Record the mass in Table 1.
3. Record the mass every 3 minutes until 15 minutes have elapsed.
4. Don't discard the soda. Your teacher may have you record the mass one more time just before the period ends so be sure to note the time you first opened the soda.

Part B. Temperature versus Solubility

1. Using a 600-mL beaker, measure out approximately 150 mL of water. Place a thermometer in the beaker.
2. Place the beaker on a hot plate and heat it until the temperature is between 55 and 60°C. You will maintain this temperature during the experiment.
3. Once the temperature of the water bath is reached, open a can of soda and quickly measure its mass and record the value in Table 2.
4. Use the temperature probe and DataCollector to measure the temperature of the opened soda and record it in Table 2.
5. Carefully, place the opened can of soda into the warm water. Place the temperature probe into the can and select a new experiment on the DataCollector. Use meter mode. When the temperature reaches 25°C, remove the can, dry it, and measure its mass. Record the value in Table 2.

6. Repeat step five after every 5°C until the temperature of the soda reaches 50°C.

Table 1: Time and mass data

Time (minutes)	Mass (grams)
0	
3	
6	
9	
12	
15	

Table 2: Temperature and mass data

Temperature (celsius)	Mass (grams)
Starting temp:	
25	
30	
35	
40	
45	
50	

3 Data analysis

a. Make a graph of the data in Table 1. Place time on the *x*-axis. Put in a best-fit straight line through the data if the relationship looks linear.

b. Make a graph of the data in Table 2. Place temperature on the *x*-axis.

4 Thinking about what you observed

a. What does the first graph show?

b. Examine the data in Table 2. What effect did a rise in temperature have on the mass of carbonated beverage in the opened can? Explain this result.

c. What does your second graph indicate about the relationship between temperature and the solubility of a gas (carbon dioxide)?

d. In the summertime, there is a risk that large populations of fresh-water fish sometimes die-off. Explain this observation.

20C Electric Charge

What is static electricity?

Have you ever felt a shock when you touched a metal doorknob or removed clothes from a dryer? A tiny imbalance in either positive or negative charge on an object is the cause of *static electricity*. In this investigation you will cause objects to have charge imbalances, and then observe what happens when different objects interact. Remember, positive and negative charges attract, while like charges repel.

Materials

*   Clean glass beaker
*   Plastic rod
*   Aluminum foil
*   Silk, Fur and/or fleece fabric
*   Thread
*   18–22 gauge copper wire
*   Balloon
*   Paperclip and pencil

1 Observing electric charge

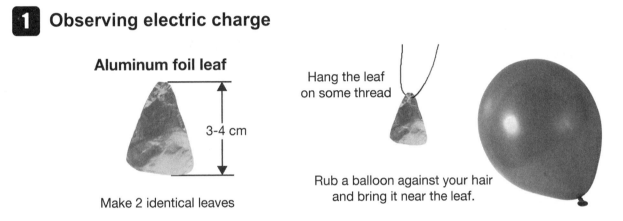

Aluminum foil leaf

3-4 cm

Make 2 identical leaves

Hang the leaf on some thread

Rub a balloon against your hair and bring it near the leaf.

1. Cut out two small "leaves" of aluminum foil and use a paperclip to make a hole in the top of each leaf. You can hold the leaf against a pencil as you poke the hole with the paperclip.
2. Suspend one leaf from a thread that you hold up in one hand.
3. Rub an inflated balloon against your hair and move it towards the foil leaf.
4. Touch the rubbed part of the balloon to something metal then bring it close to the leaf.
5. Bring other objects near the leaf before and after they are rubbed with different materials such as silk, fleece, or fur.

2 Thinking about what you observed

a. Describe what happens to the aluminum foil leaf as you move the balloon closer.

b. Explain the reaction of the leaf to the rubbed balloon using the concepts of positive and negative charge.

c. Explain why touching the balloon to a metal object changed its effect on the leaf.

3 Making an electroscope

1. Cut a piece of insulated copper wire so it is about 10 centimeters long.

2. Strip about 2 centimeters of the insulation from the wire at both ends. Be careful not to break the wire.

3. Bend the wire over the edge of the glass beaker as shown in the photo. It helps to place a small bit of clay on the side so you can anchor the wire by pressing it into the clay.

4. Make the electroscope as shown in the photo by hanging two leaves on the end of the wire that is inside the beaker.

5. Rub an inflated balloon against your hair and move it towards the end of the wire sticking out of the beaker.

6. Touch the balloon to the wire then remove it.

7. Touch the end of the wire with your finger or a metal object.

8. Bring the plastic rod near the wire. Then rub the plastic rod with the fleece and bring it near the wire again.

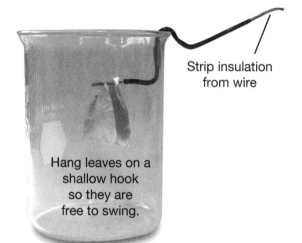

Strip insulation from wire

Hang leaves on a shallow hook so they are free to swing.

4 Thinking about what you observed

a. Describe what happens to the aluminum foil leaves as you move the rubbed balloon closer.

b. Give a reason why the leaves stay apart after the balloon is removed.

c. Explain what happens when you touch the wire with your hand or a metal object.

d. "Charge" the electroscope by touching it with a balloon that has been rubbed against your hair. Then touch the rubbed side of the balloon to something metal and bring it close to the electroscope again. Describe what happens.

e. Why does the plastic rod cause the leaves to move only after it has been rubbed with the fleece?

f. What causes the leaves of the electroscope to move apart?

21C Analyzing Circuits

How do you build and analyze a network circuit?

When both series and parallel circuits are combined into one circuit, a *network circuit* is created. In this investigation you will build and analyze network circuits. After determining the resistance of the colored resistors in the Electric Circuits kit, you will use these to build your network circuits.

Materials

- CPO Electric Circuits kit
- 5-, 10-, and 20-ohm resistors (in kit)
- Tape and a marker for labeling
- Digital multimeter with leads
- 2 "D" batteries

1 Determining the resistance of each resistor

You will use three different colored resistors in this investigation. Use tape to label the green resistors R1 and R2, the blue resistor R3, and the red resistor R4.

Use the multimeter to measure the resistance of each resistor and enter the results in Table 1.

Measuring resistance

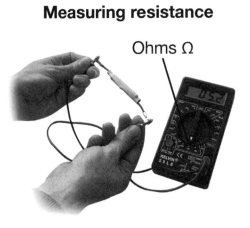

Ohms Ω

Table 1: Measured resistance values

	R1 (green)	R2 (green)	R3 (blue)	R4 (red)
Resistance (Ω)				

2 Building a network circuit

1. Use a battery; resistors 1, 2, and 3; and as many wires as necessary to construct the network circuit shown in the diagram at right.

2. Measure the voltage across the battery. This is the total circuit voltage. Then measure the voltage across each of the resistors. Record your measurements in Table 2.

3. Measure the current through each resistor. Record your measurements in Table 2. You have to break the circuit temporarily to insert the meter and make each current measurement. Be sure the meter is set to DC amps.

Build this circuit

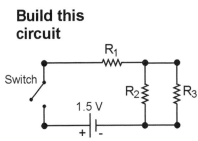

3 Analyzing the circuit

Table 2: Voltage and current measurements

	Battery (total circuit)	R1	R2	R3
Voltage (volts)				
Current (amps)				

a. Which of the two resistors is connected in parallel?

b. Which resistor is in series with the other two?

c. How does the voltage across the parallel resistors (R_2 and R_3) compare?

d. How does the voltage across the parallel resistors relate to what you learned about voltages in a parallel circuit in a previous investigation?

e. How does the current flowing through R_1 compare with the current through R_2?

f. How does the current coming out of the battery compare with the sum of the currents flowing through R_2 and R_3? Explain this relationship.

g. Use what you know about series and parallel circuits to calculate the theoretical total resistance of the circuit. The formulas for finding the total resistance are:

Series circuit	Parallel circuit
$R_{tot} = R_1 + R_2$	$\dfrac{1}{R_{tot}} = \dfrac{1}{R_1} + \dfrac{1}{R_2}$

h. Now calculate the total resistance of the circuit using Ohm's law, the battery voltage, and the total circuit current you measured.

i. How does the total resistance calculated using Ohm's law compare with the theoretical total resistance found above?

4 Predicting the effect of changing a resistor

a. Replace the 10-ohm resistor (R_3) with the 20-ohm resistor (R_4). Use what you have learned about network circuits to predict the total circuit resistance and total circuit current. Show the process you used to make your predictions.

b. Measure the voltage across the battery and each resistor and the total current in the circuit. Use Ohm's law to find the total circuit resistance. You will need to make a data table similar to Table 2.

c. How did the predicted values compare with the measured ones?

5 A circuit puzzle

Build this circuit

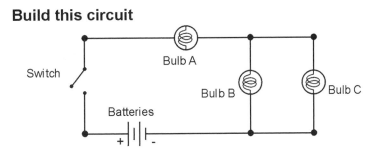

1. Build the circuit shown in the diagram above with two batteries, a switch, and three bulbs.

2. Turn the switch on and observe the brightness of each bulb.

3. Temporarily interrupt the current to bulb B by disconnecting one wire from the terminal post.

4. Observe how the brightness of the other two bulbs changes.

a. When bulb B is disconnected, does bulb A get dimmer, brighter, or stay the same?

b. When bulb B is disconnected, does bulb C get dimmer, brighter, or stay the same?

c. Use what you know about series and parallel circuits to propose an explanation for what you observed.

6 Challenge: Analyze a four-resistor network circuit

a. Build the circuit shown in the diagram at right.

b. Use what you have learned about network circuits to predict the total circuit resistance and current. Show the process you used to make your predictions.

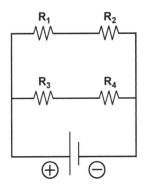

c. Use the meter to measure the voltage across the battery and each resistor and the total circuit current. Use Ohm's law to find the total circuit resistance.

d. How did the predicted values compare with the measured ones?

22C Electromagnetic Forces

How does an electric motor work?

Electric motors are found in many household devices, such as a hair dryer, blender, drill, and fan. In this investigation you will build a simple electric motor and see how it works. The concepts you learn with the simple motor also apply to other electric motors.

Materials

- 1 permanent magnet (from kit)
- 1 D-cell
- Large rubber band
- Metric ruler
- 1/2 stick of modeling clay
- Sand paper
- Varnished magnet wire
- Paper clips
- CPO Timer II (optional)

1 Making the base

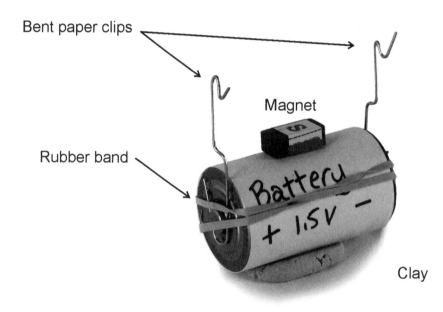

1. Bend the two paper clips so they look like the photo.
2. Fasten them with rubber bands so they contact the positive and negative terminals of the battery.
3. Break off a small lump of clay from the 1/2 stick. Set the battery on the small clay lump so it stays in one place without rolling around.
4. Use a tiny piece of clay to stick a magnet to the top of the battery.
5. Your motor base is complete!

2 Making the coil

Sand all around this end of the wire

Sand only one side of this end of the wire

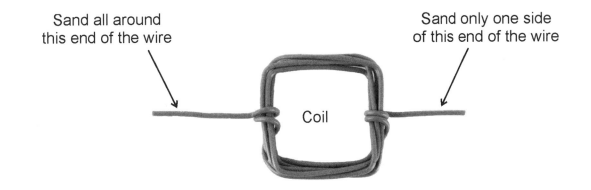

Coil

1. Cut 1 meter of magnet wire (also called varnished magnet wire). This wire has a painted insulation layer on the surface.
2. Wrap the wire around the square form of the modeling clay with one end sticking out 4 centimeters or so.
3. Keep wrapping until you have only 4–5 centimeters left.
4. Remove your coil from the form and wrap the ends of the wire a few turns around the sides of the coil to keep things together. There should be about 3 centimeters of wire on each side of the coil.
5. Take some sand paper and sand off all the varnish on one wire.
6. Sand off the varnish on *one side only* of the other end of the wire.
7. Adjust the wires until the coil balances as well as you can get it.
8. Your coil is done!

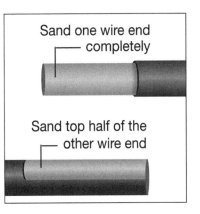

Sand one wire end completely

Sand top half of the other wire end

3 Making the motor work

1. Set the coil into the paper clips so it is free to spin.
2. Adjust the height of the paper clips until the coil rotates just above the magnet.
3. The motor should spin! Adjust the balance by bending the wires or paper clips.

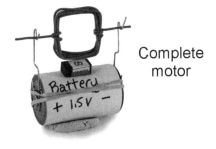

Complete motor

Troubleshooting—the main problem areas to watch out for are:

- unbalanced coil
- poor connections
- improperly sanded coil ends
- dead D-cell

4 Thinking about what you observed

a. When electricity runs through the coil of wire, what type of force is created around the coil?

b. What is the purpose of the permanent magnet?

c. What interactions cause the coil of wire to spin?

d. Try adding a second magnet. Does this make the motor go faster, slower, or about the same? What observations did you make that support your answer?

e. What else might make the motor spin faster? With your teacher's approval, try it!

5 Challenge

See if you can hold a photogate so the spinning coil breaks the light beam. With the Timer mode set on frequency, you will know how many breaks per second the spinning coil makes.

a. Describe how you set up the experiment to get frequency readings from the Timer/photogate equipment.

b. How did your spinning coil measurements compare to other groups' data?

c. Repeat the last two steps in the previous section (4d and 4e). Record your data.

d. Does the spinning coil data support your answers to 4d and 4e? Explain.

e. The basic parts of any simple DC motor like the one you made are an electromagnet, permanent magnet, commutator, and energy source. Draw a diagram of your simple motor and label these parts.

23C Waves in Motion

How do waves move?

Waves are oscillations that move from one place to another. Like oscillations, waves also have the properties of frequency and amplitude. In this investigation you will explore waves on strings and in water. What you learn applies to all other types of waves as well.

Materials

- Metal Slinky® toy spring
- Meter stick
- A length of 1" plastic pipe cut to fit the wave tray
- Food coloring
- Water
- Wave tray with wooden blocks

1 Making a transverse wave pulse

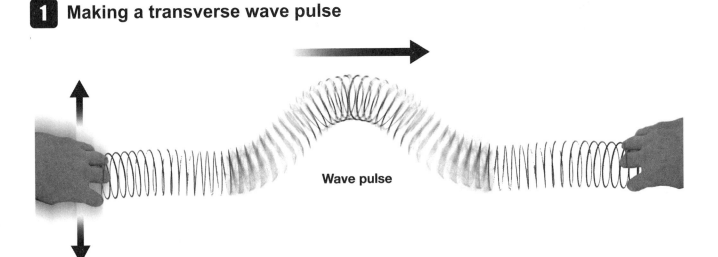

Wave pulse

1. It takes two students to do this experiment. Each student takes one end of the spring.
2. Bring the spring down to the floor. Stretch it to a length of about 3 meters while keeping the spring on the floor.
3. One student should jerk one end of the spring rapidly to the side and back, just once. Make sure both ends of the spring are held tight and do not move once the wave is in motion. A wave pulse should travel up the spring.
4. Watch the wave pulse as it moves up and back. Try it a few times.

2 Thinking about what you observed

a. How is the motion of a wave pulse different from the motion of a moving object such as a car? (*Hint*: What is it that moves in the case of a wave?)

b. What happens to the wave pulse when it hits the far end of the spring? Watch carefully. Does the pulse stay on the same side of the spring or flip to the other side? Use the word *reflect* in your answer.

c. Imagine you broke the spring in the middle. Do you think the wave could cross the break? Discuss the reasoning behind your answer in a few sentences.

d. Why does the wave pulse move along the spring instead of just staying in the place you made it?

3 Making a longitudinal wave pulse

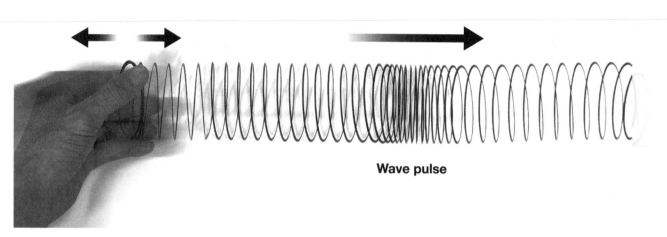

Wave pulse

1. Just like the wave you made in Part 1, each student takes one end of the spring.
2. Bring the spring down to the floor. Stretch it to a length of about 3 meters while keeping the spring on the floor.
3. One student should jerk one end of the spring rapidly forward and back, just once. Make sure both ends of the spring are held tight and do not move once the wave is in motion. A wave pulse should travel up the spring.
4. Watch the wave pulse as it moves up and back. Try it a few times.

4 Thinking about what you observed

a. How is the motion of the longitutdinal wave pulse different from the transverse wave pulse you made in Part 1? (*Hint*: How is the motion of the spring itself different?)

b. What happens to the wave pulse when it hits the far end of the spring? Does it behave like the transverse wave, or much differently? Use the word *reflect* in your answer.

c. Why do you think longitudinal waves are also sometimes called "compressional waves"?

d. Do you think a wave can be made by only stretching the spring instead of compressing it? Make a prediction then try it and see if you were right.

5 **Waves in water**

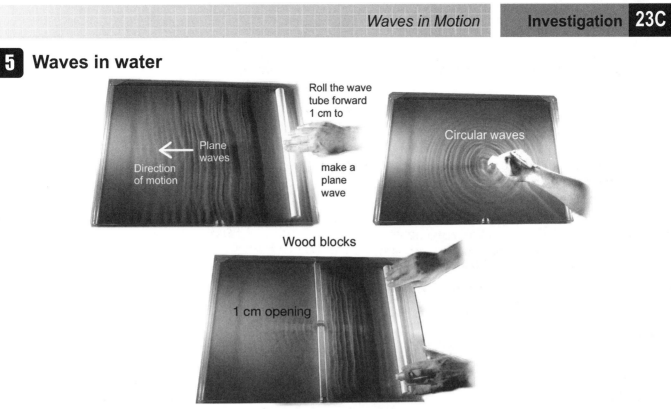

1. Fill a flat tray with about one-half centimeter of colored water. The color helps you see the waves.

2. Roll the wave tube forward about 1 centimeter in a smooth motion. This launches a nearly straight wave called a *plane wave* across the tray.

3. Next, poke the surface of the water with your fingertip. Disturbing a single point on the surface of the water makes a *circular wave* that moves outward from where you touched the water.

4. Arrange two wood blocks so they cross the tray leaving a 1-centimeter opening between them.

5. Make a plane wave that moves toward the blocks. Observe what happens to the wave that goes through the opening.

6 **Thinking about what you observed**

a. Draw a sketch that shows your plane wave from the top. Also on your sketch, draw an arrow that shows the direction the wave moves.

b. Is the wave parallel or perpendicular to the direction the wave moves?

c. Draw another sketch that shows the circular wave. Add at least four arrows that show the direction in which each part of the wave moves.

d. At every point along the wave, are the waves more parallel or perpendicular to the direction in which the circular wave moves?

e. Sketch the shape of the wave before and after passing through the 1-centimeter opening.

f. Does the wave change shape when it passes through the opening? If you see any change, your answer should state into what kind of shape the wave changes.

g. Are the waves you made in the water transverse or longitudinal waves, and why?

24C Perceiving Sound

What is sound and how do we hear it??

The ear is a very remarkable sensor. Sound waves that we can hear change the air pressure by one part in a million! Because sound is about perception, and people are different, we will have to use some very interesting techniques to make experiments reliable. In this investigation you will learn about the range of frequencies the ear can detect and also how small a difference in frequency we can perceive.

Materials

- CPO DataCollector
- CPO Sound & Waves Machine
- Pencils
- Graph paper
- At least one calculator
- Ruler or straightedge

1 How high can you hear?

The accepted range of frequencies the human ear can hear ranges from a low of 20 Hz to a high of 20,000 Hz. Actually, there is tremendous variation within this range, and people's hearing changes greatly with age and exposure to loud noises.

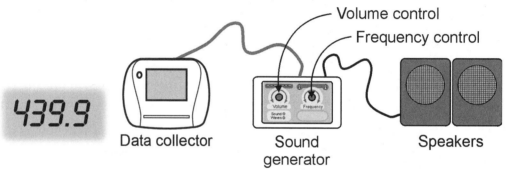

Connect your sound generator to a DataCollector set to measure *frequency*. Connect a speaker to the sound generator. When you turn the DataCollector on, you should hear a sound and the DataCollector should measure a frequency near 440 Hz.

There are two knobs for frequency and volume control. Try adjusting the frequency and see how high and low it will go.

See if you and your group can agree on a frequency where you hear the sound as low, medium, high, and very high frequency. Write frequencies of sound that you think sound low, medium, high, and very high in Table 1. Don't try to be too exact, because the words *low*, *medium*, and *high* are themselves not well defined. It is difficult to agree exactly on anything that is based completely on individual human perception.

Table 1: How we hear frequencies of sound

Description	Frequency (Hz)
Low	
Medium	
High	
Very high	

2 Testing the upper frequency limit of the ear

To start with a simple experiment, your teacher has a sound generator that can make frequencies up to 20,000 Hz. When the teacher asks, raise your hand if you can hear the sound. Don't raise your hand if you can't hear. Someone will be appointed to count hands and survey the class to see what fraction of students can still hear the sound.

a. The objective of the test is to see what fraction of people can hear a particular frequency. Once the frequency gets too high, no one will be able to hear it, or at least no humans. Cats, dogs, and other animals can hear much higher frequencies than people. Do you think the method of raising your hands is likely to give a good result? Give at least one reason why you think the method is either good or bad.

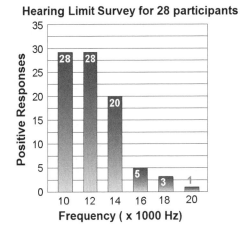

Hearing Limit Survey for 28 participants

b. Make a bar graph showing how your class responded to frequencies between 10,000 and 20,000 Hz. You should have six bars, each one for a frequency range of 2,000 Hz. The height of each bar is the number of people who could hear that frequency of sound. If someone could hear the frequency they are counted as a positive response in the graph. This kind of graph is called a *histogram*.

3 Doing a more careful experiment

Another way to do the experiment is with a hidden ballot. The researcher running the experiment will ask if anyone can hear a certain frequency of sound and you check yes or no on a piece of paper. The researcher may play or *not* play the sound. Each frequency will be played five times, and the five repetitions will be all mixed up so there is less chance for error. Every one in the class does one response survey.

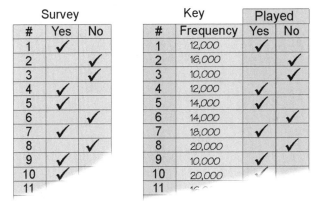

Collect the data from the survey sheets and record it in Table 2.

Table 2: Frequency survey data

# Right	10,000 Hz	12,000 Hz	14,000 Hz	16,000 Hz	18,000 Hz	20,000 Hz
5						
4						
3						
2						
1						

Plot another histogram showing only those people whose choices matched the yes/no on the key for all five times at each frequency. It is hard to fake a response or get it right by chance because you have to choose correctly five times for each frequency. This kind of experiment is called a double-blind test since neither you nor the researcher can see anyone else's response. The results from a double-blind experiment are much more reliable that other forms of surveys. Doctors use the double-blind method to test new medicines.

4 Perceiving differences in frequency

Can you tell the difference between a sound with a frequency of 400 Hz and a sound at 401 Hz? The next experiment on hearing is to test people's ability to distinguish if one sound has higher frequency than another.

In this experiment the researcher will play two frequencies and you mark which one is higher.

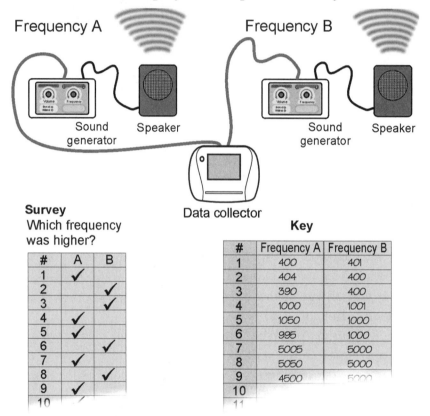

To analyze the results you need to know how many people got the right answer for each frequency range. Make a data table like the example below that is large enough to hold all of your results.

Table 3: Comparative frequency data

Frequency A (Hz)	Frequency B (Hz)	Frequency difference (Hz)	Percent difference	# of correct responses
1,000	995	5	0.5%	1
1,000	1,050	50	1%	15
1,000	1,001	1	.1%	0

a. Calculate the percent difference in frequency for each test.

b. There are two ways to look at sensitivity. In one way, we hear *absolute* differences in frequency. If the ear was sensitive to absolute differences, we would hear a 5 Hz difference no matter if the two frequencies were 500 Hz and 505 Hz, or 5,000 Hz and 5,005 Hz.

The second possibility is that we hear relative differences. We might be able to hear a 1 percent difference which would be 5 Hz at 500 Hz. But we could not hear the difference between 5,000 Hz and 5,005 Hz because the percentage difference is only 0.1 percent. To hear a similar difference at 5000 Hz, Frequency B would have to be 5,050 Hz, which is 1 percent higher.

Which model does the data support?

5 Chance and experiments

A very good way to ensure accurate results in a survey test is to make it improbable that anyone could get the correct response by guessing. A single test is almost never enough to rule out this possibility. Consider that on each test you have a 50 percent chance to guess right. That means one out of every two times you could get the right response just by guessing. This is not very reliable!

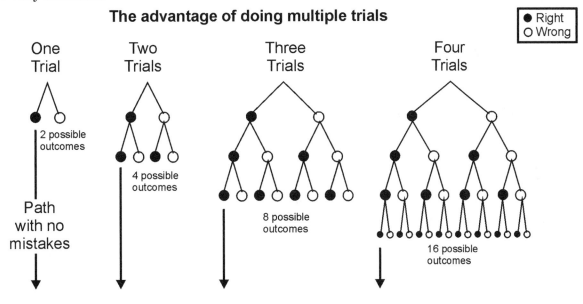

The advantage of doing multiple trials

The diagram shows a decision tree for an experiment with multiple trials. There is only one path with no mistakes. With each additional trial, the total number of possible outcomes increases by two. With two trials you have one right path out of four choices. That means there is only a one in four chance someone could guess twice correctly. With three trials there is only a one in eight chance of guessing. With four trials the chance of guessing is down to 1 in 16.

a. What is the chance of guessing correctly with five trials?

b. If 100 people did a test with five trials, and everybody guessed, how many people would be likely to make five correct choices in a row?

25C Magnification and Mixing Pigments

How is the magnification of a lens determined? What happens when you mix different colors of pigments?

In optics, lenses are optical devices that use refraction to bend light. Some lenses can be used to produce images that are larger than the object they are collecting light from. This process is called magnification and it is used in equipment like microscopes and telescopes to investigate objects that are difficult to see with the naked eye. In this investigation you will look at how distance can affect magnification, and also how mixing materials colored by pigments, paints, or dyes are different than mixing different colors of light.

Materials

- CPO Optics with Light & Color kit
- Metric ruler
- Cyan, magenta, and yellow clay

1   Finding the magnification of a lens

1. Set your light blue lens directly on the graph paper and count the number of *unmagnified* squares that cross the diameter of the lens. In the example, the lens is 10 squares wide.

2. Next, examine a section of graph paper with your lens held above the paper. Move the lens closer and farther away until you have the biggest squares you can still see clearly in the lens.

3. Count the number of *magnified* squares that cross the diameter of the lens. For example, the picture shows 4 1/2 squares across the lens.

4. The magnification can be calculated by dividing the number of *unmagnified* squares by the number of *magnified* squares. In the example, you see 10 *unmagnified* squares and 4.5 *magnified* squares. The magnification is 10 /4.5, or 2.22.

5. Try the experiment again using a ruler to measure the distance between the lens and the paper. Notice that the magnification changes with different distances.

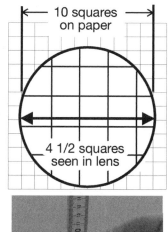

Measuring the distance from the lens to the paper

6. Fill in the table by measuring the magnification of your lens for at least four different distances. The number of squares on the graph paper will be the same for all distances.

Table 1: Magnification of a lens

Distance to paper	# of squares on graph paper (unmagnified squares)	# of squares in lens (magnified squares)	Magnification

2 Thinking about what you observed

a. Is the image in a magnifying glass inverted or upright?

b. At what distances will the lens act like a magnifying glass? What happens when the object is more than one focal length away?

c. Describe something that looks completely different under a magnifying glass than when seen with the un-aided eye.

d. Try the same activity with the dark blue lens. What happens to the image in the lens when you lift it up from the paper?

3 The subtractive color model (CMYK)

1. You have three colors of clay: cyan, magenta, and yellow. Take a portion the size of your fingertip of the both cyan and the magenta. Mix them together. What color do you get?

2. Mix equal amounts of cyan and yellow. What color do you get?

3. Mix equal amounts of yellow and magenta. What color do you get?

The subtractive color model (CMYK)

	Cyan	Magenta	Yellow	Black
Absorbs	Red	Green	Blue	Red, Green, Blue
Reflects	Blue, Green	Blue, Red	Red, Green	None

Cyan Magenta Yellow

Mix equal amounts of the three subtractive primary colors
(two colors at a time)

221

4 Thinking about what you observed

a. Explain how the mixture of magenta and cyan makes its color when seen in white light.

b. Explain how the mixture of cyan and yellow makes its color when seen in white light.

c. Explain how the mixture of yellow and magenta makes its color when seen in white light.

d. Why don't the mixed colors produce full red, green, or blue?

e. What color would you see if you looked at a mixture of magenta and cyan under a lamp that only made blue light?

f. Research how printers make colors. Do they use red, green, and blue (RGB) or cyan, magenta, yellow, and black (CMYK)? Explain why printed pictures need to use one or the other.

g. Research how computer monitors and televisions make colors. Do they use red, green, and blue (RGB) or cyan, magenta, yellow, and black (CMYK)? Explain why TVs and computer screens need to use one or the other.

h. Explain why mixing the primary colors of light is referred to as the additive color mixing process, while mixing materials colored with pigments, paints or dyes is referred to as the subtractive color mixing process.

Lab Skills and Equipment Setups

Safety Skills

What can I do to protect myself and others in the lab?

Science equipment and supplies are fun to use. However, these materials must always be used with care. Here you will learn how to be safe in a science lab.

Materials
- Poster board
- Felt-tip markers

◣ 1 Follow these basic safety guidelines

Your teacher will divide the class into groups. Each group should create a poster-sized display of one of the following guidelines. Hang the posters in the lab. Review these safety guidelines before each investigation.

1. **Prepare** for each investigation.

   a. Read the Investigation sheets carefully.

   b. Take special note of safety instructions.

2. **Listen** to your teacher's instructions before, during, and after the Investigation. Take notes to help you remember what your teacher has said.

3. **Get ready to work:** Roll long sleeves above the wrist. Tie back long hair. Remove dangling jewelry and any loose, bulky outer layers of clothing. Wear shoes that cover the toes.

4. **Gather** protective clothing (goggles, apron, gloves) at the beginning of the Investigation.

5. **Emphasize teamwork.** Help each other. Watch out for one another's safety.

6. **Clean up** spills immediately. Clean up all materials and supplies after an Investigation.

◣ 2 Know what to do when...

1. **working with heat.**

   a. Always handle hot items with a hot pad. Never use your bare hands.

   b. Move carefully when you are near hot items. Sudden movements could cause burns if you touch or spill something hot.

2. **working with electricity.**

   a. Always keep electric cords away from water.

   b. Extension cords must not be placed where they may cause someone to trip or fall.

   c. If an electrical appliance isn't working, feels hot, or smells hot, tell a teacher right away.

3. **disposing of materials and supplies.**

    a. Generally, liquid household chemicals can be poured into a sink. Completely wash the chemical down the drain with plenty of water.

    b. Generally, solid household chemicals can be placed in a trash can.

    c. Any liquids or solids that **should not** be poured down the sink or placed in the trash have special disposal guidelines. Follow your teacher's instructions.

    d. If glass breaks, do not use your bare hands to pick up the pieces. Use a dustpan and a brush to clean up. "Sharps" trash (trash that has pieces of glass) should be well labeled. The best way to throw away broken glass is to seal it in a labeled cardboard box.

4. **you are concerned about your safety or the safety of others.**

    a. Talk to your teacher immediately. Here are some examples:

       • You smell chemical or gas fumes. This might indicate a chemical or gas leak.

       • You smell something burning.

       • You injure yourself or see someone else who is injured.

       • You are having trouble using your equipment.

       • You do not understand the instructions for the Investigation.

    b. Listen carefully to your teacher's instructions.

    c. Follow your teacher's instructions exactly.

◤3 Safety quiz

1. Draw a diagram of your science lab in the space below. Include in your diagram the following items. Include notes that explain how to use these important safety items.

- Exit/entrance ways
- Fire extinguisher(s)
- Fire blanket
- Eye wash and shower
- First aid kit
- Location of eye goggles and lab aprons
- Sink
- Trash cans
- Location of special safety instructions

2. How many fire extinguishers are in your science lab? Explain how to use them.

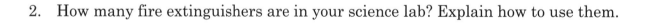

3. List the steps that your teacher and your class would take to safely exit the science lab and the building in case of a fire or other emergency.

4. Before beginning certain Investigations, why should you first put on protective goggles and clothing?

_____

_____

_____

5. Why is teamwork important when you are working in a science lab?

_____

_____

_____

_____

6. Why should you clean up after every Investigation?

_____

_____

_____

7. List at least three things you should you do if you sense danger or see an emergency in your classroom or lab.

_____

_____

_____

_____

8. Five lab situations are described below. What would you do in each situation?
   a. You accidentally knock over a glass container and it breaks on the floor.

_____

_____

   b. You accidentally spill a large amount of water on the floor.

_____

_____

_____

c. You suddenly you begin to smell a "chemical" odor that gives you a headache.

_____

_____

_____

d. You hear the fire alarm while you are working in the lab. You are wearing your goggles and lab apron.

_____

_____

_____

e. While your lab partner has her lab goggles off, she gets some liquid from the experiment in her eye.

_____

_____

_____

f. A fire starts in the lab.

_____

_____

_____

Safety in the science lab is everyone's responsibility!

4 Safety contract

Keep this contract in your notebook at all times.

By signing it, you agree to follow all the steps necessary to be safe in your science class and lab.

I, _____, (Your name)

- Have learned about the use and location of the following:
  - Aprons, gloves
  - Eye protection
  - Eyewash fountain
  - Fire extinguisher and fire blanket
  - First aid kit
  - Heat sources (burners, hot plate, etc) and how to use them safely
  - Waste-disposal containers for glass, chemicals, matches, paper, and wood
- Understand the safety information presented.
- Will ask questions when I do not understand safety instructions.
- Pledge to follow all of the safety guidelines that are presented on the Safety Skill Sheet at all times.
- Pledge to follow all of the safety guidelines that are presented on Investigation sheets.
- Will always follow the safety instructions that my teacher provides.

Additionally, I pledge to be careful about my own safety and to help others be safe. I understand that I am responsible for helping to create a safe environment in the classroom and lab.

Signed and dated,

_____

Parent's or Guardian's statement:

I have read the Safety Skills sheet and give my consent for the student who has signed the preceding statement to engage in laboratory activities using a variety of equipment and materials, including those described. I pledge my cooperation in urging that she or he observe the safety regulations prescribed.

_____   _____

Signature of Parent or Guardian   Date

Writing a Lab Report

How do you share the results of an experiment?

A lab report is like a story about an experiment. The details in the story help others learn from what you did. A good lab report makes it possible for someone else to repeat your experiment. If their results and conclusions are similar to yours, you have support for your ideas. Through this process we come to understand more about how the world works.

1 The parts of a lab report

A lab report follows the steps of the scientific method. Use the checklist below to create your own lab reports:

- ☐ **Title:** The title makes it easy for readers to quickly identify the topic of your experiment.

- ☐ **Research question:** The research question tells the reader exactly what you want to find out through your experiment.

- ☐ **Introduction:** This paragraph describes what you already know about the topic, and shows how this information relates to your experiment.

- ☐ **Hypothesis:** The hypothesis states the prediction you plan to test in your experiment.

- ☐ **Materials:** List all the materials you need to do the experiment.

- ☐ **Procedure:** Describe the steps involved in your experiment. Make sure that you provide enough detail so readers can repeat what you did. You may want to provide sketches of the lab setup. Be sure to name the experimental variable and tell which variables you controlled.

- ☐ **Data/Observations:** This is where you record what happened, using descriptive words, data tables, and graphs.

- ☐ **Analysis:** In this section, describe your data in words. Here's a good way to start: *My data shows that...*

- ☐ **Conclusion:** This paragraph states whether your hypothesis was correct or incorrect. It may suggest a new research question or a new hypothesis.

2 A sample lab report

Use the sample lab report on the next two pages as a guide for writing your own lab reports. Remember that you are telling a story about something you did so that others can repeat your experiment.

Name: Lucy O.   **Date:** January 24, 2013

Title: Pressure and Speed

Research question: How does pressure affect the speed of the CPO air rocket?

Introduction:

Air pressure is a term used to describe how tightly air molecules are packed into a certain space. When air pressure increases, more air molecules are packed into the same amount of space. These molecules are moving around and colliding with each other and the walls of the container. As the number of molecules in the container increases, the number of molecular collisions in the container increases. A pressure gauge measures the force of these molecules as they strike a surface.

In this lab, I will measure the speed of the CPO air rocket when it is launched with different amounts of initial pressure inside the plastic bottle. I want to know if a greater amount of initial air pressure will cause the air rocket to travel at a greater speed.

Hypothesis: When I increase the pressure of the air rocket, the speed will increase.

Materials:

CPO air rocket   CPO photogates

CPO timer   Goggles

Procedure:

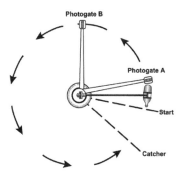

1. I put on goggles and made sure the area was clear.
2. The air rocket is attached to an arm so that it travels in a circular path. After it travels about 330°, the air rocket hits a stopper and its flight ends. I set up the photogate at 90°.
3. My control variables were the mass of the rocket and launch technique, so I kept these constant throughout the experiment.
4. My experimental variable was the initial pressure applied to the rocket. I tested the air rocket at three different initial pressures. The pressures that work effectively with this equipment range from 15 psi to 90 psi. I tested the air rocket at 20 psi, 50 psi, and 80 psi. I did three trials at each pressure.
5. The length of the rocket wing is 5 cm. The wing breaks the photogate's light beam. The photogate reports the amount of time that the wing took to pass through the beam. Therefore, I used wing length as distance and divide by time to calculate speed of the air rocket.
6. I found the average speed in centimeters per second for each pressure.

Data/Observations:

Table 1: Air pressure and speed of rocket

Initial air pressure	Time (sec) at 90°	Speed (m/sec) at 90°	Average speed cm/sec
20 psi	0.0227	2.20	216
	0.0231	2.16	
	0.0237	2.11	
50 psi	0.0097	5.15	510
	0.0099	5.05	
	0.0098	5.10	
80 psi	0.0060	8.33	794
	0.0064	7.81	
	0.0065	7.69	

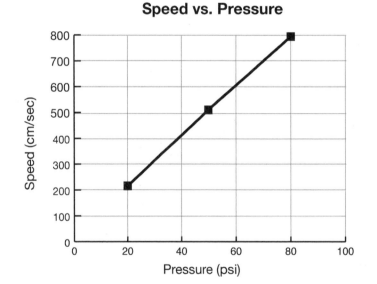

Speed vs. Pressure

Analysis:

My graph shows that the plots of the data for photogates A and B are linear. As the values for pressure increased, the speed increased also.

Conclusion:

The data shows that pressure does have an effect on speed. The graph shows that my hypothesis is correct. As the initial pressure of the rocket increased, the speed of the rocket increased as well. There is a direct relationship between pressure and speed of the rocket.

Measuring Length

How do you find the length of an object?

Size matters! When you describe the length of an object, or the distance between two objects, you are describing something very important about the object. Is it as small as a bacteria (2 micrometers)? Is it a light year away (9.46 × 10^{15} meters)? By using the metric system you can quickly see the difference in size between objects.

Materials

- Metric ruler
- Pencil
- Paper
- Small objects
- Calculator

 Reading the meter scale correctly

Look at the ruler in the picture above. Each small line on the top of the ruler represents one millimeter. Larger lines stand for 5 millimeter and 10 millimeter intervals. When the object you are measuring falls between the lines, read the number to the nearest 0.5 millimeter. Practice measuring several objects with your own metric ruler. Compare your results with a lab partner.

 Stop and think

a. You may have seen a ruler like this marked in centimeter units. How many millimeters are in one centimeter?

_____

_____

b. Notice that the ruler also has markings for reading the English system. Give an example of when it would be better to measure with the English system than the metric system. Give a different example of when it would be better to use the metric system.

_____

_____

_____

Example 1: Measuring objects correctly

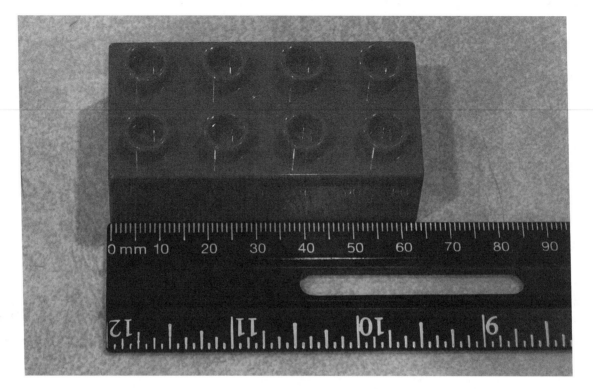

Look at the picture above. How long is the building block?

1. Report the length of the building block to the nearest 0.5 millimeters.
2. Convert your answer to centimeters.
3. Convert your answer to meters.

_____

_____

_____

_____

_____

_____

_____

_____

_____

_____

_____

_____

4 ▲ Example 2: Measuring objects correctly

Look at the picture above. How long is the pencil?

1. Report the length of the pencil to the nearest 0.5 millimeters.
2. Challenge: How many building blocks in example 1 will it take to equal the length of the pencil?
3. Challenge: Convert the length of the pencil to inches by dividing your answer by 25.4 millimeters per inch.

5 ▲ Example 3: Measuring objects correctly

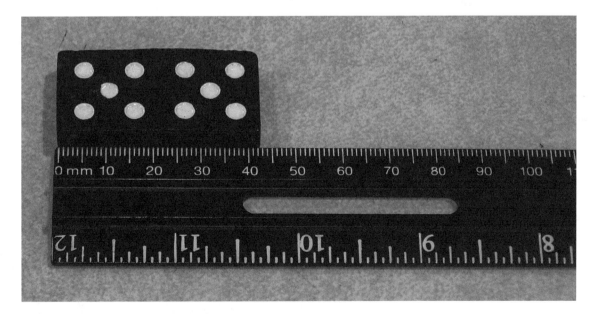

Look at the picture above. How long is the domino?

1. Report the length of the domino to the nearest 0.5 millimeters.
2. Challenge: How many dominoes will fit end to end on the 30 cm ruler?

◢6 Practice converting units for length

By completing the examples above you show that you are familiar with some of the prefixes used in the metric system like milli- and centi-. The table below gives other prefixes you may be less familiar with. Try converting the length of the domino from millimeters into all the other units given in the table.

Refer to the multiplication factor this way:

- 1 kilometer equals 1000 meters.

- 1000 millimeters equals 1 meter.

1. How many millimeters are in a kilometer?

1000 millimeters per meter ∞ 1000 meters per kilometer = 1,000,000 millimeters per kilometer

2. Fill in the table with your multiplication factor by converting millimeters to the unit given. The first one is done for you.

1000 millimeters per meter ∞ 10^{-12} meters per picometer = 10^{-9} millimeters per picometer

3. Divide the domino's length in millimeters by the number in your multiplication factor column. This is the answer you will put in the last column.

Prefix	Symbol	Multiplication factor	Scientific notation in meters	Your multiplication factor	Your domino length in:
pico-	p	0.000000000001	10^{-12}	10^{-9}	pm
nano-	n	0.000000001	10^{-9}		nm
micro-	μ	0.000001	10^{-6}		μm
milli	m	0.001	10^{-3}		mm
centi-	c	0.01	10^{-2}		cm
deci-	d	0.1	10^{-1}		dm
deka-	da	10	10^{1}		dam
hecto-	h	100	10^{2}		hm
kilo-	k	1000	10^{3}		km

Measuring Temperature

How do you find the temperature of a substance?

There are many different kinds of thermometers used to measure temperature. Can you think of some you find at home? In your classroom you will use a glass immersion thermometer to find the temperature of a liquid. The thermometer contains alcohol with a red dye in it so you can see the alcohol level inside the thermometer. The alcohol level changes depending on the surrounding temperature. You will practice reading the scale on the thermometer and report your readings in degrees Celsius.

Materials
- Alcohol immersion thermometer
- Beakers
- Water at different temperatures
- Ice

Safety: Glass thermometers are breakable. Handle them carefully. Overheating the thermometer can cause the alcohol to separate and give incorrect readings. Glass thermometers should be stored horizontally or vertically (never upside down) to prevent alcohol from separating.

1 ◣ Reading the temperature scale correctly

Look at the picture at right. See the close-up of the line inside the thermometer on the scale. The tens scale numbers are given. The ones scale appears as lines. Each small line equals 1 degree Celsius. Practice reading the scale from the bottom to the top. One small line above 20 °C is read as 21 °C. When the level of the alcohol is between two small lines on the scale, report the number to the nearest 0.5 °C.

2 ◣ Stop and think

a. What number does the large line between 20 °C and 30 °C equal? Figure out by counting the number of small lines between 20 °C and 30 °C.

b. Give the temperature of the thermometer in the picture above.

c. Practice rounding the following temperature values to the nearest 0.5 °C: 23.1 °C, 29.8 °C, 30.0 °C, 31.6 °C, 31.4 °C.

d. Water at 0 °C and 100 °C has different properties. Describe what water looks like at these temperatures.

e. What will happen to the level of the alcohol if you hold the thermometer by the bulb?

3 ▲ Reading the temperature of water in a beaker

An immersion thermometer must be placed in liquid up to the solid line on the thermometer (at least 2 and one half inches of liquid). Wait about 3 minutes for the temperature of the thermometer to equal the temperature of the liquid. Record the temperature to the nearest 0.5 °C when the level stops moving.

1. Place the thermometer in the beaker. Check to make sure that the water level is above the solid line on the thermometer.

2. Wait until the alcohol level stops moving (about three minutes). Record the temperature to the nearest 0.5 °C.

4 ▲ Reading the temperature of warm water in a beaker

A warm liquid will cool to room temperature. For a warm liquid, record the warmest temperature you observe before the temperature begins to decrease.

1. Repeat the procedure above with a beaker of warm (not boiling) water.

2. Take temperature readings every 30 seconds. Record the warmest temperature you observe.

5 ▲ Reading the temperature of ice water in a beaker

When a large amount of ice is added to water, the temperature of the water will drop until the ice and water are the same temperature. After the ice has melted, the cold water will warm to room temperature.

1. Repeat the procedure above with a beaker of ice and water.

2. Take temperature readings every 30 seconds. Record the coldest temperature you observe.

Calculating Volume

How do you find the volume of a three dimensional shape?

Volume is the amount of space an object takes up. If you know the dimensions of a solid object, you can find the object's volume. A two dimensional shape has length and width. A three dimensional object has length, width, and height. This investigation will give you practice finding volume for different solid objects.

Materials
- Pencil
- Calculator

 **Calculating volume of a cube**

A cube is a geometric solid that has length, width and height. If you measure the sides of a cube, you will find that all the edges have the same measurement. The volume of a cube is found by multiplying the length times width times height. In the picture each side is 4 centimeters so the problem looks like this:

$$V = l \times w \times h$$

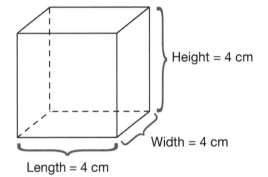

Height = 4 cm

Width = 4 cm

Length = 4 cm

Example:

Volume = 4 centimeters × 4 centimeters × 4 centimeters = 64 centimeters^3

2 Stop and think

  a. What are the units for volume in the example above?

  b. In the example above, if the edge of the cube is 4 inches, what will the volume be? Give the units.

  c. How is finding volume different from finding area?

  d. If you had cubes with a length of 1 centimeter, how many would you need to build the cube in the picture above?

3 ◣ Calculating volume of a rectangular prism

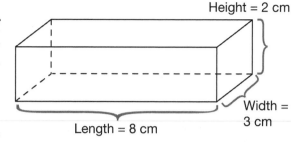

Height = 2 cm

Rectangular prisms are like cubes, except not all of the sides are equal. A shoebox is a rectangular prism. You can find the volume of a rectangular prism using the same formula given above $V = l \times w \times h$.

Width = 3 cm

Length = 8 cm

Another way to say it is to multiply the area of the base times the height.

1. Find the area of the base for the rectangular prism pictured above.

2. Multiply the area of the base times the height. Record the volume of the rectangular prism.

3. PRACTICE: Find the volume for a rectangular prism with a height 6 cm, length 5 cm, and width 3 cm. Be sure to include the units in all of your answers.

4 ◣ Calculating volume for a triangular prism

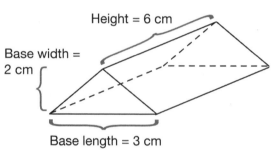

Height = 6 cm

Base width = 2 cm

Base length = 3 cm

Triangular prisms have three sides and two triangular bases. The volume of the triangular prism is found by multiplying the area of the base times the height. The base is a triangle.

1. Find the area of the base by solving for the area of the triangle: $B = \frac{1}{2} \times l \times w$.

2. Find the volume by multiplying the area of the base times the height of the prism: $V = B \times h$. Record the volume of the triangular prism shown above.

3. PRACTICE: Find the volume of the triangular prism with a height 10 cm, triangular base width 4 cm, and triangular base length 5 cm.

5 ◣ Calculating volume for a cylinder

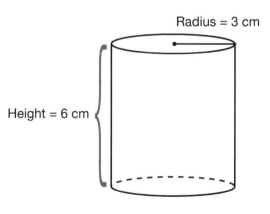

Radius = 3 cm

Height = 6 cm

A soup can is a cylinder. A cylinder has two circular bases and a round surface. The volume of the cylinder is found by multiplying the area of the base times the height. The base is a circle.

1. Find the area of the base by solving for the area of a circle: $A = \pi \times r^2$.

2. Find the volume by multiplying the area of the base times the height of the cylinder: $V = A \times h$. Record the volume of the cylinder shown above.

3. PRACTICE: Find the volume of the cylinder with height 8 cm and radius 4 cm.

◢ 6 Calculating volume for a cone

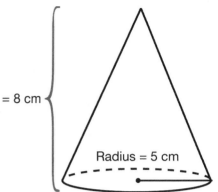

An ice cream cone really is a cone! A cone has height and a circular base. The volume of the cone is found by multiplying $^1/_2$ times the area of the base times the height.

Height = 8 cm

Radius = 5 cm

1. Find the area of the base by solving for the area of a circle: $A = \pi \times r^2$.

2. Find the volume by multiplying? times the area of the base times the height: $V = {}^1/_2 \times A \times h$. Record the volume of the cone shown above.

3. PRACTICE: Find the volume of the cone with height 8 cm and radius 4 cm. Contrast your answer with the volume you found for the cylinder with the same dimensions. What is the difference in volume? Does this make sense?

◢ 7 Calculating the volume for a rectangular pyramid

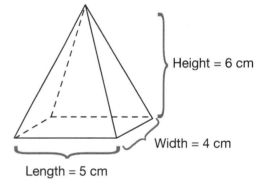

A pyramid looks like a cone. It has height and a rectangular base. The volume of the rectangular pyramid is found by multiplying $^1/_2$ times the area of the base times the height.

Height = 6 cm

Width = 4 cm

Length = 5 cm

1. Find the area of the base by multiplying the length times the width: $A = l \times w$.

2. Find the volume by multiplying $^1/_3$ times the area of the base times the height: $V = {}^1/_3 \times A \times h$. Record the volume of the rectangular pyramid shown above.

3. PRACTICE: Find the volume of a rectangular pyramid with height 10 cm and width 4 cm and length 5 cm.

4. EXTRA CHALLENGE: If a rectangular pyramid had a height of 8 cm and a width of 4 cm, what length would it need to have to give the same volume as the cone in practice question 3 above?

8 ◣ Calculating volume for a triangular pyramid

A triangular pyramid is like a rectangular pyramid, but its base is a triangle. Find the area of the base first. Then calculate the volume by multiplying $1/3$ times the area of the base times the height.

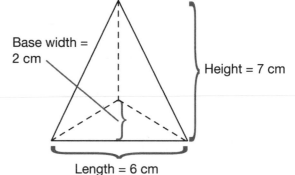

Base width = 2 cm

Height = 7 cm

Length = 6 cm

1. Find the area of the base by solving for the area of a triangle: $B = 1/2 \times l \times w$.

2. Find the volume by multiplying $1/3$ times the area of the base times the height: $V = 1/3 \times A \times h$. Find the volume of the triangular pyramid shown above.

3. PRACTICE: Find the volume of the triangular pyramid with height 10 cm and width 6 cm and length 5 cm.

9 ◣ Calculating volume for a sphere

To find the volume of a sphere, you only need to know one dimension about the sphere, its radius.

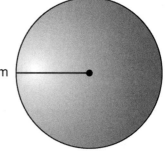

Radius = 4 cm

1. Find the volume of a sphere: $V = 4/3 \pi r^3$. Find the volume for the sphere shown above.

2. PRACTICE: Find the volume for a sphere with radius 2 cm.

3. EXTRA CHALLENGE: Find the volume for a sphere with diameter 10 cm.

Measuring Volume

How do you find the volume of an irregular object?

It's easy to find the volume of a shoebox or a basketball. You just take a few measurements, plug the numbers into a math formula, and you have figured it out. But what if you want to find the volume of a bumpy rock, or an acorn, or a house key? There aren't any simple math formulas to help you out. However, there's an easy way to find the volume of an irregular object, as long the object is waterproof!

Materials

- Displacement tank
- Water source
- Disposable cup
- Beaker
- Graduated cylinder
- Sponges or paper towel
- Object to be measured

 Setting up the displacement tank

Set the displacement tank on a level surface. Place a disposable cup under the tank's spout. Carefully fill the tank until the water begins to drip out of the spout. When the water stops flowing, discard the water collected in the disposable cup. Set the cup aside and place a beaker under the spout.

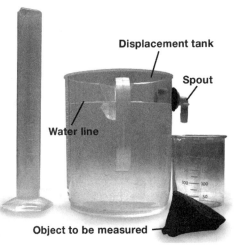

Displacement tank

Spout

Water line

Object to be measured

Stop and think

a. What do you think will happen when you place an object into the tank?

b. Which object would cause more water to come out of the spout, an acorn or a fist-sized rock?

c. Why are we interested in how much water comes out of the spout?

d. Explain how the displacement tank measures volume.

Measuring volume with the displacement tank

1. Gently place a waterproof object into the displacement tank. It is important to avoid splashing the water or creating a wave that causes extra water to flow out of the spout. It may take a little practice to master this step.

2. When the water stops flowing out of the spout, it can be poured from the beaker into a graduated cylinder for precise measurement. The volume of the water displaced is equal to the object's volume.
Note: Occasionally, when a small object is placed in the tank, no water will flow out. This happens because an air bubble has formed in the spout. Simply tap the spout with a pencil to release the air bubble.

3. If you wish to measure the volume of another object, don't forget to refill the tank with water first!

Measuring Mass with a Triple Beam Balance

How do you find the mass of an object?

Why can't you use a bathroom scale to measure the mass of a paperclip? You could if you were finding the mass of a lot of them at one time! To find the mass of objects less than a kilogram you will need to use the triple beam balance.

Materials

- Triple beam balance
- Small objects
- Mass set (optional)
- Beaker

1 ▲ Parts of the triple beam balance

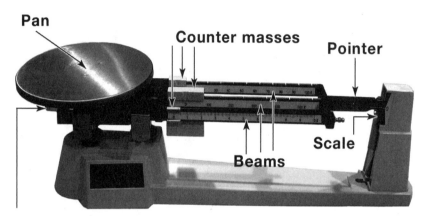

2 ▲ Setting up and zeroing the balance

The triple beam balance works like a see-saw. When the mass of your object is perfectly balanced by the counter masses on the beam, the pointer will rest at 0. Add up the readings on the three beams to find the mass of your object. The unit of measure for this triple beam balance is grams.

1. Place the balance on a level surface.

2. Clean any objects or dust off the pan.

3. Move all counter masses to 0. The pointer should rest at 0. Use the adjustment screw to adjust the pointer to 0, if necessary. When the pointer rests at 0 with no objects on the pan, the balance is said to be zeroed.

3. Finding a known mass

You can check that the triple beam balance is working correctly by using a mass set. Your teacher will provide the correct mass value for these objects.

1. After zeroing the balance, place an object with a known mass on the pan.

2. Move the counter masses to the right one at a time from largest to smallest. When the pointer is resting at 0 the numbers under the three counter masses should add up to the known mass.

3. If the pointer is above or below 0, recheck the balance set up. Recheck the position of the counter masses. Counter masses must be properly seated in a groove. Check with your teacher to make sure you are getting the correct mass before finding the mass an unknown object.

4. Finding the mass of an unknown object

1. After zeroing the balance, place an object with an unknown mass on the pan. Do not place hot objects or chemicals directly on the pan

2. Move the largest counter mass first. Place it in the first notch after zero. Wait until the pointer stops moving. If the pointer is above 0, move the counter mass to the next notch. Continue to move the counter mass to the right, one notch at a time until the pointer is slightly above 0. Go to step 3. If the pointer is below 0, move the counter mass back one notch. When the pointer rests at 0, you do not need to move any more counter masses.

3. Move the next largest counter mass from 0 to the first notch. Watch to see where the pointer rests. If it rests above 0, move the counter mass to the next notch. Repeat until the point rests at 0, or slightly above. If the pointer is slightly above 0, go to step 4.

4. Move the smallest counter mass from 0 to the position on the beam where the pointer rests at 0.

5. Add the masses from the three beams to get the mass of the unknown object. You should be able to record a number for the hundreds place, the tens place, the ones place, and the tenths place and the hundredths place. The hundredths place can be read to 0.00 or 0.05. You may have zeros in your answer.

◤5 Reading the balance correctly

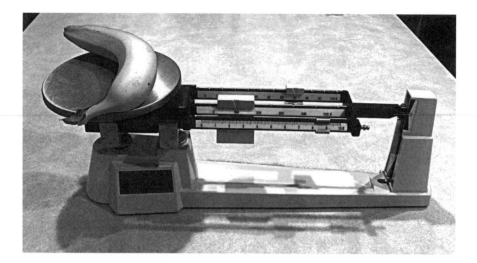

Look at the picture above. To find the mass of the object, locate the counter mass on each beam. Read the numbers directly below each counter mass. You can read the smallest mass to 0.05 grams. Write down the three numbers. Add them together. Report your answer in grams. Does your answer agree with others? If not, check your mass values from each beam to find your mistake.

◤6 Finding the mass of an object in a container

To measure the mass of a liquid or powder you will need an empty container on the pan to hold the sample. You must find the mass of the empty container first. After you place the object in the container and find the total mass, you can subtract the container's mass from the total to find the object's mass.

1. After zeroing the balance, place a beaker on the pan.

2. Follow directions for finding the mass of an unknown object. Record the mass of the beaker.

3. Place a small object in the beaker.

4. Move the counter masses to the right, largest to smallest, to find the total mass.

5. Subtract the beaker's mass from the total mass. This is the mass of your object in grams.

Recording Observations in the Lab

How do you record valid observations for an experiment in the lab?

When you perform an experiment you will be making important observations. You and others will use these observations to test a hypothesis. In order for an experiment to be valid, the evidence you collect must be objective and repeatable. This investigation will give you practice making and recording good observations.

Materials
• Paper
• Pencil
• Calculator
• Ruler

 Making valid observations

Valid scientific observations are objective and repeatable. Scientific observations are limited to one's senses and the equipment used to make these observations. An objective observation means that the observer describes only what happened. The observer uses data, words, and pictures to describe the observations as exactly as possible. An experiment is repeatable if other scientists can see or repeat the same result. The following exercise gives you practice identifying good scientific observations.

Exercise 1

1. **Which observation is the most objective? Circle the correct letter.**
    a. My frog died after 3 days in the aquarium. I miss him.
    b. The frog died after 3 days in the aquarium. We will test the temperature and water conditions to find out why.
    c. Frogs tend to die in captivity. Ours did after three days.
2. **Which observation is the most descriptive? Circle the correct letter.**
    a. After weighing 3.000 grams of sodium bicarbonate into an Erlenmeyer flask, we slowly added 50.0 milliliters of vinegar. The contents of the flask began to bubble.
    b. We weighed the powder into a glass container. We added acid. It bubbled a lot.
    c. We saw a fizzy reaction.

3. **Which experiment has enough detail to repeat? Circle the correct letter.**

   a. Each student took a swab culture from his or her teeth. The swab was streaked onto nutrient agar plates and incubated at 37 C.

   b. Each student received a nutrient agar plate and a swab. Each student performed a swab culture of his or her teeth. The swab was streaked onto the agar plate. The plates were stored face down in the 37 C incubator and checked daily for growth. After 48 hours the plates were removed from the incubator and each student recorded his or her results.

   c. Each student received a nutrient agar plate and a swab. Each student performed a swab culture of his or her teeth. The swab was streaked onto the agar plate. The plates were stored face down in the 37 C incubator and checked daily for growth. After 48 hours the plates were removed from the incubator and each student counted the number of colonies present on the surface of the agar.

◤3◥ Recording valid observations

As a part of your investigations you will be asked to record observations on a skill sheet or in the results section of a lab report. There are different ways to show your observations. Here are some examples:

1. **Short description:** Use descriptive words to explain what you did or saw. Write complete sentences. Give as much detail as possible about the experiment. Try to answer the following questions: What? Where? When? Why? and How?

2. **Tables:** Tables are a good way to display the data you have collected. Later, the data can be plotted on a graph. Be sure to include a title for the table, labels for the sets of data, and units for the values. Check values to make sure you have the correct number of significant figures.

Table 1: U.S. penny mass by year

Year manufactured	1977	1978	1979	1980	1981	1982	1983	1984	1985
Mass (grams)	3.0845	3.0921	3.0689	2.9915	3.0023	2.5188	2.5042	2.4883	2.5230

3. **Graphs and charts:** A graph or chart is a picture of your data. There are different kinds of graphs and charts: line graphs, trend charts, bar graphs, and pie graphs, for example. A line graph is shown below.

Label the important parts of your graph. Give your graph a title. The x-axis and y-axis should have labels for the data, the unit values, and the number range on the graph.

The line graph in the example has a straight line through the data. Sometimes data does not fit a straight line. Often scientists will plot data first in a trend chart to see how the data looks. Check with your instructor if you are unsure how to display your data.

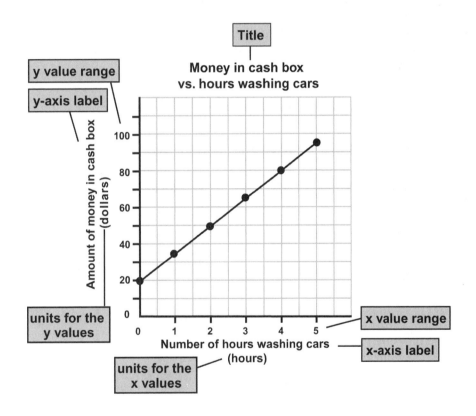

4. **Drawings:** Sometimes you will record observations by drawing a sketch of what you see. The example below was observed under a microscope.

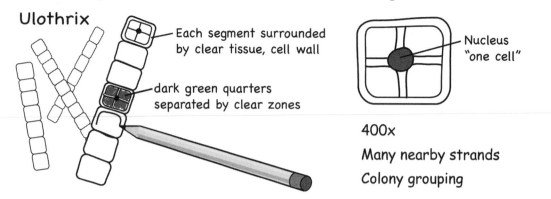

Give the name of the specimen. Draw enough detail to make the sketch look realistic. Use color, when possible. Identify parts of the object you were asked to observe. Provide the magnification or size of the image.

Exercise 2: Practice recording valid observations

A lab report form has been given to you by your instructor. This exercise gives you a chance to read through an experiment and fill in information in the appropriate sections of the lab report form. Use this opportunity to practice writing and graphing scientific observations. Then answer the following questions about the experiment.

A student notices that when he presses several pennies in a pressed penny machine, his brand new penny has some copper color missing and he can see silver-like material underneath. He wonders, "Are some pennies made differently than others?" The student has a theory that not all U.S. pennies are made the same. He thinks that if pennies are made differently now he might be able to find out when the change occurred. He decides to collect a U.S. penny for each year from 1977 to the present, record the date, and take its mass. The student records the data in a table and creates a graph plotting U.S. penny mass vs. year. Below is a table of some of his data:

Table 2: U.S. penny mass by year

Year manufactured	1977	1978	1979	1980	1981	1982	1983	1984	1985
Mass (grams)	3.0845	3.0921	3.0689	2.9915	3.0023	2.5188	2.5042	2.4883	2.5230

Stop and think

a. What observation did the student make first before he began his experiment?

b. How did the student display his observations?

c. In what section of the lab report did you show observations?

d. What method did you use to display the observations? Explain why you chose this one.

Physics Stand

You will need:

- Physics stand pole
- Physics stand washer
- Physics stand base
- Physics stand bolt

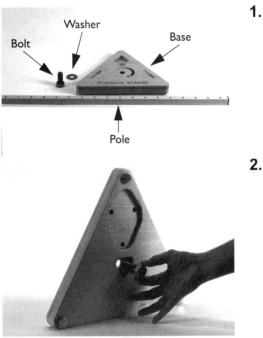

Washer
Bolt
Base
Pole

1. **Identifying the parts of the physics stand**

There are four parts to the physics stand; the base, the pole, the washer and the bolt.

2. **Placing the bolt into the base**

From the bottom of the base slide the large bolt through the hole.

3. **Sliding the washer onto the bolt**

Be sure to push the bolt into the cut-out triangle on the bottom of the stand. The washer will fit over the threaded part of the bolt.

4. **Attaching the pole to the base**

The pole screws onto the threads of the bolt. The bolt will not spin when you hold the bolt into the cut-out triangle on the bottom of the base. Spin the pole until it screws down snug onto the washer.

251

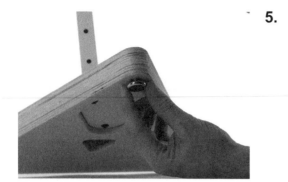

5. **Leveling the stand**

There are three adjustable feet on the bottom of the base. These feet screw into the base. They can be extended by unscrewing them a few turns.

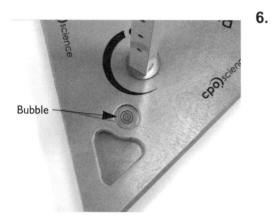

6. **Using the leveling bubble**

When the bubble is directly in the center of the small circle, the stand is level. By adjusting the feet on the bottom of the base by small amounts, the stand can be brought into level.

Energy Car

You will need:

- 2 sections of track
- Rubber bands
- Some string
- A small bubble level

- Three blue knobs
- 2 Energy Cars
- Some modeling clay
- 3 steel balls (3/4" dia.)

- 2 Stops
- 1 Sled
- Physics Stand

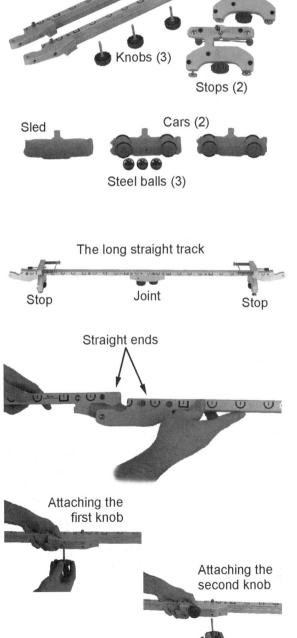

Track sections (2)

Knobs (3)

Stops (2)

Sled

Cars (2)

Steel balls (3)

The long straight track

Stop   Joint   Stop

Straight ends

Attaching the
first knob

Attaching the
second knob

1. Parts of the Energy Car set.

You will also need some rubber bands. #33 rubber bands work well but other sizes will also work. A small ball of modeling clay about 2 cm in diameter is also necessary.

The sled is the same as the energy car, but without wheels.

2. Setting up the long straight track

The long straight track is used for many experiments.

3. Joining the track sections

The two sections of the track join together with two blue knobs.

Notice that the ends of the track sections are different. One end is straight and the other has a slight curve. Join the two straight ends together to make the long straight track. The curved ends are for making a hill.

Screw one blue knob into each of the two holes on the bottom of the joint where the two track sections meet.

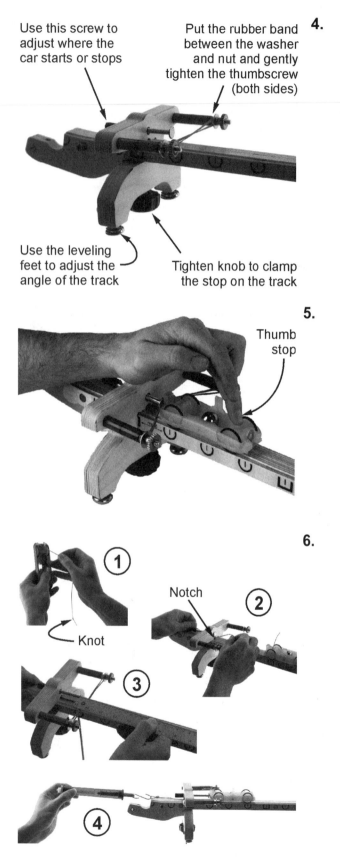

Use this screw to adjust where the car starts or stops

Put the rubber band between the washer and nut and gently tighten the thumbscrew (both sides)

Use the leveling feet to adjust the angle of the track

Tighten knob to clamp the stop on the track

Thumb stop

① Knot

Notch ②

③

④

4. Attaching the stop and making a car launcher

The stop is used to both start and stop the car on the track. There are two stops, one for each end. They are identical.

To make the stop into a launcher, loosen the two thumbscrews by a few turns. Stretch a rubber band between the two screws. The rubber band should fit behind the washer. Give the rubber band one twist so it makes an "X" between the posts. The X helps provide even force when launching the car.

5. Launching the car

To launch the energy car, rest your hand on the top of the launcher and catch the thumb stop on the car with your finger (diagram).

Pull the car back until it hits the screw. Change the adjustment of the screw to get different speeds.

Flick your finger back and off the thumb stop with a quick motion to launch the car. With practice you can get speeds that are repeatable to within 1%.

6. Measuring the force on the car

(1) Tie a knot on the end of a length of string. Thread the string through the small hole in the end of the car so the knot is on top the car.

(2) Thread the string through the notch just below the screw on the wooden stop. Tie a small loop on the free end of the string about 20 cm away from the wooden stop.

(3) Use a ruler to set the distance from the front of the screw to the front of the rubber band. Distances from 1 cm to 5 cm can be obtained.

(4) Attach a force scale to the loop on the string and pull the car back until it just touches the screw. The scale reads the force on the car at the measured deflection of the rubber band.

Clay ball

7. Stopping the car

Squish a small ball of modeling clay on the end of the screw to make a stop for the car. The clay prevents the car from bouncing.

Adjust the leveling feet on one or both ends until the bubble is exactly centered

8. Leveling the track

Some experiments require that the track be level. A small bubble-level works very well for this purpose. Adjust the leveling feet until the bubble is exactly in the center between the marking lines on the level.

Attaching the photogate

The marks are 5 cm apart. Use them to position the photogate.

Flag (1 cm wide)

9. Using the photogates

The car has a small flag on top that breaks the light beam in the photogates. The flag is one centimeter wide.

Attach photogates as shown in the diagram. The flag breaks the light beam when the photogate is snug against the bottom of the track.

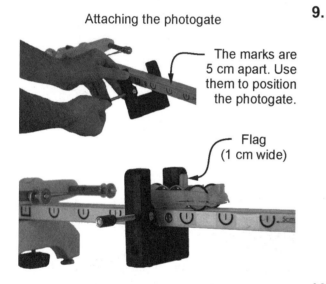

Add mass to the car so the steel balls are evenly spaced around the center of the car,

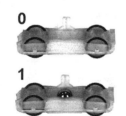

0

1

2

3

10. Adding mass to the car

The steel balls add mass to the car. Each ball is 50% of the mass of the empty car. That means adding one ball increases the mass by 50%. Adding two balls doubles the mass.

The car is designed so the center of mass stays in the same place if the balls are added symmetrically around the center (diagram).

SETUP

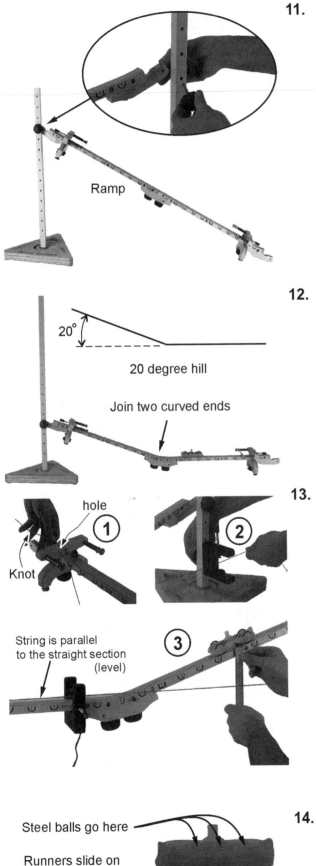

Ramp

20°

20 degree hill

Join two curved ends

hole

①

②

Knot

String is parallel
to the straight section
(level)

③

Steel balls go here

Runners slide on
the track

11. Making a straight ramp

The long straight track can be attached to the Physics Stand to make a ramp. Insert a blue knob through a hole in the stand and screw the threaded end into the end of the ramp.

12. Making a flat section with a hill

You can join the two sections of the track to make a 10 degree hill or a 20 degree hill. To make the 10 degree hill join one curved end to one straight end. To make a 20 degree hill joining both curved ends together.

Use the Physics Stand to support the track at the top of the hill.

13. Measuring height on the hill

A level string can be used as a reference to measure the height of the car on the hill.

(1) Make the horizontal section of the track level. Tie a knot in one end of a string and thread the string through the small hole in the stop.

(2) Use a photogate and a knob to clamp the other end of the string against the Physics Stand. Adjust the position until the string is parallel to the horizontal section of the track.

(3) The string is now level and at the same height as the center of mass of the car! You can easily make height measurements on the hill by measuring the vertical distance between the center of the car and the string.

14. Using the sled

The sled is just like the car, but without wheels. The sled is used for friction experiments.

Ropes and Pulleys

You will need:

- Physics Stand
- 1 set of weights
- Tape measure

- Upper and lower pulley blocks attached by red safety string
- 1 set of spring scales
- Blue knob

- Yellow string with cord stops
- Black knob

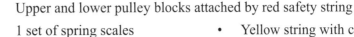

Lower pulley block

Weights

Blue knob

Red safety string   Upper pulley block   Black knob

1.

Identifying the parts of the ropes and pulleys

The ropes and pulleys set is an ideal way to learn the basic principles behind how simple machines work. The upper and lower pulley blocks each contain three pulleys. The number of pulleys through which the string passes can be varied by passing the string through the desired number. The force of the bottom pulley block can be varied by adding or subtracting weights. The pulleys contain low friction bearings for accurate force measurements.

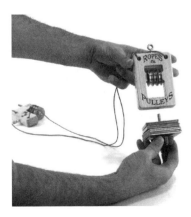

2.

Attaching the upper pulley block

Slide the threaded rod attached to the upper pulley block through the top hole of the physics stand. Secure the pulley block with the black knob. You should now have the upper pulley block secured, while the lower pulley block hangs below on the two red safety strings.

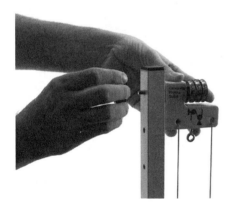

3.

Weighing the bottom block

Add weights to the bottom block using the blue knob with the threaded stud. Slide the threaded stud through the hole in the weight and screw it into the bottom of the lower pulley.

After the weights have been secured, weigh the lower pulley block by hanging it onto a spring scale using the eyelet on top.

4. **Stringing the pulley blocks**

The yellow string is the one you will use to move the lower pulley block up and down. The red strings are the safety strings that hold the bottom block while you arrange the yellow strings. The cord stops are used as reference markers for measuring the length of string needed to raise the lower block a given distance.

The first step to stringing the ropes & pulleys is to choose where to connect the brass clip on the end of the yellow string. The clip can either be attached to the upper pulley block or the lower pulley block using the eyelet on either block.

If the string is connected to the lower pulley block a mechanical advantage of 1, 3 or 5 can be obtained (1, 3, or 5 supporting strings). The diagram to the right shows a mechanical advantage of 1.

Connect string to the lower pulley block for mechanical advantage of 1,3, or 5.

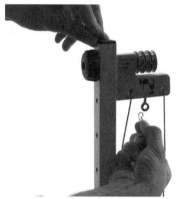

Connect string to the upper pulley block for mechanical advantage of 2,4, or 6.

If the string is connected to the upper pulley block a mechanical advantage of 2, 4, or 6 can be obtained (2, 4, or 6 supporting strings). The diagram to the right shows a mechanical advantage of 2.

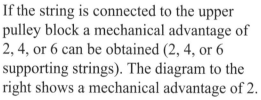

Lever

You will need:

- Physics Stand
- 1 set of weights
- 1 set of spring scales
- 1 thumb screw
- Loop strings
- Lever
- 1 black knob

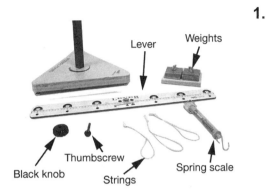

1.

Identifying the parts of the lever

The lever is attached to the stand with a thumb screw and a knob. Loops of string are put through weights and the weights are hung from the lever. Spring scales can be attached to the lever to measure the force created by hanging weights.

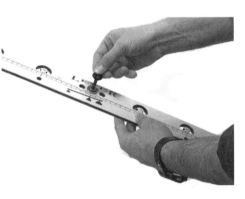

2.

Place thumb screw through lever

Slide the thumbscrew through a hole in the lever. The screw should be inserted from the side of the lever that has the scale printed on it.

3.

Attaching the lever to the stand

Select the desired hole in the Physics Stand and slide the thumbscrew, with the Lever on it, through the hole. Secure the assembly using the black plastic knob.

4. **Securing the weights**

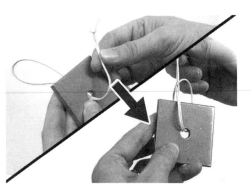

Weights can be hung on the lever in a variety of combinations. The variables are the position and the number of weights on the lever. To secure the weights to the lever, slide one end of a string loop through the hole(s) in the weight(s). Loop around one edge and slip the string back through itself.

5. **Hanging the weights**

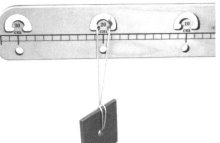

Hang the weight to the lever by placing the loop of string attached to weights securely around one of the mushroom shaped slots. Weights may be hung from more than one location on the lever.

6. **Using the spring scales**

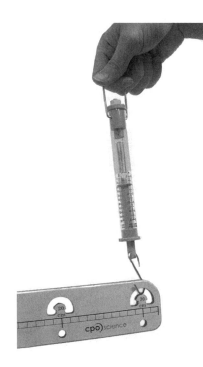

Loop the hook part of a spring scale through one of the holes used to attach weights. Hold spring scale from the top using the metal loop. Slowly lift the scale upward, take a reading while in motion and then slowly lower, also taking a reading. The scale will only need to be lifted and then lowered 3-4 inches for a reading. The true reading will be the average of the two readings.

Atom Building Game

You will need:

- Atom game board
- 1 tube yellow marbles
- Laminated periodic table

- 1 tube blue marbles
- Nuclear Reactions cards
- Game booklet

- 1 tube red marbles
- Photons and Lasers cards

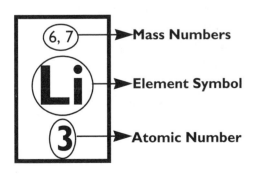

1. **Identifying the parts of the game.**

The Atom Building Game comes with an atom game board, blue, red, and yellow marbles, game cards, a laminated periodic table, and an instruction booklet.

The game cards include Nuclear Reactions cards and Photons and Lasers cards. You will learn how to use these cards in the Investigations.

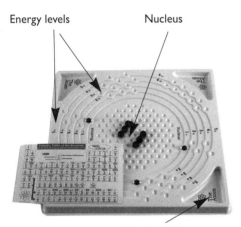

Energy levels   Nucleus

Marble Pocket

2. **Using the atom game board.**

The Atom game board is designed to sit on a table top with four players (or teams) around it. Each player (or team) is assigned to one of the four marble pockets.

The center of the board represents the nucleus. This is where the protons (red marbles) and neutrons (blue marbles) are place during the activities.

The steps around the nucleus represent the energy levels that are occupied by the electrons (yellow marbles).

(6, 7) ➤ **Mass Numbers**

Li ➤ **Element Symbol**

(3) ➤ **Atomic Number**

3. **Using the periodic table.**

The periodic table is used for many of the activities. The atomic number is the number of protons (red marbles) in the nucleus.

The atomic number determines what element the atom is. The mass number is the total number of particles (protons plus neutrons) in the nucleus.

Isotopes are atoms with the same number of protons but different numbers of neutrons. You can figure out the number of neutrons by subtracting the atomic number from the mass number. For example, lithium-6 has 3 protons and 3 neutrons ($6 - 3 = 3$).

Neutral atoms have the same number of electrons as protons. The atom in step 2 is lithium-6.

Pendulum

You will need:

- Physics Stand
- Pendulum bob and string assembly
- Pendulum body
- 10 washers
- 2 blue knobs
- DataCollector and photogates

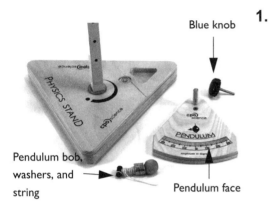

Blue knob

Pendulum bob, washers, and string

Pendulum face

PHYSICS STAND

1.

Identifying the parts of the pendulum.

The pendulum experiment allows you to change three variables: the length of the string, the mass of the pendulum, and the angle of the swing (amplitude). The length of the string can be varied from 15 cm to nearly 1 meter. The pendulum has a hardwood face with an angle scale for easy determination of the amplitude. Washers can be added to or subtracted from the pendulum bob to change the mass.

2.

Attaching the pendulum face to the physics stand.

Slide the threaded stud on the blue knob through the desired hole in the physics stand.

Turn the blue knob to thread the stud into the back of the pendulum face, securing it to the physics stand. Make sure that it is levelled.

3.

Attaching the pendulum bob and string

Select the length of string for the pendulum bob by sliding the string into the slot in the peg on the pendulum face. Check the length of the string by measuring from the bottom of the slotted peg to the bottom of the stack of washers on the pendulum bob. You can add or subtract washers from the pendulum bob to change the mass.

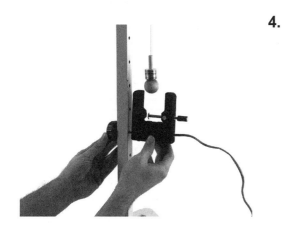

4. **Mounting the photogate to the physics stand.**

To mount the photogate to the physics stand, you will need another blue knob with threaded stud. Place the outer edge of the photogate to against the hole that allows you to align the opening with the pendulum bob. Do not overtighten. Make sure the pendulum bob breaks the beam in the photogate each time it swings.

5. **Aligning the photogate**

Be sure to align the two small holes in the photogate with the center of the round portion of the pendulum bob.

Attach the photogate to the Photogate A port of the DataCollector using the red or blue photogate cord. Make sure the DataCollector is set to the period function of the CPO timer mode.

Sound and Waves

You will need:

- Physics Stand
- Sound & waves console
- Elastic string
- Wiggler
- Blue or red photogate cord
- 2 black knobs
- Fiddlehead
- Black stereo wire
- DataCollector

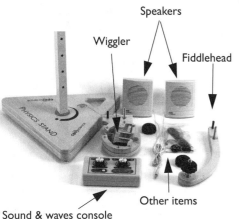

Speakers

Wiggler

Fiddlehead

Other items

Sound & waves console

1. **Identifying the parts of the kit.**

The sound and waves kit contains a wiggler for creating standing waves on a string and a sound synthesizer that can make pure tones at frequencies ranging from 20 to 25,000 hertz. The components in the kit are shown at the right.

2. **Attaching the wiggler and fiddlehead.**

Attach the wiggler by placing the two threads through the bottom two holes on the physics stand. Secure the wiggler with a black knob.

Attach the fiddlehead by placing the threaded rod and peg on the head through the top two holes on the physics stand. Secure with another black knob. Be sure the black knobs for each piece are on the same side of the physics stand pole. The top of the fiddlehead will be higher than the physics stand pole when it is attached.

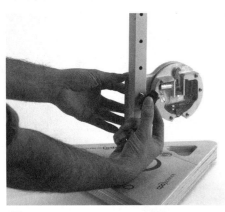

3. **Attach the string to the wiggler and fiddlehead.**

The wiggler arm is a narrow metal strip shaped like an arrow. The tip of the wiggler arm protrudes from the wiggler about 2 cm. If the string is not already attached to the wiggler, locate the hole in the wiggler arm and thread the elastic string through the hole. Knot the string at the end. This knot will create a stop so that the string can be pulled tight.

Attach the free end of the string to the fiddlehead by pulling it to the top knob on the fiddlehead. At this point there should be no slack in the string. Now tighten the string by stretching it a little (5-10 cm). Then, wrap the end around the back of the knob - sliding it between two of the washers. Lightly tighten the black plastic knob, securing the string between the washers.

4. **Connect the sound and waves console.**

Connect the black phono wire into the bottom of the wiggler. Connect the other end of the black phono wire into the round jack on the sound and waves console.

5.

Connecting to the DataCollector.

Turn on the DataCollector and set to CPO timer mode and use the frequency function. Plug one end of the phone cord into the **A** slot on the timer and the other end into the square jack in on Sound & Waves console.

While in sound mode, press and hold the mode button for 1 second to switch the Sound & Waves console to *waves* mode.

Change the frequency on the sound and waves console by turning the frequency knob left or right.

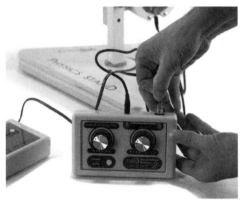

6.

Using the sound mode.

Unplug the black stereo wire from the Sound & Waves console and connect the end of the wire from the speakers into the round jack.

Set the Sound & Waves console to *sound* mode by pressing the button until the *sound* light is illuminated.

Connect the Sound & Waves console to the timer using the square jack and set the DataCollector to the *frequency* function.

Adjust the frequency by turning the frequency knob. Adjust the volume by turning the volume knob.

Electric Circuits

SETUP

You will need:

- Electric circuits table
- 6 light bulbs and 3 holders
- 2 brown (long-length) wires
- 1 red (20-ohm) resistor

- 1 potentiometer
- 6 green (short-length) wires
- 2 green (5-ohm) resistors
- 2 knife switches

- 2 battery holders
- 2 blue (medium-length) wires
- 1 blue (10-ohm) resistor

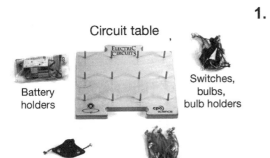

Circuit table

Battery holders

Switches, bulbs, bulb holders

Potentiometer

Resistors and wires

1. **Identifying the parts of the electric circuits kit.**

The electric circuits table is a wooden platform with brass posts for securely assembling electric circuits. There are 12 brass posts used in making connections between different components of the circuit

The posts are not connected underneath and there are no hidden wires. All connections are made using wires that come in a separate pack.

Circuits are made with wires, batteries, bulbs and holders, resistors, and switches.

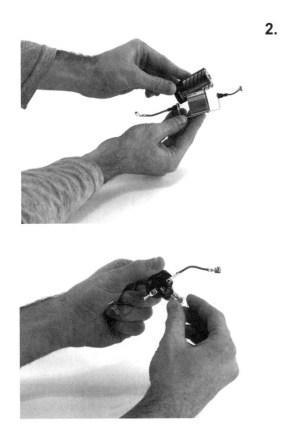

2. **Assembling the components.**

Place D batteries (1.5 volts) into the battery holders.

Place a light bulb into each bulb holder.

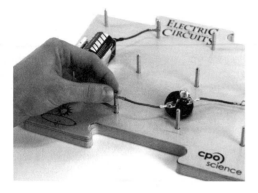

3. Adding wires and circuit elements.

Each wire has a circular connector at both ends called a hoop connector. To add a wire to the board, just place the hoop around the post and push down on the hoop. It will slide down the post, like a jewelry ring over a finger. If you need to add one or more wires to the post, simply push the first wire down the post to make room for another hoop. You can add up to 4 hoops to a post.

NOTE: Solid contact is made at any position on the post. It is not necessary to slide every wire to the bottom of the post.

A circuit element is any item that uses or affects electricity in a circuit. This includes batteries, light bulbs, resistors and switches. Each circuit element that comes with the kit has the same type of hoop connectors as the wires. To connect a circuit element to a post just place the hoop on the post and push down, sliding it down the post.

4. Closing the circuit.

A circuit is made when wires and elements are connected together making a path for electricity. Shown at left is an example of a simple circuit with a battery, a light bulb, a switch, and some wires.

5. Avoiding short circuits.

Circuits should always include a "resistor." The term "resistor" refers to a device like a light bulb or one of the resistors that comes with the kit and provides a substantial resistance to the flow of electricity. A wire alone in a circuit provides very little resistance and is not considered a resistor. A circuit without a resistor, or one in which a branch bypasses a resistor, is called a short circuit. A *short circuit* causes unsafe heating of connecting wires, batteries, and battery holders. This could result in burns and irreparable damage to the equipment. Avoid short circuits at all times!